Compulsive Exercise
AND THE
Eating Disorders

Toward an Integrated
Theory of Activity

Compulsive Exercise

AND THE

Eating Disorders

Toward an Integrated
Theory of Activity

Alayne Yates, M.D.

PROFESSOR OF PSYCHIATRY AND
ASSOCIATE PROFESSOR OF PEDIATRICS
UNIVERSITY OF ARIZONA
TUCSON, ARIZONA

BRUNNER/MAZEL *Publishers* • NEW YORK

Library of Congress Cataloging-in-Publication Data
Yates, Alayne.
    Compulsive exercise and the eating disorders : toward an
integrated theory of activity / by Alayne Yates.
        p.   cm.
    Includes bibliographical references and index.
    ISBN 0-87630-630-X
    1. Exercise addictions.   2. Eating disorders.   I. Title.
    [DNLM: 1. Compulsive Behavior.   2. Compulsive Behavior—
psychology.   3. Eating Disorders.   4. Eating Disorders—psychology.
5. Exercise.   WM 175 Y31c]
RC569.5.E94Y38   1991
616.85′2—dc20
DNLM/DLC
for Library of Congress   90-15153
                                                              CIP

Published by
B R U N N E R / M A Z E L ,   I N C .
19 Union Square West
New York, New York 10003

MANUFACTURED IN THE UNITED STATES OF AMERICA

10 9 8 7 6 5 4 3 2 1

This book is dedicated to my daughter,
MARA ARUGUETE,
for her insight and the inspiration
that she provided.

on horseback across the legendary Snowy Mountains, but they fished barramundi in Northern Territory crocodile country, raced at 155 miles per hour on the bullet train in Japan, traveled through communist China, visited the Kremlin, and crossed the Berlin Wall. During a relatively quiet moment in Australia, the parents took computer lessons while the children attended the local school.

Lamar Alexander represents the age in which he was born and raised. If he had been more inclined toward rest and relaxation, he would never have been governor of Tennessee, written a book, or perhaps had four children. Lamar Alexander, and people like him, are the mainstay of the nation: independent, productive, active, and achieving individuals. All the more reason why we should begin to examine the internal, as well as external, functions of activity.

This book is about individuals who are consumed by activity: persons who, if they are not engaged in an activity, are thinking about it, reevaluating past performance, and planning for their future endeavors. To a lesser extent, this book is about most of us.

EXTREMES OF DIET AND EXERCISE

From 1983–1989, Drs. Leehey, Shisslak, Crago, Allender, and Yates interviewed more than 150 male and female runners in depth. They found that a few of these runners carried the sport to an unusual extreme; running had become the central focus of their lives and they continued to run even when injured. The investigators called these individuals "obligatory runners" because they seemed to be unable to "not run." Obligatory runners appeared similar, in a number of respects, to eating disordered women: obligatory runners are extremely committed athletes and eating disordered women are extremely committed dieters. Individuals in both groups attempt to control the body through exercise and diet; they are well aware of the input/output equation—that they can burn up calories through exercise. Are there other similarities between eating disordered women and compulsive athletes?

Although some obligatory runners are female and some eating disordered individuals are male, for convenience we will refer to persons with an exercise compulsion as "he" and persons with an eating disorder as "she." When we speak of the eating disorders, we are referring to a category which embraces anorexia (anorexia nervosa) and bulimia (bulimia nervosa). Anorexia signifies relentless food restriction while bulimia usually implies a cycle of gorging followed by vomiting or diuretic/laxative abuse, but it also may refer to an alternating pattern of bingeing and

CHAPTER 1

Independent Activity: Exercise and Diet

On the television screen, members of the "Pepsi generation" leap, run, laugh, and gyrate, scarcely pausing long enough to relate to one another. This disconnected but enthusiastic jumble becomes a proclamation of youth, health, and the potential for success. From the chorus of "Up With People" to the welcoming ceremony at Club Med, it is the barrage of motion, of color, of sound that inspires a sense of power and vitality. Toward what goal do these persons strive, or does it really matter?

Activity, or the condition of being active, can serve as an important regulator in the intrapsychic economy, that is, individuals may not feel comfortable or of value if they are not active. Conversely, they may be distinctly uncomfortable when they face the condition of inactivity. A common example is that of the busy professional who slips a disc and is forced to rest. He is restless and irritable, but makes the best of a bad situation by catching up on his journals. When he recovers, he will not rest and, indeed, he will continue to design his life around activity.

In 1988, Lamar Alexander authored a best-selling tale, *Six Months Off*, which describes a period of time in which he put aside the heavy demands of a political career and took his wife and four children to Australia. He wished to have nothing to do, time to relax and enjoy the family he had neglected during his eight years as governor of Tennessee. Yet, as the reader browses through this pleasant volume, he realizes that the author had already agreed to write the book before the trip began. Not only did the family tour the far reaches of Australia, riding 100 miles

Part II

Clinical Issues

PART I

Clinical Issues

Acknowledgments

The obligatory runner research team, Marge Crago, Ph.D., Catherine Shisslak, Ph.D., and Jim Allender, Ph.D., together with an earlier member, Kevin Leehey, M.D., deserve a large share of the credit for this book. Walter Wolman, Ph.D., warrants a special acknowledgment for his inspired library research and editorial assistance, in conjunction with my intrepid secretary, Karen Sasek. My thanks also to Syd Arkowitz, Ph.D., and Peter Lusche, M.D., for their sage comments after carefully reviewing the tortuous first draft to the bitter end.

Contents

starving. These entities are regarded as different expressions of the same underlying process: many eating disordered women are known to move back and forth between the two categories. Anorexia and bulimia have many more likenesses than they have differences (Garner, Garfinkel & O'Shaughnessy, 1985; Mitchell, Pyle et al., 1986) and the validity of separating the two diagnoses is questionable (Beumont, George & Smart, 1976; Casper et al., 1980; Garner et al., 1985).

THE "NEW" EATING DISORDERED WOMAN

There has been a significant shift in the level of pathology that is associated with the eating disorders. Forty years ago the typical eating disordered woman was the "classic" anorexic patient. She was an immature, severely disturbed adolescent who drastically restricted her food intake, remained bound within the family, and was socially isolated and unlikely to marry (Crisp, 1965a; Russell, 1970).

Of particular interest are the "new" eating disordered women of the 70s, 80s and 90s. These women are quite distinct from the "classic" eating disordered women who still present in the clinic. The "new" eating disordered women are far more likely to be bulimic and they are unlikely to be emaciated, immature, and bound within an enmeshed family. They seem relatively well adjusted and they may have been raised in an apparently normal family (Turnbull et al., 1989). They are more apt to have become eating disordered at an older age, to be married (Heavey et al., 1989) and to function very well in educational and vocational spheres. A non-clinic sample of bulimic women seems most like a sample of professional women (Teusch, 1988) and professional women are distinctly independent.

The apparent health of many eating disordered women suggests that there may be a relatively non-pathological route to the eating disorders. Yet our understanding of these women continues to be largely based upon studies of poorly functioning women, often hospitalized patients.

Eating disordered women who are educated, high achieving, and relatively healthy are the ones who seem most like the obligatory runners in our study. The obligatory runners, like the well-functioning eating disordered women, are relative newcomers on the scene.

EXERCISE AND DIET: FACTS AND FIGURES

The number of people involved in exercise activity has increased substantially over the past several decades. Forty-nine percent of the population in the United States exercise daily, according to a 1987 Gallup poll. Twice as many persons exercise regularly now as did 25 years ago. The numbers continue to rise: in 1988, 8.5 million people ran or jogged frequently; this was a half a million more than had engaged in that form of exercise the year before (American Sports Data Survey, 1989).

Individuals are more likely to be involved in a fitness program if they are young, male, better educated, have a higher income, and are involved in a professional or business occupation. In 1987, some 7 million young and middle-aged individuals spent 5 million dollars on health club membership fees (*Time*, 6/24/88). There are an estimated 17 million sports injuries each year. The increase in athletic activity seems to be a reflection of self dissatisfaction: 61 percent of the population were satisfied with their health in the 1970s but only 55 percent were satisfied with their health in the mid 1980s. (Glassner, 1988).

Dieting is a current cultural phenomenon which, like exercise, focuses on the control of the body. Six-year-old children have already acquired a preference for bodies that are long and lean (Kirkpatrick & Sanders, 1978; Feldman, Feldman & Goodman, 1988) and 37 percent of grade school children have already tried to lose weight (Maloney, McGuire & Daniels, 1988). Fully 78 percent of adolescent girls now wish to weigh less (Eisele, Hertsgaard & Light, 1986) and 70 percent have attempted to lose weight in the past year (Wadden et al., 1989). Three-quarters of the women who attend college are dieting in order to control their weight (Jacobovits et al., 1977). Seventy-six percent of respondents to a survey by a popular women's magazine considered themselves too fat, including the 45 percent of those classified as underweight (Wooley & Wooley, 1985). Dieting has become normative behavior for women in the culture (Polivy & Herman, 1987).

The importance of diet and exercise in contemporary culture can be appreciated by the extent to which these activities are elaborated. Individuals who wish to diet can readily immerse themselves in dietary supplements, calorie counters, magazines, recipes or "fat farms." In 1988, Americans spent 74 billion dollars on diet foods—a third of the nation's food bill (*Time*, 7/25/88). Those who wish to exercise may choose among nautilus machines, stop watches, fitness magazines, and health clubs. In 1987, some 7 million Americans bought 738 million dollars worth of exercise machines for the home, when a decade earlier they had spent only 5 million on such equipment. Individuals who are not somewhat interested in dieting and/or exercise may be at odds with cultural or group expectations.

A DEFINITION OF ACTIVITY

Dieting and exercise are activities—but so are a host of other pursuits. The concept of activity may seem to be "as big as all outdoors," i.e., so broad that it becomes meaningless. To be alive is to be active. However, this book is not concerned with any and all activities; it is concerned with those independent, goal-directed activities that people engage in above and beyond the usual family and work activities—like dieting and running. This definition does not exclude "workaholism," i.e., cognitive activity that is above and beyond the usual work activity but it is more concerned with nonessential endeavors that are pursued in the name of self development or self satisfaction.

INVOLVEMENT OF THE BODY

When individuals wish to control the body, to make it stronger, prettier, fleeter, or fitter, they may become involved in an exercise or diet program. Because these activities are designed to change and control the body, they will be called "body-based activities." Aerobic dance, special diets, and working out are examples of socially condoned, body-based activities. The involvement of the body distinguishes these activities from non-body-based self improvement activities such as painting, woodworking, gardening, building a model car, etc. Body-based activities inevitably focus on what the body takes in, such as food, and what the body can produce, such as running a five-minute mile. The translation is apt to be immediate and direct; improvement can be measured in concrete units such as pounds, inches, time, and distance. Diet and exercise are the most common body-based activities.

AN INTENSE COMMITMENT

When individuals pursue an activity such as diet or exercise, they often have a goal in mind: to fit into a size 10 dress or to become physically fit. When they accomplish the goal, they cast about for some other avenue of self development. A few individuals are different: once they commit themselves to a diet or exercise program they stay committed. They simply reset their goals. One can never be too thin or too fit.

Persons who make an unusually intense commitment to diet or exercise are similar to one another in certain respects (Yates, Leehey, & Shisslak, 1983). They are generally intelligent, high-achieving individuals from well-to-do families. They are self-reliant persons who have a tendency to be dissatisfied with themselves; they inhibit their anger and spend a good deal of time thinking about who they are and where they stand in life. They are concerned about self worth and they have explored various avenues of self development in an attempt to see what fits best. They are hardworking, task oriented, and persistent. In brief, these individuals tend to be successful and well adapted to the demands of life in an industrialized culture.

Any activity can become problematic if it assumes too central a position in the life of the individual. Photography and computer "addiction" are examples of the overuse of non-body-based activities. The eating disorders and compulsive athleticism are examples of the overuse of body-based activities. These persons spend most of their free time either engaged in, or thinking about, diet or exercise. Their emotional investment in the activity becomes more intense and significant than the investment in family or in work.

When runners push themselves to the limit, this can precipitate a variety of muscular, joint, and tendon injuries. Some runners become so caught up in the sport that they continue to run after they injure themselves, even when they are in pain or when they have been told that they risk permanent debility (Little, 1969; Morgan & Costill, 1972; Yates et al., 1983). Running in spite of contraindications such as a cardiac arrhythmia can result in sudden death (Thompson et al., 1979). Coronary heart disease is said to be the major killer of conditioned runners aged 40 years and older who die while running (Waller & Roberts, 1980). The demise of Jim Fixx, the marathoner, is a notable example. A less obvious consequence occurs when runners restrict their intake relative to their output; they may be consuming quite a lot of food but not enough to compensate for the massive expenditure of energy. This may cause them to enter a state of physical deprivation.

Like the extremes of running, the extremes of dieting can be harmful to the body. Bulimic women who vomit can erode the enamel on the teeth, suffer from osteoporosis, parotiditis, edema, electrolyte imbalance, cardiac irregularities, and gastric dilatation (Herzog & Copeland, 1985; Garner, Garfinkel & O'Shaughnessy, 1985), but these complications are rarely lethal. Anorexia is the most malignant form of the eating disorders. Schwartz and Thompson (1981) estimate the mortality rate in anorexia at six percent. Anorexic and bulimic women regularly restrict or manipulate their food intake relative to output and they not uncommonly enter a state of physical deprivation.

When obligatory runners continue to run in spite of clear contraindications, they have lost control over the athletic process (Yates et al., 1983) much as eating disordered women have lost control over the process of dieting. When serious athletes are injured so that they can no longer run, they suffer severe tension, depression, anger, and a sense of bodily deterioration (Chan & Grossman, 1988; Smith et al., 1990). These are "withdrawal" symptoms that are similar to the symptoms that eating disordered women experience when they are prevented from dieting or purging (Pillay & Crisp, 1977).

ORGANIZATION AND INTENT

This book presents clinical case studies of obligatory runners and eating disordered women and attempts to integrate this information with data obtained from sociocultural, psychologic, and biologic research to generate a more comprehensive understanding of these conditions. It relies more upon the research on the eating disorders than upon the investigations of compulsive athleticism, simply because there has been a great deal more accomplished in the field of the eating disorders.

In the next several chapters we will draw a number of parallels between the eating disorders and compulsive athleticism. We will suggest that these conditions have enough features in common so that both could be subsumed under a larger category, the activity disorder. This is not meant to imply that an "activity disorder" is or should be a recognized diagnostic category. There is no activity disorder in the Diagnostic and Statistical Manual of psychiatric diagnoses. The activity disorder is simply a concept that will allow us to explore the overlap between compulsive athleticism and the eating disorders.

The book is divided into three sections. Part I presents sociocultural and historical perspectives, case material from our research on obligatory running, and case material from the eating disorder service. We explore the many points of correspondence between these conditions and the relationship to other forms of compulsive activity. Part II examines current perspectives and research on the eating disorders and compulsive athleticism and how current biological and psychological data would or would not support the concept of an activity disorder. Part III attempts to integrate these and other findings to advance a theory that could explain the etiology, symptomatology, and course of a common entity, the activity disorder. Last, we will suggest a therapeutic approach to these disorders.

CHAPTER 2

Historical and Cultural Perspectives

HISTORICAL

ASCETICISM

The term "asceticism" is derived from a Greek word that means training for the attainment of an ideal or goal (Yates, 1987). The goal may be one of soldiery, athleticism, learning, work, or religion. Asceticism is a denial of the pleasures of the flesh in favor of these laudable activities. As there are only so many pleasures of the flesh (chiefly eating, drinking, sleeping, socializing, resting, making love), asceticism has tended to assume a certain format regardless of the age in which it occurs. Fichter (1987) portrays the association between fasting, extreme exertion, and other forms of deprivation in the life of the contemporary poet Franz Kafka. Kafka, who died at age 40, depicted himself as "the thinnest man I know." He dieted rigorously, lived in an unheated room, and took cold baths even in the winter. Isolated and perfectionistic, he denied himself sexual gratification and did not eat meat, drink alcohol, or smoke. Even when he was in a weakened condition, "with some kind of happiness" he would throw himself into swimming naked, performing gymnastics, making wild jumps up the stairs, and running and hiking long distances. His extreme devotion to writing was very much a part of his ascetic adaptation.

At the very least, the eating disorders and obligatory running can be viewed as ascetic practices. When the pattern involves the denial of many pleasures, the dieting or exercise becomes but one aspect of a broader picture of asceticism.

Across the centuries, asceticism has most often been linked with Christianity. The penance of the monks and the self starvation and flagellation of the nuns in certain religious orders provide us with examples of individuals who adopted an ascetic existence in order to become exceptionally pure in the eyes of the Lord. Although the chronicle of these events is intermittent and somewhat speculative, clearly individuals have starved or overexerted themselves to the point of permanent disability in the past as well as in the present. Unfortunately, many of the accounts are distorted because at the time the ascetic practices were accepted as an indication of virtue or religious ardor.

HOLY ANOREXIA

The quest for slimness by today's upwardly mobile young women had its counterpart in the quest for spiritual purity in medieval times. Habermas (1986) presents the case of Friderada, an especially hardworking serf who lived in A.D. 895. Friderada developed a voracious appetite after she recovered from an unidentified illness. Her hunger caused her to gorge and when she gorged, she suffered from shame and sadness. The illness prompted her master to donate Friderada to a monastery. There her ferocious hunger was gradually translated into a disgust for food. She began to fast, although she continued to eat a little in secret. The fasting persisted for years, but even as Friderada neared death, she continued to work as diligently as possible. Her fierce independence, denial of debility, refusal of aid, piousness, and overactivity are highly suggestive of anorexia.

Bell (1985) describes thirteenth-century women who starved themselves to become more acceptable in God's eye. These women rebelled against rigid societal mores and the patriarchal family by "out-sainting" the pillars of the church. One of these women, Catherine Benincasa, defied church authorities in order to starve herself. She would vomit after ingesting but a mouthful and would induce emesis by inserting stalks of fennel and other plants into her stomach. She slept very little and even when she was close to death she vigorously outwalked her companions, never seeming to tire. Once, while dressing the cancerous breast sores of a patient, she felt repulsed at the horrid odor. She was so intent on denying her physical needs that in an effort to reestablish control, she carefully gathered the pus into a ladle and drank it all.

Catherine's asceticism began at age 16, as she was resisting her parents' plans to marry her off. She foiled her parents by vowing to remain a virgin, walling herself off from the world, flagellating herself thrice daily with an iron chain, wearing a hair shirt, sleeping on a board, and subsisting on bread, vegetables, and water. From that time on, she remained fiercely independent—always ready to care for others, but never willing to accept anything for herself.

Catherine and other holy anorexics proved that they needed no one—that they were completely in charge. Yet, as they continued to starve themselves, their obvious plight caused others to take control of their bodies and to care for them as if they were young children. When Catherine was starving, sleeping on a board, and flagellating herself, her mother became so distraught that she took Catherine back into her bed.

Today's anorectic patients rarely offer religious reasons to rationalize their avoidance of food. Nonetheless, their view of themselves and their diet is as simplistic and fraught with distortions, dichotomous thinking, and overgeneralizations as was the holy anorexics' view of themselves and their regimen. In each instance, the women strive toward an ideal which in their view is the only direct route to total happiness or acceptance. The more restrictively they diet, the more deprived they become; the deprivation serves to enhance the cognitive distortions and the simplistic perception of the self (Neimeyer & Khouzam, 1985; Garner, 1985).

The women who pursued holiness through fasting in the middle ages were similar to today's eating disordered women in their perfectionism, overactivity, fierce autonomy, persistent self dissatisfaction, and high self expectations (Bell, 1985). They fought for complete control of the body and its needs. They renounced the protection and care of the family in order to challenge the male-dominated society of the church. Their many talents and the manner in which they struggled to be independent are suggestive of the "new," well-functioning, eating disordered women of today.

As times change, so do the symptomatologies characteristic of a given disorder. The first case of anorexia in the current medical literature was that described by Richard Morton (1714) in 1694. His patient was a young woman who presented with amenorrhea, starvation, and a devotion to study rather than to exercise. She refused all treatments and eventually starved herself to death. In that day, physical exertion was viewed as unladylike and upper class women were encouraged to study. Now, exercise is viewed as a valuable activity for women and it is common for anorexic women to overexercise (Kron et al., 1978).

ASCETICISM IN THE MONASTERY

From the time of Constantine, ascetic monks abandoned their worldly possessions and fled to monasteries or solitary abodes in deserts or on barren isles. They abjured the use of wine and refused to marry. They chastised the body, mortified their affections, and embraced a life of misery, all for the chance of eternal happiness in the hereafter (Gibbon, 1900). The hermit monks sank under the weight of crosses and chains, and they confined themselves in collars, bracelets, and gauntlets of massive iron. They aspired to reduce their bodies to misery, a state kindred with the animals. They passed many days without food, many nights without sleep, and many years without speaking. In the monastery, the actions, words, and thoughts of the monks were judged by an inflexible rule. A capricious superior assigned penalties of confinement, extraordinary fasts, or bloody flagellation for the slightest offense. He tested the virtue of the monks by commanding them to walk into a fiery furnace. The monks wore the coarsest materials, wrapped their heads in cowls to escape the sight of profane objects, and kept their legs and feet naked except in the coldest winter. They slept on the ground on a hard mat or a rough blanket and were awakened frequently to pray. They found by experience that rigid fasts and an abstemious diet were an effective defense against the impure desires of the flesh. They passed their lives without personal attachments, in a group which had been formed by accident. Even when they sat close to one another at meals, they were silent, enveloped in their cowls, inaccessible, and almost invisible to each other.

Religious ascetics were viewed as exceptionally virtuous persons who were superior to other men. They made a certain connection with God by walking long distances, wearing crowns of thorns, sleeping without blankets, kneeling for hours on bare stone floors to pray, and laboring past the point of exhaustion in the garden and the fields. The monks did this not to lose weight or become physically healthy, but to establish their worth in the eyes of the Deity.

PHYSICAL DEPRIVATION

The state of physical deprivation is a common denominator in the religious asceticism of yesteryear and the extremes of diet and exercise today. The monks intentionally incurred a state of physical deprivation so that they could experience an altered state of consciousness, a vision of holiness. Deprivation brought an exaltation of spirit, a sense of power and of oneness with God. Today's emaciated anorexic women speak of feeling filled with energy and with a sense of power, strength, and control. Gaunt long distance runners describe the "runner's high" as a state in which they feel omnipotent and indestructible (Morgan, 1979). They report sensations of floating above the ground, primitive bliss (Altshul, 1978), of being one with the seashore (Bannister, 1973), of being renewed and revitalized (Sacks, 1979), and of fusion, timelessness, and mystical awe (Sacks, 1981).

Physical deprivation may provide a sense of power, but it also creates hostility and depression. The holy anorexics became more obstinate, more determined to persist, more overly active, more self hurtful, more alone, and more profoundly independent. Gibbon (1900) noted that the rigors of the monks must have "destroyed the sensibility of both mind and body. . . . A cruel, unfeeling temper has distinguished the monks of every age and country: their stern indifference which is seldom mollified by personal friendship, is inflamed by religious hatred; and their merciless zeal has administered the holy office of the Inquisition."

COMMENTS

Asceticism is a central element in the accounts of holy anorexia in the middle ages, in the penance of the monks, and in the self flagellation of certain nuns. At the present time, asceticism has lost the religious flavor but it is asceticism nonetheless. Stein (1982) suggests that "in the 1960s and early 1970s, many believed in salvation through sex. Since the late 1970s, many have come to believe in salvation from sex. Abstinence, a lean diet, and regular, vigorous exercise promise to keep the temptations of the flesh at bay" (p. 167). The new ideal is belt-tightening asceticism, not indulgence.

For centuries, intentional self deprivation was closely linked to religious beliefs. In recent years this has changed; ascetic practices now have to do with appearance, physical fitness, and personal best. Asceticism has become largely divorced from religion. This may be because religion no longer supports self-harm; because religion is a less persuasive influence in the culture; or because values such as health and fitness have eclipsed the more traditional, religious beliefs.

In the past, asceticism involved goals above and beyond the self: to compose a symphony, to serve the Lord, to become a great soldier, etc. Holy anorexics abstained from food in order to serve the Lord, not to improve their appearance. The marathon runners of ancient Greece ran in order to protect the country or to support the reputation of the city, not to become fit or to establish a personal best. It is only in recent times that the goals have come to involve the self rather than an organization or ideal. Athletic and dietary excess in the name of self development is a truly contemporary phenomenon.

PHYSICAL FITNESS

In the United States, we tend to assume that the movement toward physical fitness is a late 20th Century phenomenon. Yet, in the years following 1860, this country witnessed an even more intense athletic crusade, one that linked moral strength to physical vigor. (Green, 1986). This was the movement for "Muscular Christianity" which began in England and spread rapidly to the United States. This crusade espoused the perfection of the body through gymnastics, calisthenics, and competitive sport. Fitness was viewed as a cornerstone of Christian morality.

Muscular Christianity took hold at a time when a large portion of the population had migrated off the farm to the town or city, and many people had settled down in sedentary occupations. With less vigorous physical activity, some individuals began to complain of lethargy, and some were said to be suffering from "neurasthenia." Perfection of the body through athleticism became the prime method by which people could increase their energy and sense of self worth. A great many gymnasiums and athletic fields were constructed. The gymnasium became a central gathering place for the community, much as our health clubs function now. Physical education classes were adopted into the school curriculum and graduation was made contingent upon the acquisition of athletic skill. Women were encouraged to exercise so that they would have a sound nervous system, without any tendency to mental irritability or hysteria, and so that they could produce healthy progeny. The influence of Muscular Christianity persisted well into the 20th Century.

As Muscular Christianity became a guiding force in the increasingly sedentary middle class, physicians began to note an association between anorexia and exercise or "hyperactivity." In the mid to late 19th Century Sir William Gull (1874) in England and Charles Lasegue (1873) in France clearly described the refusal to eat, extreme weight loss, amenorrhea, constipation, and low pulse rate of anorexia. They were singularly impressed with these women's intense commitment to exercise. Gull (1874) wrote, "it seemed hardly possible that a body so wasted could undergo the exercise which seemed so agreeable." Gull assumed that the patients exercised to lose weight and prove that they were not sick. In the first decade of the 20th Century, Janet (1920) was especially intrigued by the heightened activity associated with anorexia. He described a driven "physical and moral activity, a strange feeling of happiness, a euphoria" which abolished fatigue and the need to eat. He viewed the activity and the euphoria as central in the disease process.

In the late 19th Century, Muscular Christianity was supplemented by an emphasis on dietary righteousness (Green, 1986). The rationale behind this had to do with the concept of the body as a machine. The body was viewed as a vehicle that needed to be finely tuned and developed if it were to run efficiently. Exertion, especially in the outdoors, was pre-scribed to build strength and to supplement the body's store of energy. The proper fuel was necessary if the body were to function proficiently and so the prescription soon came to include healthy foods and the avoidance of "bad" foods such as red meat. If they were to function smoothly, "brain workers" would need pure and natural foods so that their nerve centers could be repaired and rebuilt. The breakfast food industry—the health food of its time—was created in 1878. John Harvey Kellogg, a vegetarian and an Adventist, produced "Granula," which later became Granola. Granola was followed by shredded wheat and various forms of wheat flakes. These foods were marketed almost exclusively as remedies to counteract the deleterious effects of living in an industrial-ized civilization.

Exercising properly and eating nutritious food do not necessarily imply asceticism. Like the fitness movement of the late 20th Century, Muscular Christianity was primarily an organizing, energizing force within the culture, one which benefited many individuals. However, a few indi-viduals did use the rationale of Muscular Christianity as a framework for asceticism.

In the 19th Century, people ate the proper foods and exercised to maintain the body in top condition so that they would be better workers, better spouses, and in some cases better Christians. Yet, in spite of the expression of other-directedness, the body clearly had become the center of attention. Perhaps the focus on enhancing the body for the good of the family or community was a forerunner of today's concern with en-hancing the body for self development.

PURGING

When a society is concerned with diet and exercise, it is apt to be concerned about excretion, or the avoidance of constipation, as well. Purging is one method of balancing the input/output equation, of ridding the body of undesirable substances. Bowel function was a prominent concern late in the crusade for Muscular Christianity. At that time, people talked about their bowel habits and many articles were written on the benefits of a regular internal cleansing. People went to great lengths to insure intestinal purity through enemas, laxatives, a customary bowel routine, regular exercise, and the correct diet. Health food ads about the turn of the century took aim at the businessman too exhausted to be effective and the woman who had the potential to be beautiful if it were not for the fatigue caused by "auto-intoxication." Young women were cautioned to attend to their internal bathing so that they would not carry about putrefactive matter in the intestines.

The turn of the 20th Century certainly was not the first time in history in which people tended to focus upon the evacuation of the bowels. Pliny in A.D. 77 related the legend of the ibis, a bird that was thought to have administered enemas to itself and to have originated the practice of self purging. In the 15th Century, enemas were common: an apothecary's sign depicted a buxom young lady with bare buttocks about to receive the solution. Louis XIV of France was said to have had more than 2000 enemas in his lifetime; he sometimes received court visitors during the procedure (Bockus, 1974).

Although people today are concerned with the body and its functions, there seems to be less overt interest in evacuation than there has been at times of heightened body interest in the past. Purging by laxative abuse is chiefly of note in the context of the eating disorders, where 25 percent of bulimic women are said to abuse cathartics (Freeman et al., 1988; Yates & Sambrailo, 1984). Coovert and Powers (1988) report four cases of older, more seriously disturbed bulimics who abuse enemas. These women are uncomfortable with inducing emesis and so they abuse laxatives and administer frequent enemas. Laxative use is not infrequent among today's youth: 3.5 percent of a non-clinical adolescent sample use (and may abuse) laxatives (Lachenmeyer, Muni-Brander & Belford, 1988). Laxative use is distributed in the same pattern as the eating disorders in that twice as many upper socioeconomic strata (SES) adolescents as lower SES adolescents use laxatives. Fifty-five percent of the users reveal an eating disturbance, especially the use of other pills (diuretics, diet pills) to lose weight.

At present, laxative abuse is not identified as a significant problem except in its association with the eating disorders. Yet laxatives are utilized to change and control the body, just as diet and exercise are used. The same forces that prompt a person who diets to become eating disordered and a person who exercises to become compulsively athletic could operate to transform laxative use into laxative abuse.

FEEDING PRACTICES

Parents perceive infant hunger and respond to it in a fashion that reflects the philosophy of the age. In English-speaking nations, infant feeding practices have swung through four separate phases during the last century. Pratt (1984) characterizes these periods as "the harmful effect of too much," "the harmfulness of too little" (the vitamin era), "how it should be done" (strict vs demand feedings, when to start solid foods, wean, etc.), and "the search for perfection" (how to provide an optimal nutritional state).

The current "search for perfection" in infant feeding mirrors the search for perfection and high self expectations of individuals in the upper SES. These parents want the best for their children and they want their children to grow up to do their best also. The striving for a perfect body through diet and/or exercise must be evaluated against current cultural mores and expectations.

HISTORY IN THE MAKING

Interpretations of health and illness have changed radically in the course of history. At present, the culture tends to categorically underwrite exercise as beneficial. The person who runs in spite of pain and exhaustion is idealized as a true athlete by the media. The runner who continues to run on a stress fracture finds little resistance and much encouragement from other runners and the population at large. The same could be said of dieting, but to a lesser extent since the public has become more aware of anorexia. Yet anorexic women are admired by women and they may be seen as more sexually attractive by men (Branch & Eurman, 1980).

The tenor of reform, of making things different and better, pervades the health movement today just as it did the Muscular Christianity movement. Stein (1982) comments that among wellness advocates there is "that same ardor and reformist zeal one finds among rehabilitated drug addicts and alcoholics for whom proselytizing against their erstwhile waywardness is their means of preventing their own backsliding. What one cannot prohibit in others, one can at least feel, and certainly act, self-righteous about." Perhaps salvation has been redefined as getting in shape and being aware of calories.

The United States is viewed by other countries as a nation of the worried well where people are perpetually dissatisfied with how they look and how their bodies function. This dissatisfaction has spawned a billion dollar "health" industry, which caters to well-heeled but self-dissatisfied citizens who search for a special state of being or some concrete talisman of worth.

CULTURAL

A STANDARD OF SLIMNESS

Throughout recorded history, beautiful women were pleasingly plump —corpulent by present-day standards. Artists of the past depicted attractive women as anything but tubular. By today's standards, women were fit but fat in the era of Muscular Christianity. The reason for the association of beauty with corpulence is clear: only the wealthy could afford to be overweight. A moneyed man proved his worth by keeping his spouse (and/or mistress) fat and fruitful. Moneyed men were rotund also: in the Edwardian age, it was said that anyone who could afford it was as stout as His Majesty. The idealization of slimness commenced during the 1920s and spread with Wallis Simpson's well-known dictum that a woman cannot be too rich or too thin (Ristich, personal communication).

In this culture, the ideal shape for women has become slimmer and more "tubular" over the past decades. The weight of Miss America contestants and the women in *Playboy* centerfolds declined significantly from 1959 through 1978 (Schwartz, Thompson & Johnson, 1982). During that same period, there was a significant increase in the number of articles on dieting and weight loss published in women's magazines (Garner, Garfinkel et al., 1980). Some authors suggest that the bias toward slimness fostered the upsurge in the eating disorders. That this could indeed be the case is suggested by a study which indicated that the photographs of women published in popular women's magazines became notably more tubular or uncurvaceous in the mid-1920s, and from the mid-1960s to the present (Silverstein, Peterson & Perdue, 1986). The eating disorders apparently increased during the same intervals.

The association between the idealization of slimness for women and the increase in the eating disorders has prompted the suggestion that the fashion conscious media have caused the increase, i.e., the magazine articles on dieting inspire women to overcontrol their weight. Articles on diet probably do reenforce some women's resolve to diet. However, if women were not interested in diet to begin with, the articles on diet would not exist. A woman who is dissatisfied with her body, who wishes to be more attractive or able to compete with other women, may select a magazine on diet and she may be inspired to diet as she reads the material. Although the media may reinforce the need to diet, they are not the sole reason for the increase in the eating disorders.

SOCIAL STATUS AND BODY SIZE

A woman's weight is important not only in how she evaluates herself but in how she is evaluated by other people. Women who are overweight are viewed by others as weak and unable to take care of themselves (Wooley & Wooley, 1979). A woman's job performance may be judged in part on the basis of her body size. Women in pictures that have been manipulated to increase the bust size are rated as less intelligent and as less competent than when they are shown having smaller busts (Kleinke & Staneski, 1980). Personnel consultants are less likely to appraise women as independent, as potential managers, and as interested in work if their grooming is feminine (Cash & Janda, 1984). Women who value nontraditional roles prefer a thin female form; they associate a more ample female figure with "wife and mother" (Beck, Ward-Hull & McLear, 1976).

In Western culture, thinness in women is equated with a higher educational and vocational status. A review of 144 studies (Sobal & Stunkard, 1989) reveals a strong inverse relationship between socioeconomic status and weight among women in developed societies. Highly educated women are more likely than less educated women to diet and to be slim. Women who stress academic achievement, higher education, and professional careers prefer a less curvaceous body (Beck et al., 1976). Women from lower class backgrounds are six times more likely to be obese than are upper class women (Milkman & Sunderwirth, 1987). Given the association between thinness and social class, it is not surprising that the eating disorders are most commonly found among upper SES women (Szmulker et al., 1986). The association of anorexia and class commences at age 15 and the percent of women who are eating disordered increases with socioeconomic strata (Jones et al., 1980).

Ballet dancers (Hamilton, Brooks-Gunn & Warren, 1985; Garner, Garfinkel et al., 1987), models (Cosinas et al., 1986), gymnasts (Calabrese, 1985; Rosen et al., 1986; Blue, 1987), and perhaps cheerleaders (Lundholm & Littrell, 1986) are more likely than other women to suffer from an eating disorder. These women are successful competitors and they have high achievement expectations for themselves. They are under pressure to be slim, and their bodies are always on display and presumably open to criticism. Because there is a relatively high incidence of eating disorders among women in these occupations, there is a tendency to blame the occupation for the disorder. While it is true that the demands inherent in being a ballet dancer or a model reinforce the importance of appearance, these women are likely to have had high self expectations and to have been concerned about the body before they chose the career. The high self expectations, coupled with the striving toward perfection, are what enabled these women to succeed in a highly competitive field.

EARLY INFLUENCES

The cultural bias toward slimness commences at an early age. Six-year-old children rate pictures of the chubbier endomorphic body more negatively than they do the long and lean ectomorphic body (Kirkpatrick & Sanders, 1978; Feldman et al., 1988). Children view other youngsters who are overweight as weak, as "wanting to be fat," or even as having a masochistic desire for rejection. These anti-fat attitudes fuel the self hatred of those who are, and who are not, overweight (Wooley & Wooley, 1979). Given these attitudes, it is not surprising that children are beginning to diet at an early age. Almost 7 percent of 8–13-year-old children score in the anorexic range on the new child version of the Eating Attitudes Test, a percentage which closely matches that found among adolescents and young adults (Maloney, McGuire & Daniels, 1988). In grades 3–6, 45 percent of the children want to be thinner and 37 percent have already tried to lose weight, mostly by exercise (Maloney et al., 1988). By the time they reach adolescence, a number of these youngsters will resort to serious bingeing, highly restrictive dieting, or purging (Kagan & Squires, 1984).

If grade-school children are already weight, diet, and exercise conscious, they are not deriving that bias from the women's magazines. Peer group influences and television are important, but the most likely source is from within the family itself. Many children have diet-conscious mothers and workout-conscious fathers. Even when this is not the case, most middle class children are already beginning to have high self expectations for independent achievement.

ACCULTURATION AND THE EATING DISORDERS

When a person moves away from a less developed culture into an industrialized setting, the transition, or acculturation process, is stressful. When traditional ways and familiar community supports vanish, the individual becomes more autonomous, whether he likes it or not. In an industrialized nation, the person must not only exist apart but he or she must redefine the self through independent achievement. There are no elders or grandparents to offer counsel.

The eating disorders, which rarely arise in the context of a stable, traditional society, are more likely to occur as women move away and attempt to conform to the expectations of a strange, more complex, society. The pattern of disturbed eating which these women begin to present is indistinguishable from the typical case of an eating disorder as we know it. The emergence of an eating disorder seems to be related to the women's separation from traditional values—which may include comfort with extra weight (Pumariega, 1986). They adopt the biases about body size and acceptability that are characteristic of the new culture: Kenyan women who have moved to Great Britain rate large bodies negatively, a value judgment that is far removed from the native Kenyan's view of an acceptable female figure (Furnham & Alibhai, 1983). In addition, they seem to develop significantly more abnormal attitudes toward food and eating as they push themselves toward independence and achievement in a more developed nation (Pumariega, 1986).

The desire for independent achievement and the need to compete in alien territory seem to increase the likelihood of an eating disorder. Kope and Sack (1987) describe three Southeast Asian girls with eating disorders. These were compulsive, perfectionistic girls from achievement-oriented families who were striving to succeed in a strange setting. The same factors can precipitate an eating disorder in Black and Hispanic girls when they move into a different social or ethnic group. Silber (1986) describes upper SES black adolescents who developed an eating disorder after they were enrolled in highly competitive, exclusive schools in which there was no Black peer group. The girls were striving to achieve in a strange and unreceptive society. We have observed the same issues in Native American patients in our eating disorders clinic. These girls are the children of high-achieving parents who have moved off the reservation. They are struggling to succeed in an Anglo school system where there are very few Native American students.

When a person moves from a less developed to a more developed nation, certain forces seem to foster the emergence of an eating disorder. These are: female gender, the pressure to achieve and to be independent, high self expectations, and the loss of traditional mores and group supports. The same factors could place women who have grown up in this culture at risk for the development of an eating disorder.

FROM COMMUNITY ADVANCEMENT TO SELF DEVELOPMENT

Less developed nations tend to value the group over the individual because the group is important for survival. Adults remain connected within the family, the clan, and the community; they are likely to spend their lives in the same geographic area. In some countries, the roles of community members may be clearly specified even from birth. In India, the little village girl knows what clothes she will wear in the future, what duties she will have, whom she will marry, and where she will be cremated. As her role is clearly defined, she does not need to grapple with the ambiguities of self definition. In addition, she does not need to develop herself apart from the family so that she may achieve (leave home to attend college or to work) as she will remain in close contact with her family and her husband's family for the rest of her life. If she were to attempt to individuate in adolescence—by wearing unconventional clothes or by eating different food than her parents—she would be severely disciplined and her entire family would be disgraced. If she were to continue this behavior, she would be cast out of the community.

In less affluent nations, there is no such thing as self development through diet and exercise. If individuals diet or exercise, they do so for reasons other than appearance or fitness. For instance, the Nandi in Kenya are famous for their distance runners, but these men run for their people; when they return they are not put on a pedestal but are absorbed back into the community. They don't have a great fear of losing because the loss is distributed over the group (Moore, 1990). The men of the Masai run in order to carry messages and to warn of danger rather than to demonstrate their prowess. The eating disorders and compulsive athleticism are the hallmarks of industrialized, affluent societies where independence and achievement are emphasized and where individuals are not narrowly defined by political, social, economic, or family constraints. The eating disorders and compulsive athleticism are found in most English-speaking nations and in West Germany, but rarely in East Germany, in the Soviet Union, or in most of Africa or Asia.

Compulsive athleticism and the eating disorders are found in cultures where there is considerable pressure on individuals to demonstrate a personal best. In industrialized nations, citizens are encouraged to define themselves, to chart a life course, and to move away from the family so that they may achieve to the best of their ability. "What to become" and the best way to become it are issues which are left up to the person to decide. This places an enormous burden on the shoulders of the individual to become "worth something"—a something which is unique and special.

Women who attempt to define themselves as "worth something" in the highly competitive business or professional world present a substantially greater incidence of eating disorders than do those who are less achievement oriented. Fifteen percent of women medical students have a lifetime history of an eating disorder (Herzog et al., 1985) and there is five times the incidence of bulimia among university women than there is among working women (Hart & Ollendick, 1985). Men who face the same issues rarely develop an eating disorder; they may be more likely to develop a condition that is consonant with their gender, such as compulsive athleticism.

Becoming a success usually entails being independent—moving away from home to be educated and to begin a career. The pressure to leave the family and community of origin is especially intense for upper SES individuals and for women who wish to define themselves in a traditionally male arena. These persons tend to expect a great deal from themselves and because their self expectations may be quite unreasonable, they tend to be unhappy with themselves and dissatisfied with their performance.

In developed nations, moving away from home is an event which commonly occurs in adolescence or young adulthood, but there are many other events which demand greater independence in the early years of life. Infants and toddlers often are separated from their parents and placed in day care facilities. These youngsters learn to remain apart from their parents at an early age. They are praised for becoming self sufficient as they learn to dress, toilet, and feed themselves. When they enter school, they are rewarded for developing competencies that are important in the classroom but which may not be recognized or useful in the home. These skills are designed to equip the child to become an autonomous, productive adult. These are a few of the ways in which an industrialized society begins to foster independence at a very early age.

When individuals with high self expectations are dissatisfied with themselves, they have the option of becoming someone special by becoming thinner or able to run faster or farther than others. These are independent achievements, a statement of personal best. They provide measurements of self worth in concrete, easily definable units—by pounds, inches, miles, and minutes. Regardless of how unsuccessful individuals may feel in school or in their chosen occupations, they may taste success, in a tangible form, through a body-based activity.

CHAPTER 3

Obligatory Running

Our paper entitled "Running: An Analog of Anorexia?" was published in the *New England Journal of Medicine* in 1983. The article suggested that extreme athleticism (obligatory running) and the eating disorders are parallel conditions which develop in similarly predisposed individuals. Men are more likely to become compulsively athletic and women are more likely to become eating disordered. We, the authors, were all from the University of Arizona: Alayne Yates, M.D., Chief of Child Psychiatry; Kevin Leehey, a Child Fellow in the same program; and Catherine Shisslak, Chief of the Eating Disorders Service and consultant to the Sports Medicine Clinic. All of us were involved in sports activities—trail running, marathon running, hiking, and swimming.

The project on the eating disorders and extreme athleticism began with Kevin Leehey's astonishment at the achievement of a 45-year-old man who ran down and up the North Rim of the Grand Canyon in two and a half hours. It took Dr. Leehey twice as long to cover the course even though he was in his 20s, ran every day, and had competed successfully in distance races. He began to ask other trail runners about their lives, their training, and their relationships. Eventually he shared this information with his program chief, Dr. Yates. Together, they generated a hypothesis on the similarity between running and anorexia. Shortly thereafter, Leehey and Yates invited Catherine Shisslak, who had just run in the New York Marathon, to join them in setting up a pilot study. Dr. Shisslak had access to the runners in the sports medicine clinic, some of whom had been injured and could no longer run.

The three investigators began to interview men who ran an average of more than 50 miles a week. They contacted runners at races, in the sports medicine clinic, and through other runners. They found that many of these athletes were middle-aged, high-achieving men who were some-what dissatisfied with themselves in spite of their substantial academic and vocational accomplishments in life. The running made them feel better about themselves and it contributed substantially to their emotional balance or adaptation.

The vast majority of the men who were interviewed were healthy, productive individuals who were involved in running as one of a number of activities which contributed to their well-being. A few of the men stood out from the rest and were identified by other runners as different. Instead of the sport contributing to their adaptation, running had become their adaptation. They seemed locked into and controlled by the activity. These men were dubbed the "obligatory" runners.

After the paper was published, a number of runners contacted the authors or wrote letters to the editor of the *New England Journal of Medicine*. Most of the writers stated that they knew another runner who fit the description of the obligatory runner. A few spoke of their own desperate struggle with anorexia or bulimia, and wondered how they might be helped. The following are excerpts from these letters:

"I am an obligatory runner as described in your article, meeting all of the characteristics described and running seventy to eighty miles weekly . . . You may be interested to know that I am also a former anorexic male, which occurred when I was twenty through twenty-two years of age. I am currently thirty-four, and became an obligatory runner about five years ago, following a marital annulment."

A 25-year-old man writes of his initiation to running in high school: "I immediately joined in the 10-mile daily workout and was expected to run no less than 70 miles a week. This was a challenge at first, but very soon I began to relish it. I began to keep a record of my weight and how long it would take me to run 12 miles." After attending college and immersing himself in Buddhism, he continues: "I was so in love with fasting that I went for 31 days drinking only liquids and using an enema. My body was strong and clean and I had so much energy and peace that I soon became very attached to feeling high and at peace. I found that the less I ate, the stronger and more content I became. My unusual life-style and ideology brought me great loneliness and I found that the ritual of eating and vomiting helped to purge my emotions as much as good sex might . . . now I'm so deeply a part of this habit that it's all I do. I have no job, no friends, nothing but the aisles of the supermarket and dream worlds of oral fantasy and nightmare."

A physician runner who disagreed with the article writes about training for a marathon: "You must train 60 to 100+ miles a week with most fast middle-aged people doing 70 to 90. Low body weight is essential and not an irrational quest. Carbohydrates are eaten in very large amounts and enjoyed. The muscle just won't work without them. Fixation on diet is important because it really matters what you eat if you run a 90-mile week. Since running is a constant injury-prone sport, one must train through injury or you just won't be there at the start line of the race. . . . I have raced bicycles, ran 13 competitive marathons until I really tore a knee up twice, did mountain hiking and climbing and now am forced because of the knee into long distance swimming."

A 32-year-old male graduate student writes: "I began running to get back in some kind of decent physical condition. Over the next four years, I gradually increased my mileage, began adding calisthenics and weight training to my regimen, became more nutrition and weight (calorie) conscious, etc. . . . have run the marathon in 2:42 and would like to run under 2:40. . . . Right after finishing my master's thesis, I had my first binge-eating episodes . . . since then this has become a progressively worsening cycle of living at one extreme or another. Binge eating would last 2–6 weeks with corresponding weight gains of 15–50 pounds. In between there would be 3–6 months of fanatical adherence to running and lifting routines. . . . I would work my mileage back up to 80–100 miles a week (I would cease my exercise during the binge periods), ride my bike 75 miles a week, and lift weights 3 times a week for my upper body and twice a week for my legs. I became totally obsessed with looking lean and muscular."

From a university professor: "I've been a runner myself for about 20 years. I've also been a caver, and was much more committed to caving than I've ever been to running. They are obsessive activities, just as is scholarship."

A 23-year-old woman writes: "As we got closer and closer, I started becoming interested in his hobby: body-building. I guess it follows, I began lifting weights and jogging. About that time I found out he was taking steroids. . . . I began taking steroids too. I now take what I know is too many pills. My breasts have gotten smaller and I've started to get hair. I don't like it—I don't seem to be able to quit. What would probably interest you is that I am now obsessed with jogging. Every day—10 miles. It's like someone else is making me do it. At Easter my parents came; each day I made our schedule around my run. My vacation time from work is centered around marathons. At least I'm eating now. Ironically, the most important thing in my life is my intake."

The next step was to commence a larger, in-depth study of both male and female distance runners. Obligatory runners were defined as individuals who will not or who cannot moderate their running in spite of clear contraindications such as a stress fracture or threatened divorce. By this definition, the obligatory runners were comparable to eating disordered women who continue to diet or binge and purge despite clear contraindications.

The new study employed a semistructured interview and a number of standardized instruments designed to assess the personality, mood, and eating attitudes of the runners. The battery included the Minnesota Multiphasic Personality Inventory (MMPI), the Beck Depression Inventory, the Eysenek, and the Eating Attitudes Test (EAT). Over the next several years, we recruited 95 male and female distance runners. Each subject contributed five to eight hours to complete the semistructured interview and standardized tests.

There were some runners whom we would have liked to have included in our study but were unable to interview. We always inquired of our subjects if they knew of any other serious runners who might be interested in participating in the study. They often described individuals who always ran alone, who rarely were involved in clubs or other groups, and who would "never" take time away from their run to be interviewed. They described these runners as aloof, distrustful, and sometimes quite hostile. When we were able to contact these persons, they always refused to participate. Our obligatory group probably does not include the most zealous or "obligatory" runners.

When the interviews and tests were complete, independent raters identified the obligatory subjects: those individuals who had harmed themselves by running on injuries and/or incurred serious personal, vocational, or social difficulties because of their need to run and/or their rigidly restrictive lifestyles. In general, the male and female runners resembled one another. We discovered that the miles run per week did not necessarily distinguish the obligatory from the non-obligatory group although the obligatory group averaged many more miles per week than the non-obligatory group. As we expected, the obligatory runners did not look especially pathological on the standardized measurements. These individuals appeared healthy and they were functioning in the superior range academically and vocationally.

Our study sample could be criticized in several respects. We recruited the runners in whatever way we could: at races, by referral from the Sports Medicine Clinic, through newspaper ads, word of mouth, Roadrunners Club, and from the other runners that we interviewed. Some of the subjects were aware of the original article and they either agreed or disagreed with it. We were unable to pay the subjects for the 5–8 hours it took them to complete the interview and the standardized tests. Because of these difficulties, our sample is not likely to be representative of the population of runners as a whole and we can make no estimate of the percent of runners who would fit the description of obligatory.

THE OBLIGATORY RUNNER

An example of an obligatory runner is a 45-year-old emaciated male who races 210 miles a week—and never misses his run in spite of gale winds, sleet, or lightning. Each evening he consumes an 8000-calorie meal, not because he enjoys it but because he needs a carbohydrate load for the night's exertion. After sleeping a few hours, he awakens to begin his race at 1:30 A.M. He runs through city streets out to a national monument 15 miles away and back again. He always runs on exactly the same course and he reaches each milepost on schedule. He checks his time by the clocks which are visible in the windows of the all-night bars and diners along the way. He has been injured by stumbling on rocks in the dark, hit by a car, struck by a bottle as he was passing a bar fight, and harassed by passing motorists and the police. He completes his run at 4:30 A.M. and goes to work at eight. He avoids parties or relationships because they might interfere with his running. Needless to say, his life revolves about the run. He states, "I never felt better in my life."

Obligatory runners are individuals who know pain. They compromise their bodies by continuing to run when injured. They forfeit jobs, marriages, friends, and other pleasures because of their running regimen. They plan vacations around running and when they are not running they ruminate endlessly about time, distance, food, and the proper shoes. They restrict certain foods and they follow a rigidly structured diet. They work toward a lower percentage of body fat so that they can run faster or farther. They retire early in the evening and may begin running well before dawn. They almost always run alone. There is nothing in their lives that can equal the experience of running.

Although the description of an obligatory runner suggests that such individuals pay a price, the price is well worth it to the runner. These runners explicitly state that they are *not* sick in any way and that they feel great because they are able to run. Clearly they would fight tigers in order to continue. They appear energetic and intent—so passionately engrossed in the sport that other endeavors are insignificant in comparison. They are proud of their physical ability. They no longer need to be concerned about their weight; they can eat anything they want as long as they continue to run. Running gives them a sense of freedom, power, and control over the body.

Runners who are not obligatory share many of the characteristics of the runners who are obligatory. They are generally independent, healthy, high-achieving persons who are goal directed and enthusiastic. They are proud of their performance and relieved that gaining weight is not a problem when they run. They are concerned about diet and weight, although somewhat less so than the obligatory runners. They may have felt dissatisfied with themselves, depressed, or without direction before they commenced running.

The non-obligatory runners differ from the obligatory runners in that they do not build their lives around running; they continue to enjoy many other activities. They are not as rigid in their training or as extreme in their self expectations. They seldom think about running when they are otherwise engaged. They are more sociable and less likely to run alone. When they are sick or hurt, they stop or cut down on their running. Most of the differences between obligatory and non-obligatory are a matter of degree rather than kind.

We did not include in the study runners who were unable to run because of injuries. However, most of our obligatory runners had been forced not to run for a period of weeks or months because of injury and they vividly recalled their emotional state. They described intense anxiety and depression, a feeling that the body was deteriorating, and a sense of fragmentation or bloatedness. If they were unable to resume running, the dysphoria could persist for months or even a year.

CASE EXAMPLES

The case descriptions that follow are taken from the semistructured interviews completed by the male and female obligatory and near-obligatory runners in the study. The first three subjects are men and the second three subjects are women.

DICK

Dick is a 37-year-old physician who runs 70 miles per week, more than 280 miles per month. In the past 10 years he has fractured his toe, pulled his hamstrings several times, and had an operation to repair the cartilage in his knee. He is often in pain from chronic Achilles tendinitis. When he runs, he monitors pace, speed, distance, his heart, lungs, knees, feet, etc., thus turning running into a pseudoscientific experience. Running is not recreation for Dick; it is imperative that he achieve his time and distance goals.

At the time of the interview, Dick had been running for 10 years. He began to run because he felt "fat and flabby" after a masseur had commented that he had the softest body he'd ever massaged. Once he began to run, he steadily increased his goals, and at one time, when his practice was less demanding, he ran 400 miles a month. He prefers to run alone so that he can concentrate. He always runs 15 times around the same .7 mile loop, which is within beeper range of his office.

After his knee operation, Dick could no longer run. This was a catastrophe, as nothing—not even cycling—could replace the feeling of power, control, and well-being he gained from running. He felt mean, fat, and worthless; he even found that he was missing the orthostatic hypotension that came with the dehydrated state after a run.

Dick weighs 153 pounds and stands at 5'9". When he was a senior in medical school, Dick weighed 192 pounds. He crash dieted and lost 40 pounds in 40 days. Now, as long as he runs, he can eat and drink whatever he wants. In spite of this, he follows a vegetarian/fish diet, eating one meal a day (dinner), and occasionally breakfast.

Dick was reared in a traditional family, although both parents were physicians. As a child, his self esteem depended upon what others thought of him. His parents let him know that he could do whatever he wanted as long as he didn't make a mistake. He was most afraid of "messing up." In school, he was an overachiever who absolutely had to get good grades. He was a loner and he toyed with many different activities and roles. He kept his feelings to himself and didn't have much fun.

At present, Dick describes himself as a workaholic who has trouble sitting down and relaxing. He has earned his J.D. as well as his M.D. degree and he has been through a family practice and a surgical residency. Although his practice is flourishing, he wonders if another career might be more to his liking.

Dick has been married three times. He has been in counseling because of depression, anger, and problems with relationships. These difficulties improved once he began to run. As he increased his running, his need for therapy diminished; he felt mellower, and his relationships became more comfortable and more meaningful. He describes his present wife as wonderful; she is also a runner.

Discussion

Dick had always been a hard worker, an independent achiever who was anxious about his performance. These traits contributed to his success in law school and in medicine. Dick is a good runner; running harnesses his restlessness and stabilizes his emotional state. The activity of running is critical in maintaining his adaptation, just as being able to struggle through graduate school had been critical some years earlier. His description of himself as a workaholic suggests that he recognizes a style of intensive, task-oriented or goal-seeking behavior which may be focused in different directions at different times.

Dick initiated his exercise program in response to the comments of the masseur about his body. At the time, Dick was already experiencing low-grade dissatisfaction with himself and the remark simply crystallized and intensified his unrest to the point where he could launch himself into a new activity. The ease with which he could assume a major new direction is mirrored by the many differing career and marriage choices he has made in the past and his fantasy of a new career for the future. Committed runners often provide a history of having assumed a number of roles and made major commitments to different activities during their lives. They pursued the other activities with the same vigor and persistence with which they pursue the running.

Although Dick qualified as an obligatory runner, the raters questioned whether he was truly obligatory because he clearly stated that getting his practice established was as important as his running. It seemed that he could be as much invested in his profession as in athleticism.

CLINT

Clint is a 42-year-old man who is a physical education teacher. He lifts weights and runs 50–60 miles every week; at one time he ran 80 miles a week. He developed plantar fasciitis from overuse of the feet and Achilles tendinitis from overtraining. The most time he has taken off because of injury is three days because "if you don't use it you lose it." He began to run because he had friends who ran and because he wanted to lose weight as he felt "pudgy in the middle." Now Clint runs alone, in part because there are very few people who run as fast or train as hard as he does.

Clint has always been a very optimistic and active person; before he ran he played basketball and rode his bike. Now he gets up well before dawn and he tries to arrange his other activities around the running. He is less sociable now because he dozes off in company and he has sex less frequently as he is very tired when he goes to bed. Sometimes he wonders if he has control of the running or if the running has control of him. On the other hand, he is uncomfortable with his tendency to procrastinate.

After reading *Fit for Life* (Diamond, 1985) Clint changed his diet to correspond with that recommended in the book. He doesn't mix meats and carbohydrates. He eats fruit in the morning and salad at lunch. For protein he eats chicken or turkey almost exclusively. He does not like to overeat because he feels "stuffed." Before he began to run, he weighed 145; at present he weighs 135 and is 5'9" tall. As long as he runs, he does not need to worry about his weight, yet he is trying to reduce his body fat from 10 percent to 7 or 8 percent.

Clint wonders about his career and what he should do with his life. Although he enjoys coaching, he might prefer a vocation such as wildlife management. He defines himself as successful because he is still employed and still married. He is a born again Christian; his two children attend a Christian school.

As a child, Clint was very active; he played every sport, but could have worked more diligently in his classes at school. He describes his early life in generalities. His parents were good people who taught him a good set of values—right from wrong. Although he felt close to his younger brother, each of them "did our own thing."

Discussion

At 135 pounds, Clint is well below the expectable weight for his height and age. He exercises because of a fear of procrastination and he diets so that he will not feel stuffed. He engages in these activities because they provide a sense of control of his body and of his life, but he wonders if the running might be controlling him instead. Clint's homeostasis is delicately balanced between feeling strong and potent and weak or lazy. Each and every day he struggles to maintain a positive sense of self. He does this through running and by denying himself many pleasures such as eating, taking days off, and spending time with friends.

MAX

Max is a 33-year-old divorced man who is a dispatcher for a truck line. He runs 40 miles each week. He has had a number of minor injuries such as stone bruises and a hamstring pull. Once he bruised his kneecap so badly he could not walk; he was told to stay off it for a week. After three days, he was back running. It would take having his leg in a cast for him not to run, but then he would "probably walk it." He is able to separate himself from pain when he runs and he regularly experiences a runner's high in which he enters his own world and seems to float over the earth effortlessly. His greatest fear is that he would be injured so that he could never run again; if this were the case, he would want to kill himself. He runs regardless of the weather or of how he may be feeling, and he always runs alone.

For a number of years, Max was a dedicated swimmer who also ran. When he moved where there was no swimming pool, he began to escalate his mileage and he continued to increase it over the next three years. He would like to run 60 miles a week. Through running, he has become more controlled and he has a greater degree of control over his life. Running compensates for his lack of mastery over his job and relationships. If he is upset, increasing his mileage or pace makes him feel good again. He can push his problems out by running and then he feels cleansed.

Max never eats breakfast and he almost never eats red meat. His two meals and three snacks a day consist of the same foods, day after day. He can easily go without eating, and this is his preferred method of losing weight. Standing at 5'8", he weighs 140 lbs. and would like to weigh 130. He estimates his body fat at 12 percent, but he would like to get it down to 8 percent. He weighs himself three times weekly at his health club; if he's a pound over, he can sweat it off. He may add miles if he eats too much.

Max describes himself as always lonely and shy, friendly but afraid. He is independent and does not ask others for help although he may manipulate them into offering help when he has already decided what he wants to do. Running has made him more intense. Now he takes the initiative more often and he is less accommodating to others. He portrays himself as a social animal who hasn't been able to interact. The friends that he has he doesn't want any more. Lately, coworkers have been critical of Max and he thinks that this may be because the running has made him less social. "They wanted to go eat, I wanted to run—I won the battle."

Although Max would like to be married again, he worries that it might interfere with his running. He has a girlfriend, but he is angry because she questions the value of his running and thinks that he uses it to avoid issues. He has not been faithful, but she is not aware of this. Sometimes he wants to make love, but then he thinks that he has to run. Sometimes he wants to get lovemaking over with so he can have a run. He would really like to find a woman to support him for a year so that he could spend all of his time training.

As a child, Max describes himself as a "cute little bugger." He was delighted by his mother's affection, but angered and saddened by the emotional absence of his father. His father always had the final say. Max was a compliant child who was whipped only once or twice but his parents controlled him through mental strictness or "Jewish guilt." The parents were respectful of one another but not very affectionate. In high school he failed math and chemistry because his mother wanted him to be an accountant and his father wanted him to be a pharmacist. At present he does not enjoy visiting his family, although he feels obliged to do so. He is less religious than his parents would like him to be and he tells them that he cannot attend Friday night services because he is not through running by 8 P.M.

Discussion

Max describes substantial, long-term problems within himself and in interpersonal relationships. He often feels angry. Running is an obstacle to building or maintaining relationships and it sets him apart from other people. On the other hand, running provides him with a workable adaptation and it enables him to fashion his life more as he would like it.

Of the male runners described above, Clint demonstrates firm religious convictions. A few of the obligatory runners—men and women—are devoutly religious; indeed, they are devout runners also. An interrelationship between athleticism and religion is illustrated by the following case history.

MARILYN

Marilyn is a 44-year-old woman who spent five years in a convent as a young adult. She has been married for 17 years and has three children. She has been running for two years. She runs six miles per day, starting at 4:30 A.M.. She keeps a log which carefully records her time and the distance run. She often feels guilty about the time she takes for running, but she never forfeits a day of running because she is afraid that she might lose a week and then quit. It would take a "car accident which would put me in the hospital" for her not to run. She prefers to run alone and to meditate as she runs.

Marilyn runs in order not to get fat, to maintain her self discipline, and to avoid becoming depressed again. Twenty years ago she was hospitalized for a depression. She was in therapy and taking medication intermittently before she became a serious runner; now she is not depressed as long as she runs. She is obsessed with not becoming fat. If she does not maintain tight control, she is afraid she would weigh 200 pounds. She is 5′4″ and weighs 116. She would like to weigh 110. Once she did diet down to 110, and then she decided that 108 would be ideal. After reaching 108, she wanted to diet further but became afraid that she couldn't stop dieting. Now she follows a stringent diet in addition to running. She always eats four ounces of chicken for dinner. She loves sugar but cannot eat dessert because she will lose control and be unable to stop. She has used laxatives and diuretics to lose weight, but states that she has never abused them. She is concerned about the lines in her face and about growing old, but she likes it when she is told that she is doing well for a woman her age.

There have been times in Marilyn's life when she has been quite isolated, but she thinks that the running enables her to be more sociable. She feels close to her husband, who also runs, but feels guilty because she may be less interested in making love when she is tired from running. The relationship was strained when she became increasingly compulsive about running more miles in a shorter time. If she were forced to choose between sex and running, she would give up sex because it doesn't offer her that much satisfaction.

Marilyn was reared in a strongly religious, Catholic home as one of nine children. Her father was the decision maker and was very strict. He often criticized the children and he ordered her mother about. Her mother acted as a buffer between the children and their father. Marilyn felt close to her mother, who was able to give all the children much love and acceptance. When Marilyn became an adolescent, she was proud of her excellent coordination and of the fact that she could outrun the boys. However, she was shy and embarrassed about the fact that she was chubby.

Marilyn has always been a devout Catholic. When she began to run, she became more compulsive about her religion as well as about running. Now she attends mass daily, prays with her family, and spends an hour or so reading the scriptures. She is afraid that if she stops she may quit altogether.

Discussion

Marilyn began to run at a period in her life when her children were older and presumably she could have had more time to relax and to meditate. Instead she took up running and she meditated as she ran. She increased her religious activity at the same time. An increase in several activities at a time when there was less need to be busy would suggest that Marilyn was uncomfortable with inactivity.

In spite of the fact that Marilyn does not need to diet when she runs, she tightly restricts her intake because she is terrified that she might lose control of her voracious appetite. Although Marilyn would not qualify for an eating disorder diagnosis, her struggle against the desire to eat suggests that she has the potential to develop an eating disorder.

At one time, Marilyn reinforced her self discipline by joining a religious order; presently she maintains it by diet and exercise. It is through diet and exercise that she alleviates her depression. Yet her balance appears quite fragile: Marilyn is afraid that she will stop and afraid that she can't stop. She must relentlessly drive herself toward her goals, or she may fail completely. Marilyn is locked into running, and she gives a history of having been locked into dieting.

The female obligatory runners in the study closely resembled the male obligatory runners. However, more of the women runners had a history of having suffered from an eating disorder and the women who did were somewhat more likely than the male runners to score in the pathological range on the psychometric indices. There was one unexpected difference between the sexes: all the women who ran and who scored in the pathological range on the EAT were obligatory runners. We were unable to find women runners who exhibited disturbed attitudes about eating who were not obligatory runners. It seemed that if the women were intense and compulsive about dieting they were intense and compulsive about running. The following case is that of a bulimic runner.

LENORE

Lenore is a 20-year-old, single woman who teaches aerobics. She began to run this past year after she started dating a man who ran. She wanted her body to look like his. She runs 25–30 miles a week, usually by herself. When she is depressed, she prefers to run alone. At one point, she began to measure her running time and increase her distance; she found that she couldn't let herself stop. She "felt lousy but kept pushing myself." She wished that she might break a bone so that she wouldn't drive herself so hard. At present, she continues to run and to be ambivalent about her running; like eating, it is a way to avoid feelings and provides a sense of control. She used to block out problems by eating and now she does so through running. Eventually, she would like to run just for enjoyment.

Lenore has been in treatment for about a year for anorexia, which may have helped her to make the connection between running and eating activities. Her eating disorder has improved considerably; now she follows a 1200-calorie diet and weighs slightly more than 100 pounds (height 5'2"). The eating disorder began at age 16 when she desperately wanted to lose weight; she began to binge and vomit at least five times a week. The following year she resorted to chewing the food and spitting it out. When she was finally hospitalized, she was eating only one apple a day and some lettuce. Eating is still problematic for Lenore. She ruminates about food and calories, and worries about gaining weight.

Lenore describes her family as having been caring and concerned. Her parents were quite religious and Lenore continues to attend church and to have a strong faith in God. She describes her father as perfectionistic and a workaholic. He had high expectations for his children and was a strict disciplinarian. As a child, Lenore felt as if she couldn't function without her mother, who was "always there." She was helpful, a child who tried to please others. She was an A student who blamed herself for any problem and who worried about what others might think. She watched a great deal of television and would "eat for fun." Now she does not watch television at all, and eating is a source of conflict.

Lenore views her ability to run and to diet as independent achievements, just as were her good grades in school and her success on the job. She is proud of her ability, but well aware of the fact that once she starts in an activity she may not be able to stop.

Discussion

Lenore's achievement orientation, need to please others, obsessive traits and ambivalence about food are often found in eating disordered women. She clearly identifies dieting and athleticism, the control of intake and the control of output, as sister mechanisms which she can use to block out problems. She knows that she can control her body through these activities, but also that she can be controlled by the activities.

Lenore's eating disorder improved when she began to run and it improved when she commenced therapy. Some of the women runners seemed to be able to extricate themselves from a rigid diet after they began to run, apparently because the exercise kept them from gaining weight so that they no longer needed to worry about their diet.

Lenore's account demonstrates the use of dieting and athleticism as equivalent mechanisms to maintain a metabolic and emotional homeostasis. Running also can be employed in the same manner as purging: to rid the body of unwanted calories, as the following case will illustrate.

PATTY

Patty is a 31-year-old married woman who describes herself as "a serious runner who does not know enough to quit." She runs more than 200 miles a month and also bicycles 200–250 miles a week. She has sustained two serious stress fractures. Before her tibula broke, she had been in pain for months but continued to run. She carefully measures time and distance and resets her goals so that they are greater than her current performance.

Patty became a serious runner in part because the faster she became, the more weight she lost. She is 5'7" and once weighed 150 lbs, at which time she felt "gross." Now she weighs 115 and would like to get down to 110. She runs at least eight miles every day in order to balance out the food she ate the day before. If she overeats, she runs extra miles to get it off. She may use laxatives or give herself an enema before a race. Until six months ago, she was inducing emesis at least once a week because she was afraid of gaining weight, but now she uses only exercise and feels in total control of her body.

Members of Patty's family did not touch one another or express their affection. Both parents worked outside the home and were not very sociable. Patty was closest to her mother, who "told me what I could or could not do." She described herself as a child as lazy and immature. She would meet someone and want to be just like them, so she would play that role. Then she would meet someone else. . . . In adolescence, she smoked marijuana, drank, smoked cigarettes, partied, and didn't really have any goals. With running, Patty became motivated, "more of a type A personality," and harder on herself.

Now Patty wishes to become a sports massage therapist and an Olympic bike racer. She is deeply religious, reads the scriptures daily, and tries to live by the Bible. Her husband is just as religious and he also runs, covering 50 miles a week. Patty seldom menstruates and they do not have children. Running is more gratifying and more important than sex for both of them. Sex is "no big thing in our lives."

Discussion

Patty's history illustrates the use of athleticism to organize, motivate, and redirect. In adolescence, she had little sense of who she was or where she wanted to go in life. She did many things, such as using drugs and alcohol, that made her feel even worse about herself. In early adulthood, she began to diet and to vomit, then began to run. Through running, she met her husband; he reinforced her religion and her athleticism. Eventually, she was able to replace "caloric output by vomiting" with "caloric output by athleticism." Now she has a positive sense of self and concrete goals for the future.

GENERAL COMMENTS

Although a few of the obligatory runners do demonstrate psychopathology, most of them are healthy, well-functioning individuals. If anything, they seem to be even more active, independent, and high achieving than the non-obligatory runners. In some instances, the problems that do exist seem to have emerged after they began to run.

When obligatory runners begin to run, they are more intense and they pursue the sport more persistently than do non-obligatory runners. Their lives and their thoughts begin to revolve about running. They are delighted with their increase in stamina, leanness, and muscularity; the running becomes self reinforcing. They begin to avoid social engagements which could interfere with the sport.

One of the questions asked of the runners in our semistructured interview is "What would you do if you were unable to run?" Responses ranged from "I'd kill myself" or "I'd run on crutches" to "I'd rejoice." Non-obligatory runners would search for a reasonable substitute so that they could keep in shape. Bicycling or swimming might suffice. Obligatory runners insisted that there could be no substitute for running.

When obligatory runners are committed to running, they seem always to be poised in flight toward an elusive target. Although they set specific goals such as running five miles, they never seem satisfied with their progress. They increase their self expectations so that success is always just beyond their reach. Step-wise goal setting is one of a number of strategies which they use to keep themselves on course. One runner described this as a means of maintaining himself at "maximum thrust" so that he would not "get lazy." If he kept success a hairbreadth away, he could sustain his motivation to run.

Obligatory runners are as concerned about weight and body fat as they are about time and distance. They run long distances and they rigidly restrict their diet. They calculate their caloric expenditure and they monitor their body fat. They want to be thin because lean athletes make better runners—but they don't know how to stop. They inflate their percentage of body fat goals in the same systematic manner as they do their time and distance goals. They continue to restrict their diet even when they are already painfully gaunt.

Other than their penchant to run when injured, on ice, and when the spouse is threatening divorce, obligatory runners may best be distinguished from other runners by the fact that running is the central focus of their lives. Running has become a deadly serious endeavor; they cannot afford not to run. The sport has become a jealous mistress. Because of this, they appear overly serious, rigid in their adherence to schedule, and constricted in their interests.

Obligatory runners continue to run in part because they derive substantial benefit from the sport. This is the case even when the running is painful and driven. They are soothed and invigorated when they run; they feel proud of the body and in command of their future. Max describes the runner's high as enormously satisfying, a sensation of floating through space. Dick describes running as providing a sense of power, control, and well-being. His body seems alive with grace and vigor.

The pleasurable sensations of running are no match for the misery of a stress fracture or an Achilles tendinitis. Yet athletes on crutches continue to extol the virtues of running. Runners like Max and Clint, who have been injured but continue to run, seem to celebrate the sport more loudly and longer than anyone else. Perhaps they must rationalize the activity while they bolster the resolve to carry on. Why would they be willing to endure pain if running were not a consummate experience?

A few obligatory runners report an improvement in their relationships after they began to run. They relate this to an overall increase in their well-being and self esteem. The body looks better, they feel better, and they have the opportunity to make contact with other runners. They can build a fresh alliance around a mutual interest, running. If they make a match, the perception of the partner may be fused with the idealization of running. "I never felt better in my life" is extended to "This is the best relationship of my life."

Most obligatory runners seem rather disinterested in maintaining close relationships. The extent of their commitment to the sport seems to preclude any other investment: they choose to run rather than to be with others. Perhaps the running restricts their field of interest or perhaps the relationships were problematic before they began to run. Perhaps they are more comfortable when they are engaged in a solitary activity. In any case, their stake in the activity seems somehow related to the scant gratification that they derive from relationships.

Obligatory runners prefer to run alone. In part, this is because no one else runs as fast or as far as they do. Few persons would choose to maintain as spartan a schedule or be willing to train as relentlessly. Yet, like Marilyn who meditates as she runs, obligatory runners prefer to be alone. If they happen to run with another, they may run silently. When they are by themselves, they think special thoughts, make unique calculations and comparisons, and immerse themselves in the sensations of body and mind. Solitary activity provides them with the chance to reflect, to problem solve, to savor the run, to visualize themselves in action, and to regroup for the challenge ahead. Running alone is one method of resolving the resentments which stem from being misunderstood by the boss or being taken advantage of by the spouse or children.

Obligatory runners wish to be alone so that they can concentrate on their performance; if they "psych" themselves up, they may make their time or distance mark. The autonomy extends to their performance at school and on the job. If they work independently, they will be neither distracted nor corrupted. They seem to be saying, "If you want something done right, do it yourself." They strive for perfection and they become irritated at persons who are less committed, less perfectionistic, or more fallible than they are. Because of this, obligatory runners seem to be more independent, more alone, and more comfortable in being alone than are most other persons.

GENDER DIFFERENCES IN APPETITE DESCRIPTION

Male and female runners are concerned about diet and weight; they are relieved that the exercise stabilizes their weight. Yet they express these concerns differently: the men speak about acute, immediate, hunger, the "I could eat a horse!" response, but they seldom speak of the nagging insistence of appetite. They talk about hunger, but not about appetite. This may be because the men view wanting to eat (when there is not a physiologic basis) as frivolous, as a sign of weakness, or as a feminine trait. This may be because they associate the desire to eat with dependency and loss of control. Men (more than women) need to see themselves as independent, in control, and able to take care of themselves.

Male runners seldom say that they are dieting in order to lose weight even when they are closely monitoring their intake and are distressed about their percentage of body fat and their girth. Instead, they speak of diet and exercise as a means to become fit. One way to become fit is to lose weight. Yet they justify their diet in a manner which does not invoke the "feminine" concepts of appearance, appetite, and weight control.

ANOREXIC AND BULIMIC FORMATS

Obligatory runners use running to control their weight. They employ running in place of dieting, to make dieting more effective, and as an antidote to eating. When emaciated runners progressively increase their running and their dieting so that they can diminish, even further, their percentage of body fat, they could be said to be following an anorexic format. When they counter the amount of food they consume by boosting the distance they run so that they will not gain weight, they could be said to be following a bulimic format. In both formats, the need for absolute control of the body is similar to that found in the eating disorders. The next chapter will address the relationship between compulsive athleticism and the eating disorders.

CHAPTER 4

Obligatory Running
and the Eating Disorders

In this chapter, we will present the histories of four well-functioning, eating disordered women. We will identify a number of similarities between these women and obligatory runners. Then we will suggest a more comprehensive entity, the activity disorder. Finally, we will discuss some clinical and theoretical considerations.

CASE EXAMPLES

BETSY

Betsy was the youngest of three children. She was born to a mother who taught history part-time at a prestigious college and a father who was a busy physician. The family lived in Boston. The first-born child, Pamela, arrived 10 years before the next child, a boy named Brad, followed by Betsy four years later. All the children attended private schools, and Pamela consistently achieved honor grades. Brad was a disappointment to his parents because, although he was bright, he never did well in school.

Betsy's mother enjoyed having children, and she especially liked "fussing over" little girls. In contrast to her older brother, Betsy was never a behavior problem. Brad would hit Betsy and Betsy would run to her mother, crying loudly in protest. The mother always found some activity to distract and quiet her. Betsy had many interests which her mother fostered, including art, crafts, cooking, swimming, taking care of animals, and reading. When Betsy's mother would depart for her teaching job, she would leave Betsy with plenty of activities so that she wouldn't be lonely. Betsy performed well in school, in spite of the fact that she would forget to bring her pencils and papers. She seemed like a happy child who continued to need her mother to structure her day and keep her organized.

When Betsy was 12 years of age, her mother began an extramarital affair with an English professor in the college where she taught. Betsy's parents separated and reconciled. When her mother was away, Betsy seemed lost; she ate a lot and gained considerable weight. Her father encouraged her to take on some household responsibilities and during the next several years she seemed able to adapt. Brad began to drink and to abuse drugs and he eventually dropped out of school. He began working for a landscape company and eventually became the manager.

When Betsy was 14 years old, her parents divorced, her mother moved to Great Britain, and she was placed in a boarding school near Boston. She did not see her mother although they corresponded. She stayed with her father on school holidays and continued to progress academically. Eventually, she was accepted at the University of Minnesota. She moved to Minneapolis, made a few friends, and began to date another student.

When Betsy was a college junior, her father suggested that she think seriously about her future and a career. Betsy visited her mother for the first time since the divorce. She had hoped that an interesting job might be available in Great Britain, but she was disappointed. Her mother offered her little support. When she returned to school, she still didn't know what she wanted to become. She took a part-time job in merchandising and began to jog every morning, rain or shine. She studied even more diligently and earned straight A grades for the first time. In the six months prior to her graduation, she embarked on a diet along with several of her friends. She was delighted that she was finally able to lose weight. She began to weigh herself daily and to carefully monitor calories.

Shortly after her graduation, Betsy assumed a position as an apprentice buyer in a large department store. She followed a demanding schedule, worked diligently, and soon was promoted to an assistant buyer. She continued to diet; it seemed easier now because she was busier. She subsisted on carrots, canned vegetable soup, and an occasional business lunch. At first she was proud that she was shaped more like the models with whom she had contact, but as she continued to lose weight, she began to hide her gaunt appearance in baggy clothes. She continued to run 15 miles a week regardless of weather conditions.

After several years had passed, Betsy ended her first long-term, sexual relationship with a married man at the store where she worked. She began to binge, put on several pounds, and became terrified that she would continue to gain weight. She taught herself to vomit and soon was spending most of her free time bingeing and vomiting. In spite of this, Betsy continued to do extraordinarily well on the job. She took on extra duties and often worked during the weekend. She became the youngest buyer ever in her department store and then moved on to a better position in one of the most prominent firms in the city.

When Betsy was 28 years of age, she nearly committed suicide because of her inability to extricate herself from the bingeing and purging. She continued to enjoy her work, but had no close relationships and little time to develop them. She entered long-term psychotherapy.

Discussion

Betsy is fairly typical of the "new" eating disordered women in that she functions well in a demanding position. She is able to live alone (although many of these women are married) and her progress in life is marked by her resourcefulness and responsibility. Her day revolves about her work and the binge/purge activity. She has no intimate relationships and she spends most of her free time alone.

When Betsy was small, her mother had been the center of her life. Staying apart at the time of her parents divorce was difficult for Betsy. When she was at boarding school, it seemed as if she was still waiting for her mother to return to comfort her and keep her organized. In college she demonstrated a strong drive toward independence and achievement and because of this she eventually managed to establish herself in a highly competitive field.

Of note is Betsy's style of heightened activity. This pattern became apparent in adolescence when she was separated from her mother. She involved herself in many different activities and was uncomfortable when she had nothing to do. As an adult, she selected a demanding job which required long hours of work if she were to be successful. She found many other things to do after work; eventually she filled her spare time with binge eating and vomiting.

Betsy's many activities began "at her mother's knee," so to speak. Her mother provided the materials, encouraged Betsy's explorations, and rewarded her for her accomplishments. Later on, Betsy continued to be involved in activities and to draw comfort from them. The skills which she had acquired as a child contributed to her achievements later on.

JAN

Jan is a 28-year-old graduate student in English Literature. She writes stories and hopes to become a college professor. She developed anorexia five years ago when she was employed as a grade-school teacher. She is 5′10″ tall and weighs 115 pounds. One year ago she collapsed while lifting weights at a health club. She tells her therapist that she is terrified of becoming fat. She weighs herself daily, counts calories, and allows herself to fluctuate a half pound of "water weight."

Jan describes her early life as an only child as pleasant. Her mother is a nurse practitioner and her father a certified public accountant. Both parents worked when she was small, but one or the other was always available to stay home with her if she was sick. When she was old enough to attend school, they saw to it that she had piano and dance lessons and could attend a children's drama camp. She was an avid reader and well liked by peers, but a "klutz" in competitive sports. She progressed well in school and, with her parent's encouragement, applied to several Ivy League colleges. When she was accepted by one of them, she was pleased and excited.

In college, Jan had looked forward to becoming a school teacher. She enjoyed children and expected that teaching would bring its own rewards. Unfortunately, her first job after graduation was in an inner city school where the teachers were demoralized and there was little support from the parents or the administration. It was all she could do just to keep order in the classroom. This was when she began to diet.

Discussion

Jan, like Betsy, developed an eating disorder after a crisis of self worth at a time when she was attempting to live apart and achieve in a challenging environment. Neither Jan nor Betsy provided a history of childhood trauma, difficulty in separation, or enmeshment in the family. The parents were high-achieving persons with many independent interests; they were not described as rigid or overcontrolling.

PAT

Pat is 20 years old and a junior at a state university. She does not know what she wants to become, but she does want to contribute something to society. She is the youngest of two girls; her mother is a nurse who is a consultant on breast feeding. Pat has no memory of her father, who died when she was two years of age. She is close to her mother and her sister.

Pat describes herself as the only person in the family for several generations who is not blue eyed, blonde, and petite. Pat was chubby as a teenager; now she is of average weight but feels fat. While Pat's sister graduated with honors from a prestigious university, Pat's grades have always been "only" somewhat above average. She remembers no great difficulties when she was growing up, although her mother always worked and sometimes took courses as well. She remembers her early life as happy.

Pat's bulimia began when she was a junior in high school. She was trying to become a cheerleader and she believed that she was overweight. She watched a Jane Fonda tape in which Fonda described her bulimia as "having her cake and eating it too." Pat soon taught herself to purge. This pattern continued until her sophomore year in college when one of her friends became aware of her habit.

At the present time, Pat is in therapy and only occasionally vomits. She attributes some of her improvement to living in a sorority house where there are so many things happening that she has less time to think about eating. She continues her efforts to diet, and she runs every day.

NICOLE

Nicole was raised as the middle child of three children in an affluent, strongly Catholic, traditional family. Both parents had earned graduate degrees. Nicole's mother was a homemaker until Nicole was a teenager. Nicole described herself as a generally happy, industrious youngster. She began to take on baby-sitting jobs when she was 10 and by the time she graduated from high school she was employed full-time at a bakery.

Although Nicole had dieted intermittently for years, she did not develop an eating disorder until she had graduated from college, taught school for three years, married, and was pregnant with her first child. Her husband was a lawyer who was struggling to establish his career. He needed Nicole's emotional support. Nicole's bulimia began during pregnancy when her appetite increased and she experienced morning sickness. At the time, she was wondering how she would be able to care for a baby, continue to teach, do the housework, and minister to her husband. The bulimia continued over the next 10 years and worsened with each of her four pregnancies. She invariably binged and purged when she was "stuck at home" alone, minding the children.

The eating disordered women just presented are from high-achieving, upper SES families. They appear to have been well cared for as children and their lives were reasonably stable. They were close to, and dependent on, their mothers but they developed a strong drive toward independence. They were talented and achieved well; they were involved in many activities outside the home. In each instance, the eating disorder began at the time of a crisis of self worth, in a situation which demanded greater independence and achievement. Even after they developed an eating disorder, they continued to do well in life. These young women are fairly representative of the "new," well-functioning, eating disordered women.

OVERLAP BETWEEN DIET AND EXERCISE

Diet and exercise are interrelated methods of managing the body; therefore, it is not surprising that obligatory runners are concerned about weight and that eating disordered women are likely to exercise. Becoming fit usually means losing weight. Exercise helps a person to diet, speeds the burning of calories, and trims the contours of the body. It diminishes hunger and can remove the person from the source of food. Lean runners are better runners. Athletes watch what they eat and strive for a lower percentage of body fat. Obligatory runners are as concerned about their weight as some eating disordered patients. They often begin to run because they dislike their size and weight. Dick once crash dieted and lost 40 pounds. Now, as long as he runs, he can eat whatever he wishes— but he still consumes only one meal a day. Clint began to run because he was getting pudgy in the middle, and he continues to run because running stabilizes his weight; Max adds miles if he eats too much; Marilyn runs in order not to get fat; Patty runs strenuously because the faster she has run, the more weight she has lost. If these athletes are not running to lose weight, they are running in order not to gain weight.

In some sports, such as gymnastics and running, athletes are encouraged to lose weight to improve their performance. Some athletes try to take off more weight so that they can become even better at their sport. For women, a serious commitment to any sport may increase the risk of developing an eating disorder. The Austin, Texas *American-Statesman* (8/10/89) reports that one out of 10 female athletes are diagnosed as having a serious eating disorder. Another 20–30 percent have abnormal eating behaviors, but not the full-fledged disorder. Two of the women with eating disorders surveyed were former Olympic swim team members.

Most women know that exercise facilitates weight loss, and many women feel more energetic as they lose weight and begin to exercise. When eating disordered women begin to lose weight, they become energized, enthusiastic, and less anxious and introverted than before they began to diet (Bruch, 1975; Crisp, 1977; Stonehill & Crisp, 1977). During the acute weight loss phase, they feel compelled to be active and they prefer to engage in solitary endeavors. Then the activities become more intense and driven, more diffuse and unsettled than before (Kron et al., 1978).

Excessive activity has been reported in 38–75 percent of anorexia nervosa patients (Ching, 1963; Kron et al., 1978, Crisp, Hsu et al., 1980). When Beumont, Booth et al. (1983) assessed the order of occurrence of symptoms in 25 anorexics, they found that changes in diet are followed by increased sports activity and a preference for exercising alone. However, Kron et al. (1978) found that the increase in activity is independent of the weight loss and they suggest that physical activity may be a primary feature of the disorder. In anorexia, the increase in activity most often antedates the dieting or loss of weight and it often persists even after weight recovery. It may take a number of months before the diet and activity levels normalize after the eating disorder responds to treatment (Kaye, Gwirtsman et al., 1986).

The activities which eating disordered women choose are usually goal directed, organized, and planned in advance (Kron et al., 1978). They prefer individual rather than team sports, dance (especially ballet), gymnastics or exercise routines, and jogging. They also take on multiple chores and numerous extracurricular activities. Even when these activities occur in a social context, they are always tightly scheduled and rigidly executed.

From the material presented it would seem that diet and exercise are sister activities; they are methods of controlling the body. A serious investment in one activity is likely to be accompanied by a preoccupation with the other.

OBLIGATORY RUNNERS AND OBLIGATORY DIETERS

Well-functioning, eating disordered women and obligatory runners share a number of features. They choose running and dieting in part because they are solitary trajectories. Eating disordered women keep their own counsel; the dieting or binge/purge cycle is a personal, private matter. Obligatory runners run wherever they may be, for as long as they wish. They don't need to wait for anyone; they prefer to run alone. They see themselves as free spirits in pursuit of a personal best.

Before eating disordered women begin to diet and before obligatory runners begin to run, they describe a prodromal state of dissatisfaction with the self or the body. They may be displeased with their progress in life or they suffer a blow to their self concept such as not being accepted in graduate school. They may face a personal challenge such as having a baby, retiring, or becoming a single person again. In some instances, they become dissatisfied at a time of relative ease, when there are fewer demands on their time. They decide to run to organize themselves, to set a new direction, and to feel better about themselves.

When obligatory runners and eating disordered women become involved in a diet or exercise program, they gain a concrete, clearly defined goal. They no longer feel as aimless or self dissatisfied. Through dieting and/or exercise, they enjoy a sense of comfort, efficacy, and an organization of thought and daily living. They gain emotional stability through running and dieting. When obligatory runners are upset, they "run it off"; they also run when they are anxious or excited. These benefits may or may not persist. As they become more and more wrapped up in the pursuit, they appear less pleasurably involved and more as if they are compelled to continue. They become "locked in" to the activity to the point where they seem unable to stop; this may lead to physical damage. Betsy felt so controlled by the bulimia that she considered suicide; Jan dieted to the point of collapse. Clint wondered if he had control of the running or if the running had control of him. Lenore couldn't stop running; she hoped she would break a bone so she could quit.

Obligatory dieters are uncomfortable with free time and they usually manage not to have any. When they are unoccupied, they must confront their voracious appetite. They may binge and purge or become caught up in ruminations about diet or exercise. Betsy was typical in that she binged in the evening when she was not engaged in structured activities. Pat does better in a sorority house where there are many activities, and Nicole's disorder is most troublesome when she stays at home minding the children.

Obligatory runners are as uncomfortable with leisure time as are eating disordered women. The runners quickly transform days tagged for rest and relaxation into days of small projects and exercise. If they are forced to sit still and do nothing, they feel diffusely uncomfortable, restless, bored, or hungry. When Lenore was younger, she had watched a great deal of television and had enjoyed eating and relaxing. Now she runs instead of relaxing. Watching television and eating have become problematic rather than pleasurable. Clint, who feared procrastination, and Max, who preferred running over making love, seem to be expressing the same theme. When asked about why they do not rest, they speak about the virtues of being active.

Eating disordered women who are prevented from dieting and compulsive athletes who are prevented from running suffer the same sort of "withdrawal" symptoms. When runners are injured and can no longer run, they describe severe anxiety, depression, confusion, psychic fragmentation, and a feeling of bloatedness (Morgan, 1979; Sachs & Pargman, 1979; Paxton, 1982; Chan & Grossman, 1988; Smith et al., 1990). When eating disordered women are prevented from dieting or from bingeing and purging, they panic, seem to fragment, and become acutely depressed and sometimes suicidal (Pillay & Crisp, 1977).

COGNITIVE STRATEGIES

Eating disordered women and obligatory runners employ many of the same cognitive strategies. They select short-term, readily attainable goals that will maximize their striving. When they achieve or almost achieve the goal, they choose a somewhat more difficult target. Then they continue the step-by-step escalation. Anorexic women employ this system using weight, dress size, or calorie count. When Betsy begins to diet, her aim is to lose 10 pounds. As she loses the weight successfully, she feels proud of her ability. By the time she approaches her goal, she no longer wishes to relinquish the satisfaction that the activity provides. She readjusts her goal to 15 pounds, saying to herself that she should be capable of doing even better.

Like eating disordered women, obligatory runners adjust their goals and they systematically increase their self expectations. Clint is trying to reduce his body fat from 10 percent to 7 or 8 percent; Max runs 40 miles a week but he would like to run 60 miles a week; Marilyn's relationship with her husband is strained when she becomes increasingly compulsive about running more miles in a shorter time; Patty carefully measures time and distance and resets her goals so that they are greater than her current performance. These are cognitive strategies which they use to insure their continued effort.

Anorexic women and obligatory runners place enormous value on the activity. In their minds they must make a last-ditch effort to succeed or die in the attempt. They seem poised between pressing even harder and quitting altogether—although it is equally clear that wild horses couldn't keep them from their chosen activity. Restricting anorexics feel as if one bite too many or a taste of the "wrong" food will destroy their diet. Clint always runs because "If you don't use it you lose it." He is afraid that if he stops he won't start again. Marilyn is terrified that if she forfeits a day from running she will quit; that if she eats sweets she will stop dieting. The exaggerated value they place on the activity, the penalties that they envision, and the do-or-die perceptions are strategies which they use to strengthen their resolve.

Obligatory runners and dieters monitor their progress in discrete units of measurement. This is an additional strategy designed to enhance their motivation by providing many small successes and a few small failures. Dick makes running into a pseudoscience by monitoring his pace, speed, distance, heart, lungs, knees, feet, etc. Through this, he feels proud and in control of his body. Max weighs himself three times weekly at his health club; if he's a pound over, he sweats it off. Marilyn and Patty carefully measure time and distance; Lenore did so until she found that she could not stop. Obligatory runners tend to be engrossed in elaborate logs, diaries, and calculations. Eating disordered women are involved in a similar process. When Betsy was an apprentice buyer, she counted calories and weighed herself daily; if she had lunch with clients, she would not eat again until she had used up the excess calories. Jan allows her weight to fluctuate one half pound.

RELATIONSHIPS

Obligatory runners and dieters are heavily invested in the activity—and they are somewhat disinvested in relationships. Betsy refuses social engagements because she needs to stay home so she can binge and vomit. Outside of work, her life revolves about the bulimia. The same may be said of Nicole: she derives little pleasure from her relationship with her husband. Outside of work and childcare, her life centers on bulimia. Jan spends her time studying, attending to her diet, and working out at the health club. Among the obligatory runners, Dick has trouble sitting down with the family. Clint describes himself as dozing off in company since he began to run. Max may want to make love, but then he thinks that he has to run. Max prefers to run rather than to socialize with his co-workers. Marilyn would rather give up sex than running. These individuals may prefer to be alone so that they can devote as much time as possible to the activity.

Physical deprivation may be part of the reason why obligatory runners and eating disordered women become less sociable. Starvation causes normal persons to become alienated, distrustful, and seclusive (Keys et al., 1950) and anorexic patients are more seclusive when they are emaciated (Wooley & Wooley, 1985). Physical deprivation is less likely to contribute to the picture which normal weight bulimic women present. Painfully thin Betsy withdrew from all social relationships when her eating disorder worsened. Pat, on the other hand, had never been underweight and she maintained her social relationships. Emaciated obligatory runners suffer from physical deprivation when they restrict their diet in the face of increased physical exertion. Clint describes himself as having become less sociable since he began to run and Max states that running has made him less accommodating to others. The friends that he has, he doesn't want any more.

ACTIVITY DISORDER

Because of the many points of congruence between obligatory running and the eating disorders, it would seem reasonable to propose a more inclusive category, which will be called the "activity disorder." In this volume, an "activity disorder" is a conceptual rather than a diagnostic entity. It is an abstraction which speaks to the similarities between compulsive athletes and individuals with an eating disorder and it allows us to explore certain theoretical ramifications which include diagnosis. The concept of the activity disorder would need to hold up under rigorous investigation to be considered as a diagnostic entity.

We can begin to formulate an activity disorder as distinct from the more casual use of body-based activity. The following items are proposed as the salient features of an activity disorder:

1. The use of activity in the activity disorder differs qualitatively from the ordinary use of activity.
2. The person must maintain a high level of activity and may be uncomfortable with states of rest or relaxation.
3. The individual depends upon the organizing, energizing, soothing, self-defining, and enhancing functions of the activity. The activity continues to stabilize the affective state of the individual.
4. Once instituted, the activity disorder becomes self-perpetuating and resistant to change.
5. There is an intense, driven quality to the activity. The person feels compelled to continue and unable to stop, as if controlled by the activity. This can lead to physical or social damage.
6. The physical deprivation which is secondary to exposure to the elements, extreme

exertion, rigid dietary restriction, etc. perpetuates the process and contributes significantly to the psychopathology.

7. Although a person may become locked into non-body-based activities, only the overuse of the body can produce the physiologic effects of deprivation which are an important component of the activity disorder.

8. The extent to which the person must control the self by use of the activity is inversely related to the ability to diminish control and to derive gratification from relationships. The activity disordered individual is ambivalent in all close relationships.

9. Although activity disordered individuals may have a coexisting personality disorder, there is no particular personality profile or disorder which underlies an activity disorder. These persons are apt to be healthy, high-functioning individuals.

10. Some activity disordered persons employ primitive defenses such as idealization, omnipotent control, splitting, grandiose fantasies, and devaluation to protect their involvement in the activity. This may represent a preexisting personality configuration and/or be secondary to the physical deprivation.

11. The activity disordered person's achievement orientation, independence, self control, perfectionism, persistence, and well-developed cognitive strategies can foster significant academic and vocational accomplishments.

DIFFERENCES

At the conclusion of our preliminary study, the chief difference between the eating disordered population and the obligatory runner population seemed to be that of gender and of age. The runners tended to be middle aged men, while the eating disordered women were more likely to be young women. Although the gender discrepancy remains, we now know that there are many persons who deviate from the age norms in both categories. At present, the mean age of bulimic women is in the late 20s (Turnbull et al., 1989). There is even a report of senior citizens who are eating disordered (Hsu & Zimmer, 1988) and the number of married and older eating disordered women seems to be increasing (Dally, 1984; Heavey et al., 1989). Obligatory running occurs over a wide age span also; in our larger study, the ages of the obligatory runners did not deviate significantly from that of the non-obligatory runners.

The outstanding difference between the eating disorders and obligatory running seems to be that of gender: there are more males who become compulsive athletes and there are more females who develop eating disorders. There are several possible explanations for this discrepancy. Physical factors such as the androgen-enhanced musculature in males cause men to be better runners than women. Women may perceive hunger and react to it in a different fashion than men do, thus creating a predisposition to an eating disorder. Their relatively intense craving may be hormonally determined and genetically transmitted. Social factors could be important also. Girls are taught to cook while boys are encouraged to be physically active. In adult life, women are apt to shop for and prepare food while males are involved in activities away from the house and the refrigerator.

In this culture the self esteem of young women tends to be based upon physical attractiveness while the self esteem of young men tends to be based on physical effectiveness (Lerner, Orlos & Knapp, 1976). Girls are more inclined to diet to improve their appearance and boys are more likely to exercise to augment their strength and skill.

As women mature, their physical appearance becomes a key to their success on the job and in social groups. Power, prestige, and privilege are granted to "beautiful" women (Wooley & Wooley, 1985). Women understand this principle and those who stress academic achievement, higher education, and professional careers are found to prefer a less curvaceous body (Beck et al., 1976). The fact that women are more likely to become eating disordered and men are more likely to become compulsive athletes may simply mean that, at the time of a crisis of self worth, individuals tend to express themselves along gender specific lines.

DIAGNOSTIC CONSIDERATIONS

Many healthy persons present some elements of an activity disorder. Even when individuals employ activity in a distinctly maladaptive manner, the activity can be said to be healthy in that it continues to soothe and stabilize. When we speak of an activity disorder, we are speaking of the far end of the spectrum of activity, a distinctly unusual extreme. The far end of the spectrum of eating behavior has been spelled out in anorexia and bulimia and the far end of the spectrum of athletic behavior would need to be equivalent in severity in order to be considered pathological. In order to qualify for a disorder, a person would need to reach the level of disturbance that is characteristic of disorders in general.

DSM-III-R specifies that a condition can be diagnosed as a disorder when the person's pattern of perceiving, relating to, or thinking about the environment and the self becomes inflexible and/or maladaptive in a manner which causes subjective distress or a significant impairment in social/occupational functioning. Obligatory runners and eating disordered women would qualify for the diagnosis of a disorder when their inflexible adherence to the activity (of dieting, binge eating/purging or exercise) damages their social or occupational functioning by interfering with other more productive and desirable behaviors.

Many eating disordered women and obligatory runners provide a history of a rather pacific adaptation before they become immersed in the activity—yet they appear depressed, hostile, or suspicious at the time of the interview. This suggests that a large share of the evident pathology is a result of the intense activity and the attendant physical deprivation. Unfortunately, our running study provided only incidental, retrospective data on how the runners functioned before they became obligatory. However, it is our impression that the physical deprivation did contribute substantially to the clinical picture.

In considering the existence or nonexistence of a disorder in the runners in our study, we were often struck by the strengths of these individuals rather than by their weaknesses. We were impressed by their courage and persistence in the face of notable obstacles. They were more modest than boastful, supportive rather than critical. They described a rich inner life and were deeply concerned about social and political issues. And they were harder on themselves than they were on anyone else. The conspicuous strengths of the runners reminded us once more that the Diagnostic and Statistical Manual (DSM) is designed to measure the degree of illness and not the extent of health.

Some of our obligatory runners could have fulfilled the criteria for a DSM diagnosis, but many did not. A few of them probably could have qualified for a DSM diagnosis before they began the activity. The same may be said of eating disordered women (Mitchell, Pyle et al., 1986).

The activity disorders appear to have their own characteristics—enough so that one might question whether they are disorders at all. This simply underscores the fact that, given our current knowledge, we should hesitate to apply any label until we can learn more about the entity. In any case, an activity disorder should not be considered, or any diagnosis be applied, unless the individual meets the general criteria for a disorder. In the case of obligatory athleticism or an eating disorder, the person must be locked into a joyless, rigid pattern of activity which leads to physical, personal, or social damage and which interferes with other more constructive activities. Even if a diagnosis is made, it must be remembered that the deprivation itself can contribute substantially to the pathology. Final judgment needs to be deferred until the individual can be observed under more propitious circumstances.

COMPULSION OR ADDICTION?

Are obligatory athletes and women with eating disorders compulsive or are they impulsive? Are they more like patients with OCD (obsessive-compulsive disorder) or like those who abuse or are addicted to drugs and alcohol? This is an important theoretical issue which bears upon prognosis and on the approach to treatment. Anorexia has been called an addiction to dieting, and bulimia an addiction to food or to eating. Patients with these disorders have sought treatment at Overeaters Anonymous, a 12-step program modeled after Alcoholics Anonymous. Distance runners have been said to have a positive or a negative addiction, depending upon whether the involvement in sport seems to work for or against them (Morgan, 1979).

Obligatory runners and dieters are thought to be addicted because they have a voracious desire for the chosen activity and they seem to be unable to moderate their involvement in it even when they face clear contraindications. In addition, the eating disorders and distance running seem to be associated with an increase in beta endorphins, the opiate-like substance produced in the body and the brain. However, the quantity of endorphin secreted in these instances is minuscule compared to the quantity of morphine or heroin that an addict might inject. A final reason why the activity disorders are thought to be addictive rather than compulsive is that when these persons are prevented from their chosen activity, they experience symptoms that are suggestive of withdrawal. Yet the intense physiologic changes which are characteristic of drug or alcohol withdrawal do not occur.

To call the activity disorders addictions would seem to be an oversimplification. A true addiction is ego syntonic, i.e., these persons enjoy drug use, they don't want to stop, and they are not concerned enough (by society's standards) about losing self control. Addictive persons are impulsive rather than compulsive. The goal of therapy is to create in them the motivation to stop the activity. Compulsions, on the other hand, are for the most part ego dystonic, i.e., these people do not enjoy what they are doing, although they may think that it is something they should do. They feel driven or compelled to continue the activity; they can't stop, even though they want to stop, because they are mightily afraid of losing self control. Those who are addicted "give in" to their appetite; those who are compulsive struggle against their appetite.

When these concepts are applied to the activity disorders, they highlight some important issues. Anorexia is clearly a compulsive rather than an impulsive or addictive disorder as the problem is restraint rather than overindulgence. The anorexic woman might prefer to satisfy her intense hunger, but she cannot stop dieting because she is afraid of losing control of her appetite and of becoming obese. She dislikes the self deprivation but she feels compelled to continue. Although she may say that dieting is good and she doesn't want to stop, she diets because she is terrified of becoming fat. It is not the love of diet but the compulsion to resist the impulse to eat which fuels the disorder. Her ruminations about food and calories clearly qualify as obsessional thoughts.

Bulimia is more complex; it presents a mixture of compulsive and addictive features. When bulimic patients gorge, they lose control and abandon themselves to their appetite. The pleasure they experience while gorging is quite variable; the progression from pleasure to misery tends to be rapid. The period of pleasurable gorging could be called an addictive phase. However, when these women begin to struggle against their urges, they enter a compulsive phase in which they no longer enjoy what they are doing. Although they must proceed to eat, they are more concerned with getting rid of the food. They feel compelled to continue eating and they feel compelled to purge. Bulimic women regard themselves as failed anorexics and they admire anorexics for their self control (Wooley & Wooley, 1985).

Runners often depict the sport in picturesque superlatives, as if there were no activity on earth that could supply the joy that running provides. Those who view running as an addiction cite the intense pleasure which the athletes derive from the sport. This may be an adequate picture of those who run recreationally, although even these persons seem to be running to achieve something rather than to lose themselves in pleasure. It is not an accurate picture of the obligatory runner. For him, the sport is a deadly serious endeavor and he has no choice but to drive himself forward.

There is more pain than pleasure, more compulsion than addiction, in the runner who struggles over the hill on the 21st mile of the marathon or winces as he pounds the pavement on a twisted leg. Yet these runners may claim that they run because of the sheer pleasure of running. However, obligatory runners who have been injured and can no longer run describe a different scenario. Some weeks or months post injury, they portray their running as having been strenuous and exhausting—a chore in which they forced themselves to engage for reasons that they did not completely understand.

When obligatory runners are interviewed in depth, and when they establish an affectual tie with the examiner, they tend to temper the glowing picture of the sport with a different theme. Dick, who idealized running, labors under the imperative that he achieve his time and distance goals. Clint describes pain from his injuries and no special joy in running. He feels controlled by the sport because it has made him give up so much that was pleasurable. Max is so compelled to run that he would need to have his leg in a cast in order to (possibly) quit. Marilyn describes no pleasure in running; she runs to maintain her discipline, and in order not to become depressed. Lenore has run when she felt "lousy" about it. Patty is obligated to run in order to balance out the calories she consumes. Although the running continues to provide certain benefits, it has become a driven, painful activity, one which lies much closer to a compulsion than an addiction. A study by Kagan (1987) supports this contention by demonstrating that the frequency with which individuals run is negatively correlated to measures of addiction, but positively related to measures of compulsion.

CHAPTER 5

From Gymnastics
to Bodybuilding

Obligatory runners can become compulsive dieters; they can become compulsively engaged in sports other than running. Sometimes they become locked into two activities at the same time and sometimes they manage to substitute one obligatory activity for another. The following cases illustrate the manner in which an extreme commitment to one activity can supplement, supersede, or replace an extreme commitment to another activity.

COMBINED ACTIVITIES

When an obligatory dieter begins to run compulsively, the result may be either very good or very bad. The results were good for all three of the women and two of the men who were presented as obligatory runners in Chapter 3. They had been greatly concerned with diet before they began to run, but they became less concerned after they began to run. In other instances, the combination of running and dieting can be disastrous. Men who run and who are eating disordered do very poorly indeed (Katz, 1986). The following cases speak to the deleterious effects of combining exercise and diet.

JUDY

Judy is a 35-year-old bulimic patient in our eating disorders clinic. She began to diet in her early twenties at a time when her first marriage had begun to disintegrate. She had wanted to get in shape for spring and she was delighted when she found that dieting was not difficult. She went out and bought a calorie counter, a diet cookbook, and a kitchen scale. In rapid succession, Judy decided that it would be nice if she could fit into a size 8 dress, then a size 6, and then a size 4. By this time, dieting had become a preoccupation; it made her feel effective and focused as her marriage continued to flounder. She continued to diet after she was divorced, when she needed to go back to school, and when she became employed.

After several years of self-imposed starvation, Judy taught herself to vomit and she soon was vomiting 10 times or more each day. One day when she was restless and searching for something to do, she decided to try running so that she could develop better looking legs. Judy became locked into running also; she could not stop even after she developed a severe Achilles tendinitis. She continued to diet, to vomit, and to run— even through ice and snow on the streets of Chicago. After several years, Judy decided to move to the milder climate of the southwest. Once there, she hired a trainer so that she could get in shape to compete in the 10 K races. She doubled the exercise program the trainer assigned and added her own twists, such as running up and down the stadium steps 10 times each day. She consumed only 700–800 calories a day, a fraction of what her trainer had specified. She continued to vomit, but less often than before because most of her free time was spent in training.

Eventually Judy became too weak to run and she simply collapsed. On admission to the hospital, she weighed 78 pounds. After several weeks of refeeding, the nurses found that she was running up seven flights instead of taking the elevator and was waking in the middle of the night to perform calisthenics. When she was not allowed to exercise, she became even more obsessed with thoughts of diet and exercise. It was several months before these ruminations diminished. Now, several years after her hospitalization, Judy remains on medication and in therapy. She maintains her weight in the low average range and only occasionally vomits. She no longer runs, but she organizes her life around training and showing horses—seven days a week.

MARY WAZETER

Mary Wazeter was 18 years of age when she threw herself off a railroad bridge into the frozen Susquehanna River 35 feet below. She survived, but as a paraplegic, confined to a wheelchair. Mary's case was described extensively in the media, and we were able to interview her six months following her injury. She describes her life in the book *Dark Marathon* (1989).

Mary had been ambitious, smart, and competitive. She was the youngest child in what she described as a loving, middle class family. By the time she was a junior in high school, she had already become a phenomenal runner. She placed 8th in the L'eggs Mini-marathon, ahead of some of the world's top-ranked women runners. She broke the record in a national 20 kilometer race for 17-year-olds while she maintained a straight A average in high school.

Mary wanted to look like a runner and that meant being lean. Runners were supposed to be skinny and if she were lean she could run faster. During most of her high school years, she didn't worry about weight because the running enabled her to eat anything and not gain any pounds. At age 15, she pulled a hamstring muscle in her leg and was forced to rest. Without her activity, she became terrified of becoming fat. Even though she weighed only slightly over 100 pounds, she began to diet, reducing her intake to 1000 calories a day. Her weight went from 105 to 89 pounds. She worried constantly about her weight and meticulously rationed her calories even after she had resumed her training. Each morning she would hold a 10-pound weight behind her head while she completed a hundred sit-ups. Then she would run for five miles and return to consume her 100-calorie breakfast. She was constantly tired. Running was no longer a pleasure; it had become a deadly serious pursuit.

At 89 pounds, Mary had become too weak to run in competition. Feeling like a failure, she isolated herself from others and became even more obsessed with controlling her body. She began to vomit all the food she ingested and her weight continued to drop. In spite of a profound depression, Mary managed to graduate from high school. She left home to enter college, but there she was unable to sleep or to concentrate. One night, in a daze, she was almost run down by a car as she wandered aimlessly through the streets in the rain. Several hospitalizations followed, but she did not respond to the treatment offered. She dropped out of college and—after her first day at business school—she jumped from the railroad bridge.

When we spoke with Mary, she was paralyzed from the neck down and she was understandably depressed. She was living at home, nursed by her mother, and was no longer concerned with diet or exercise. She attributed her improvement to her newfound religion and the prayers of the fundamentalist church group with whom she spent many hours each day.

Discussion

The two women described above combined dieting and exercise. They escalated both activities simultaneously as if there were no relationship between input and output. Eventually their bodies were unable to keep up with the demands and they decompensated. It was as if the world crashed in on them: Mary made a near lethal suicide attempt, but Judy entered the hospital instead. After a considerable interval had passed, they became caught up in other activities beside dieting and exercise. The new commitments helped them to maintain an internal balance.

CATHY RIGBY

Cathy provides another example of the relationship between athleticism and the eating disorders. She described her battle against binge eating and purging at the 1988 American Psychiatric Association annual meeting in Montreal. Cathy had become obsessed with losing weight while in training for the Olympics. She struggled against her overwhelming appetite and sharply restricted her intake. She became less concerned about gaining weight after she taught herself to vomit. She vomited an average of six times a day. However, it was not until after she had retired from gymnastics that the bulimia took over her life. All she was doing was eating—10,000 calories a day in junk food—and throwing up.

In her 13th year of bulimia, Cathy was able to stop vomiting with the help of her second husband and her therapist. When asked if some of the other female gymnasts on the Olympic team had suffered from a similar disorder, she stated that almost all of them had an eating disorder of one kind or another. She thought that anorexia and bulimia are probably most frequent among gymnasts, ice skaters, and wrestlers. Vomiting is a clandestine habit, a quick and easy solution to the frustration of long-term food restriction.

During this past year, Cathy has embarked on a new career as a singer. She had not been trained in voice and she needed to take many intensive lessons in order to qualify. At the same time she continued to care for her young children because she did not wish to entrust them to the care of others.

Discussion

Cathy approaches her new career in singing with the same perfectionism, persistence, and drive toward independent achievement that made her a gymnastics champion. This suggests that individuals who can become intensely and persistently committed to a goal have the propensity to become caught up in whatever activity they undertake. When they choose body-based activities, they are at risk for developing an activity disorder. Running, dieting, bingeing, and purging are not the only body-based activities which can become driven or obligatory.

GYMNASTICS

Certain sports are more apt than other sports to be associated with eating disorders. Gymnasts present the highest rate of anorexia found in any sport: an estimated 20–25 percent of gymnasts become bulimic to keep from gaining weight (Blue, 1987). Eating disorders can now be seen in seven-year-old competitors. In one study, 74 percent of college gymnasts vomited more than twice a week, used laxatives, diuretics, diet pills, or starved themselves (Rosen, McKeag et al., 1986). Cathy and many other gymnasts are able to perform in spite of a serious eating disorder.

Female gymnasts begin training as early as age six and their career peaks at age 16–17. Gymnastics is an extraordinarily competitive sport, one in which the women must practice meticulously to attain a personal best. Injuries are frequent, and the women usually continue to train in spite of the pain. Competitive gymnasts practice at least nine hours a week and many practice twice that long. In spite of the energy expenditure, gymnasts consume an average of only 1800 calories a day (Loosli et al., 1986). A short, extremely flexible body is necessary for elements such as the Korbut somersault and loop, moves which are now standard in international meets. Gymnasts fashion a slim, prepubescent shape through intensive training and by maintaining their body fat below 7 percent (Blue, 1987). The British champion Lisa Elliot has a body fat of only 5.3 percent, on a par with the Russian stars. Most competitive gymnasts fall in the 8–9 percent range while the average amount of body fat for women is 20 percent.

Female gymnasts and distance runners have the lowest body fat percentage of all women athletes (Wilmore Brown & Davis, 1977) and they are under great pressure to be slim. When the runners run, they run off the calories, but gymnasts perform in short bursts. They have no choice but to curtail their intake (Blue, 1987). When gymnasts start dieting, they may not be able to stop when they attain their goal. Sixty-three percent reset their original goals and 75 percent admit that they continue to drop weight because they are afraid they will lose control of their eating if they terminate their diets (Rosen, McKeag et al., 1986).

Rosen, McKeag et al. (1986) surveyed the eating attitudes and practices of 182 varsity-level female college students. Thirty-two percent of these women were practicing a pathogenic weight control behavior such as binge eating more than twice weekly, self-induced vomiting, or ingesting laxatives and diet pills. The highest percentages of women who did so were engaged in gymnastics, field hockey, and distance track events. These pathogenic behaviors occurred occasionally in all sports, but the women who were least likely to binge and/or purge were those who participated in basketball, golf, and swimming.

Borgen and Corbin (1987) administered the Eating Disorders Inventory to nonathletes, athletes, and athletes in sports that emphasize leanness. Six percent of the nonathletes, 10 percent of the unselected athletes, and 20 percent of the athletes in leanness sports were either exceptionally preoccupied with weight or had tendencies toward an eating disorder. Sports which emphasize leanness may create a special predisposition for an eating disorder. However, the women who value thinness may be the ones who gravitate to leanness sports.

Sports with a relatively high incidence of the eating disorders have certain elements in common. These include the competitiveness of the sport, the degree of stress placed on the body, the emphasis on form or appearance, the reliance on individual excellence rather than on team performance, and the need for the participants to be small and/or lean in order to do well. Perhaps the characteristics of the person interact with the characteristics of the sport to place the individual at risk for the development of an eating disorder.

BODYBUILDING AND POWER LIFTING

The following is an excerpt from Arnold Schwartzenegger's description of his development as a bodybuilder (Schwartzenegger & Hall, 1982).

> By the time I was 13, team sports no longer satisfied me. I was already off on an individual trip. I disliked it when we won a game and I didn't get personal recognition. The only time I felt rewarded was when I was singled out as being best.
>
> After two or three months with the bodybuilders, I was literally addicted. . . . But I didn't think that I could wait five years. I had

this insatiable drive to get there sooner. Whereas most people were satisfied to train two or three times a week, I quickly escalated my program to six workouts a week. . . . I'd always been impressed by stories of greatness and power. . . . I wanted to do something special, to be recognized as the best. . . . When I felt my lungs burning as though they would burst and veins bulging with blood, I loved it. . . . My weight room was not heated, so naturally in cold weather it was freezing. I didn't care. I trained without heat even on the days when the temperature went below zero.

I couldn't be bothered with girls as companions. My mind was totally locked into working out, and I was annoyed if anything took me away from it. . . . Whatever I thought might hold me back, I avoided. I crossed girls off my list—except as tools for my sexual needs. I eliminated my parents too.

I can lose ten to forty pounds rapidly, easily, painlessly, by simply setting my mind to it. By observing the principles of strict discipline that bodybuilding taught me, I can prepare myself for anything. I have developed such absolute control over my body that I can decide what body weight I want for any particular time and take myself up or down to meet it. . . .

I discovered that taking measurements gave me both satisfaction and incentive. I measured my calves, arms, and thighs regularly, and I'd be turned on if I saw I'd increased an eighth-inch or a half-inch. On a calendar I kept even fractional changes in measurements and weight.*

Some sports emphasize individual rather than team performance and some sports emphasize the appearance of the body more than do others. Bodybuilding, now the sixth largest international sports federation, is an example of a physical activity where the appearance of the body is essential. Bodybuilding is a kind of institutionalized exhibitionism. It is an extremely strenuous endeavor; it requires many hours each day for training and it can be harsh to the body. In order to do well, individuals must display remarkable persistence in the pursuit of an ideal form. It attracts persons who wish to achieve, to be envied, and to be known by the appearance of their bodies in spite of, or because of, the body strain which is required.

Weight lifting, or power lifting, is quite different from bodybuilding in intent. Where bodybuilding aims to change and enhance the superficial aspects of the body, weight lifting focuses primarily on the efficacy of the body. Women are less attracted to the sport and, of course, they are less likely to excel in it. Weight training improves the self concept of males, especially those who were weak or did not appreciate their bodies to begin with or those who idealize a muscular physique (Tucker, 1987). In a recent study comparing obligatory runners, weight lifters, and controls, the obligatory runners and the weight lifters demonstrated a significantly greater eating disturbance than the controls (Pasman & Thompson, 1988).

Little or nothing has been written in the psychiatric literature about bodybuilding or weight lifting. However, an anthropologist (Klein, 1985, 1987) completed his field work (1979–1985) at one of the leading bodybuilding gyms near Muscle Beach in California. He describes male bodybuilders as striving, fiercely competitive men, often from a blue collar background. Much of their anxiety and their embattled stance stems from their efforts to gain recognition in spite of a prosaic background. Women bodybuilders are not as fiercely competitive; they tend to come from a higher socioeconomic background and are more likely to have graduated from college and to hold a skilled job.

It is only in recent years that bodybuilding has become a women's as well as a men's sport. Some of the women who became bodybuilders have been aerobics instructors, others have been ballet dancers. Women bodybuilders must train longer and harder than men, they must diet more assiduously to reduce their naturally higher levels of body fat, and they must take diuretics to reduce the water content of their skin so that they will show the veined "ripped" effect that the judges prize. Steroid injection to increase muscle size is said to be standard—individuals who train without it don't win in competition.

Bodybuilding contains elements of idol or image worship, as found in the world of modeling, beauty contests, and the cinema. Women's bodybuilding sprang from the American beauty pageant (Klein, 1985, 1987) and controversy persists among judges as to how much muscle is too much for women competitors. In Klein's experience, women comprised 15 percent of the long-term membership of the gym. In common with the men, they often entered bodybuilding to compensate for a poor physical image which might include a sense of being fat and ugly. However, the women were less driven than the men and more likely to see bodybuilding as a means rather than an end in itself (Klein, 1985). The men were loners and ruthless competitors, while the women (with a few notable exceptions) were less defensive and more sociable, forthright, and concerned about one another.

In describing bodybuilders, Klein (1987) remarks on their grandiosity, underlying sense of inferiority, the prodigious need for mirroring, and the single-minded quest to become supermen and women. Bodybuilders are obsessed with developing huge, striated muscles. To this end, they spend hours each day in graded exercise and they follow a high protein, low fat, sugarless diet religiously. Above all, they must control the body: through extreme dieting, endless working out, and steroid abuse. It is the appearance of the body—not the health of the body—which the bodybuilder adulates, and, as one Mr. Universe commented, "By the time we are on stage, we are more dead than alive." The body must *look* vital and youthful; the cardinal fears of the bodybuilder are of age and physical deterioration.

Like running and dieting, bodybuilding is an independent activity in which achievement-oriented individuals engage. Bodybuilders are most often loners and their friendships tend to be undervalued and brittle (Klein, 1987). Yet, when the bodybuilder is actively engaged in training, he seems healthier, as if he is able to rise above his self doubt. His commitment to the sport provides the bodybuilder with organization, energy, concrete goals, and a positive self image—as long as he remains vigorously involved.

OBLIGATORY INDIVIDUALS

Certain individuals demonstrate the propensity to become caught up in various activities. These tend to be exceptionally active, independent, persistent, and perfectionistic individuals. They are high achievers: good workers, good students, and good athletes. They work hard and they play hard. Persons with these characteristics could be called "obligatory individuals." When they engage in diet or exercise, they attack the activity with exceptional vigor and persistence. A few of these persons may, under certain circumstances, become activity disordered.

Sports such as gymnastics, bodybuilding, and distance running tend to enhance the obligatory qualities of the persons who engage in these activities. Perhaps this is because of the competitiveness of the sport, the degree of stress placed on the body, the emphasis on form or appearance, the reliance on individual excellence rather than on team performance, and the need for the participants to be small and/or lean in order to do well. Sports endeavors that fit most of these criteria (in addition to those already discussed) are aerobic exercise, figure skating, wrestling, skiing, and diving. In most instances, the characteristics of the sport seem to interact with the characteristics of the individual to determine the risk of an activity disorder.

PART II

Theoretical Overview

CHAPTER 6

Biological Theory

Compulsive athleticism is an intriguing but largely uncharted condition. We do not know what the biologic factors are that predispose some individuals to overexert themselves or what enables them to continue to press forward in spite of pain and physical exhaustion. We know a good deal more about the biologic forces involved in the eating disorders. Over the past 10 years, research studies have identified a number of risk factors for the development of an eating disorder and several elements which can perpetuate the problem. Some of these findings might apply to compulsive athleticism as well.

In this chapter we will review important neuroendocrine, hormonal, and physiologic research on eating disordered women, on amenorrheic women runners, on male distance runners, on starving men, and on animals exposed to stress, food deprivation, and rigid scheduling. Some of this material, especially the first section of this chapter, may be difficult for the person who does not have a background in the basic sciences. There are several strategically placed summaries to aid the reader who is not biologically based.

THE SEARCH FOR A BIOLOGIC BASIS

Emaciated anorexic women display a host of neuroendocrine abnormalities along with sleep disturbance, impaired concentration, indecisiveness, withdrawal, mood lability, anxiety, apathy, and depression (Garfinkel & Kaplan, 1985). These changes are likely to be a consequence of starvation as they tend to revert to normal once the women have gained weight and/or the depression that is secondary to starvation has been relieved. The findings of elevated cortisol, diminished cortisol metabolism, and impaired responses to dexamethasone (Walsh, Katz et al., 1981; Halmi, 1987) can be attributed directly to starvation and/or metabolic instability (Strober & Katz, 1987).

Distance runners demonstrate some of the same neuroendocrine changes that have been identified in anorexic women. (Luger et al., 1987). Highly trained runners present high levels of ACTH and cortisol which are proportional to the intensity of their exercise. These changes may be secondary to the stress placed on the body by the extreme, persistent exertion. The neuroendocrine changes which occur in anorexia and in distance running suggest that the starved state is similar in some respects to the metabolic state of near exhaustion.

THE SEARCH FOR PERPETUATORS

There are biologic factors which may not cause the eating disorders but which may perpetuate them once they have begun. The two first described, serotonin and cholecystokinin, have not yet been measured in athletes, but a third element, beta endorphin, has been measured in athletes who run long distances.

SEROTONIN

Underweight anorexic women demonstrate low levels of the neurotransmitter, serotonin (Kaye, Ebert & Gwirtsman, 1984). Serotonin is important in the regulation of sleep, pain, appetite, and mood. Tryptophan, the amino acid from which serotonin is derived, is diminished also in anorexia (Clippen et al., 1976). This may be due to the inadequate diet which is characteristic of anorexic patients. Tryptophan and serotonin revert to normal when the patients reach an adequate weight (Hotta et al., 1986). A low level of serotonin could cause sleeplessness, diminished appetite, irritability, and hyperactivity, symptoms which have been noted in anorexic patients. Thus, a deficiency in serotonin could contribute to, and perhaps perpetuate, the course of the disorder. Serotonin has not been studied in distance runners, but it might conceivably be low in those runners who restrict their diet while they continue to expend a prodigious amount of energy. If the runners were deficient in serotonin, the deficiency might serve to sustain their unusually high level of activity.

CHOLECYSTOKININ

A peptide hormone, cholecystokinin (CCK), is thought to play a role in the bulimic process. CCK has been called the hormone of satiation. Normal individuals secrete CCK after they eat, when the food that they have ingested passes from the stomach to the duodenum. When individuals secrete enough CCK, they become satiated and stop eating. Both lean and obese individuals eat less when they have more CCK (Gibbs & Smith, 1985). When individuals have less CCK, they eat more (Hewson et al., 1988). Bulimic women secrete unusually low levels of CCK (Geracioti & Liddle, 1988), perhaps because the food leaves their stomach slowly—or not at all if it is vomited. It is thought that the diminished CCK keeps these women from feeling satiated so that they are always hungry. The persistent hunger could cause them to gorge repeatedly (Abell et al., 1987).

Perhaps a diminished level of CCK is one factor which sustains the appetite of bulimic women, but the low level of CCK is unlikely to cause the bulimia. Even when CCK is administered to bulimic women immediately before they begin to binge, the CCK is ineffective in terminating the binge or in diminishing the amount of food they consume (Mitchell, Laine et al., 1986). Bulimic women binge in response to a variety of precipitants, such as depression, anxiety, or anger, which are not directly related to CCK and the satiety response.

ENDORPHINS

The beta endorphins are naturally occurring, opiate-like substances secreted in the brain and in the body. The endorphins are involved in pain and temperature regulation, eating behavior, energy expenditure, and the regulation of hypothalamic-pituitary hormones. An increase in endorphins occurs when the body is severely stressed. When beta-endorphin is administered to human subjects, they become intensely hungry (Sternbach et al, 1982; Mitchell, 1987). Conversely, naloxone, a drug which counters the effect of the endorphins, decreases appetite and the amount of food ingested. The endorphins are elevated in the spinal fluid of underweight anorexia patients (Kaye, Picker et al., 1982), which suggests that this substance could be responsible for the intense appetite, food preoccupation, and other food-related behaviors of patients with anorexia. An increase in the endorphins could also produce some of the neurohormonal changes which are found in anorexia (Risch et al., 1983; Garfinkel & Kaplan, 1985).

Starving women may not react to the endorphins in the same manner as do other persons. That this may be the case is suggested by a study (Sanger & McCarthy, 1980) which shows that when rats are administered opiates while they are on a sharply restricted diet they will demonstrate a decrease, rather than an increase, in appetite. If this holds true in humans, it would suggest that starvation could remove a significant source of stress for anorexics by diminishing their appetite through an increase in endorphins. This would support the contention of many anorexic patients that they are less troubled by their appetite in the emaciated state than they were before they became emaciated. Perhaps the reaction to the endorphins is biphasic: i.e., when anorexic women begin to restrict their intake the endorphins increase and they experience a ravenous appetite, but once they enter the starved state the increase in the endorphins causes a decrease in appetite. It is not known whether this is the case as the research so far conducted does not provide an index of the women's physical state at the time of the measurements.

A substance that blocks the endorphins should counteract the clinical effect of the endorphins. Of the two uncontrolled studies using opiate blockers, one shows a tenfold increase in weight gain in anorexic patients (Moore, Mills & Forster, 1981) and the other indicates marked benefit in six out of eight patients (Luby, Marrazzi & Kinzie, 1987). The opiate blockers are said to reduce the patients' obsessive preoccupation with dieting, anxiety about weight gain, and resistance to treatment. They also decrease the exhilaration associated with losing weight. This would suggest that the opiate blockers foster weight gain by increasing the appetite (i.e., they counteract the diminished appetite which is secondary to the endorphins). On the other hand, the opiate blockers might diminish the appetite so that these women can eat more without fearing loss of control.

Bulimic patients who vomit present increased levels of plasma beta endorphin compared to those who do not vomit (Fullerton et al., 1988). This may be due to the stress of vomiting, the increased caloric intake, or changes in the distension of the gut. In the one controlled study available, the administration of an opiate blocker substantially decreased the size of the binges in bulimic patients (Mitchell, Laine et al., 1986). However, the opiate antagonist only diminished the amount eaten; the binge was not terminated. This is an expectable result as bulimic women binge for a variety of reasons which have nothing to do with appetite.

The effect of opiate blockers in bulimia is to diminish the amount eaten while the effect of opiate blockers in anorexia is to increase the amount eaten. Bulimic women react in the same manner as do normal subjects. This would suggest that bulimic and anorexic women do react differently to the endorphins: that these substances enhance the appetite of bulimic women but diminish the appetite of starving anorexic women. This probably is not due to a difference between women with anorexia and women with bulimia, as many women switch back and forth between these categories. It is more likely that the starvation itself acts to produce far reaching physiologic, as well as psychologic, effects.

The feeling of lightness or euphoria reported by some bulimic women after they vomit (or the tendency of some bulimics to gorge again immediately after they vomit) may be related to an increase in endorphins. Endorphins, and opiates in general, have calming, soothing, and pain-relieving properties. A few non-bulimic persons may intentionally induce an increase in endorphins through emesis. Some entertainers and public speakers have learned to diminish stage fright by vomiting before going on stage (Yager, 1984) and several patients in our clinic first learned to vomit to lessen the pain of menstrual cramps (Yates, 1989). Ford and Dolan (1989) describe a woman who learned to vomit at age 6 to relieve her asthma attacks.

Vigorous exercise causes an increase in endogenous opiates. Peripheral endorphin levels are markedly elevated in endurance runners after a marathon (Appenzeller et al., 1980) and runners who show such an increase are also those who report feeling "high" (Callen, 1983). Measurements of the level of endorphins in the bloodstream do not necessarily reflect the level of endorphins in the brain, but the fact that the blood level correlates with a mood change in these athletes suggests that the brain endorphins are elevated, because only brain endorphins could affect mood. This finding suggests that the endorphins could be responsible for the elation of the long distance runner. Only a tiny amount of these substances is secreted in response to stress—a fraction of that which would produce an addiction—but perhaps this is sufficient to lift the mood, to mute the pain, and to make the person resistant to change.

SUMMARY

Although the extensive investigation of serotonin and CCK has not demonstrated a causal role for these substances in the eating disorders, these naturally occurring agents could serve to intensify and perpetuate the disorders. In addition, these substances can influence the emotions and they may play a role in maintaining psychological balance. Serotonin has not been studied in distance runners, but if it were found to be low it might serve to sustain their high level of activity.

An increase in endorphins has been found in long distance runners and in eating disordered women. The increase in these morphine-like substances may allow the anorexic to tolerate starvation and to be active in spite of fatigue and it may allow runners to continue running in spite of the pain and exhaustion they experience. Although the increase in endorphins is intriguing, the significance has not been established.

RELATIONSHIP TO DEPRESSION

Anorexic and bulimic women usually are miserable and angry at themselves when they begin treatment. A number of these women do respond favorably to antidepressant medication. Because of this, some researchers have thought that the eating disorders are an expression of depression or that the eating disorders are just one symptom of depression. However, recent research indicates that the women are likely to become depressed because of the eating disorder or that they happen to be depressed and to have an eating disorder, i.e., the depression and the eating disorder are transmitted independently (Cooper & Fairburn, 1986; Strober & Katz, 1987). Patients with anorexia may be depressed because they self-starve; starvation can produce depression even in normal individuals (Keys et al., 1950). Patients with bulimia may be depressed because they are caught up in the binge/purge cycle. Bulimic women regularly become more depressed as their eating becomes more pathological (Johnson-Sabine, Wood & Wakeling, 1984). In any case, the eating disorders are not simply the symptoms of an underlying, biologically based depression.

Although depression does not cause the eating disorders, there could be an interaction between depression and diet which serves to promote and/or perpetuate the eating disorders in susceptible individuals. Women who are mildly depressed and upset with their appearance or performance may decide to diet. They may be elated at their initial success at losing weight, but as time goes on they may become tense and miserable because of the chronic dietary hardship they endure. Then they might restrict their intake even more in an attempt to feel better. If they restrict themselves sufficiently, they will encounter the further increase in depression which is secondary to starvation (Keys et al., 1950).

When men adhere to an exercise regimen, they may confront a sequence of events which is similar to that just described in eating disordered women. "Getting oneself in shape" is a socially approved, easily available mood elevator and running has become an acceptable treatment for mild or moderate depression (Brown, Ramirez & Taub, 1978; Markoff, Ryan & Young, 1982)—although involvement in other sports activities may have the same effect (Doyne et al., 1987). However, when athletes train intensively, the program can backfire and they become more depressed and anxious than before (Morgan, Brown et al., 1987). This means that certain individuals who begin an athletic program in order to feel better may overdo it and begin to feel worse. They may escalate the activity in a further attempt to feel better, only to become even more dysphoric. Presumably, this cycle could foster a locked in, compulsive adherence to exercise.

An identical sequence may occur when obligatory individuals engage in exercise or diet: they undertake the activity in order to feel better and they do feel better. However, because they are persistent and perfectionistic persons, they have a tendency to overdo the exercise or diet and then they feel worse. They try to control the dysphoria with a further increase in activity but the increase only compounds their distress.

MENSTRUAL IRREGULARITIES

An intriguing parallel between obligatory running and the eating disorders is that women in either category tend to forfeit their menses. The menses may disappear before the women increase the exercise or lose the weight. One-third to one-half of women with anorexia indicate that they ceased menstruating before they began to diet or to lose weight (Dally, 1969; Halmi, 1974; Morgan & Russell, 1975). Twenty percent of women athletes stop menstruating before they begin to run (Speroff & Redwine, 1980). The amenorrhea that these women experience must be caused by something other than weight loss or vigorous exercise. This phenomenon has never been adequately explained.

Some women will quit menstruating when they experience an emotional upset. "Psychogenic" amenorrhea occurs in 5–25 percent of women when they undergo significant life events such as leaving home (Shanan et al., 1965; Drew & Stifel, 1968; McCormick, 1975). We know that the eating disorders often commence around the time of separation—when women leave home to attend college, after a love affair ends, etc. Perhaps when certain women experience an emotional upset, often one which is related to separation, the upset interrupts the menses and it causes an increase in their self dissatisfaction because the women expect that they should be able to exist independently. Perhaps it is the self dissatisfaction which causes these women to engage in a diet or exercise program.

Women ultramarathon runners who menstruate irregularly differ from those who menstruate regularly: they are better runners, they run more, start at an earlier age, and frequently have a past history of anorexia nervosa (Van-Gend & Noakes, 1987). Women athletes who have lost their menses with exercise tend to be obsessed with diet and rigid about their training regimen (Brooks et al., 1984). We do not know if amenorrheic dieters are stricter, more obsessed with diet, or if they begin to restrict food at an earlier age, but this would be an important area to investigate.

Gadpaille, Sanborn & Wagner, et al. (1987) interviewed 13 amenorrheic and 19 regularly menstruating women runners to explore the relationship between athleticism and the eating disorders. The eating disorders and depression clustered within the amenorrheic runner group and they were virtually absent within the group of women who had retained their menses. Eight of the amenorrheic runners reported an eating disorder and 11 described major affective disorders such as depression in themselves or in first and second degree relatives. Not one of the regularly menstruating women reported an eating disorder and only one had first degree relatives with a major affective disorder. In addition, the amenorrheic group displayed low food intake, ritualized dietary habits, heightened energy and activity, and compulsive behavior. Twelve of the 13 amenorrheic runners were vegetarians, compared to three of the 19 menstruating runners. Fifty-four percent of the amenorrheic runners reported severe agitation and depression when they were unable to run compared to 5 percent of the menstruating group. If the amenorrheic runners had not developed substantial musculature from running, they would have appeared emaciated, as they had lost considerable body fat.

The association between menstrual dysfunction and abnormal attitudes toward eating is not confined to athletic or eating disordered women; it is also found among ultramarathoners, ballet dancers, and models (Rippon et al., 1988). Certain women may have a biologically based predisposition to amenorrhea, depression, obsessive thoughts, and compulsive or exaggerated behaviors. If they experience an emotional upset, any or all of these symptoms might increase. If they should gravitate toward exercise or diet, their obligatory qualities would make it more likely that they would be caught up in the activity. If this were the case, the existence of menstrual irregularities could serve as a biologic marker of risk for depression, obsessive compulsive phenomena, and the activity disorders.

The association between hormonal imbalance, extreme diet/exercise, depression, and obsessiveness is fascinating, and it invites further exploration. A sample of young adult women who are prone to menstrual irregularities could be identified, thoroughly assessed, and followed over time for the development of extreme diet/exercise patterns, compulsivity, and depression.

EARLY SEPARATION, THE ENDORPHINS, AND LATER VULNERABILITY

Little is known about the forces which predispose individuals to follow a certain course in life. Yet, on the basis of the material just presented, there do seem to be innate influences on mood and on the manner in which individuals relate to the environment. For the most part, these forces seem to be genetically programmed in that they operate, in one way or another, throughout the life span. However, an early circumstance, such as separation, may have the capacity to permanently alter the biochemical climate of the brain, thus creating a predisposition to certain mood states and patterns of behavior. This is an important area of investigation because, if it bears fruit, it might mean that the manner in which parents separate from their infants could determine the children's predisposition to various disorders later on. Primate research suggests that this indeed may be the case.

Observations of nonhuman primates in the wild by Jane Goodall (1979) and research in the primate laboratory by the Harlows (Harlow & Harlow, 1971) clearly describe the extensive, pervasive emotional damage which transpires when infant apes or monkeys are separated from their mothers. Early separation has a lifelong impact on these nonhuman primates' sexual competence, parenting ability, and relatedness to other animals. When animals that have been separated are forced in contact with other animals, they isolate themselves and respond with unpredictable aggression or terror. Even when these animals are reunited with their mothers after some time has passed, they are irritable or isolative, and unable to relate appropriately. Under natural circumstances in the wild, separated animals refuse to eat; they die, succumb to infection, or are killed by others in the tribe.

When infants of any mammalian species are separated from their mothers, they become terribly upset, engage in immediate, frantic activity, and emit what is termed a "separation-distress cry." When an infant animal emits a cry, this regularly stimulates concern or rescue behavior on the part of the parent. Both the infant cry and the maternal response are mediated by endorphins, those opiate-like substances found in the body and brain. A minuscule amount of morphine abolishes the distress call in animals (Newman, Murphy & Harbough, 1982) and the opiate blocker, naloxone, reinstates it (Scott, 1974; Panksepp, Sivey & Normansell, 1985). When infant animals are separated from their mothers, even for a brief interval, there are substantial changes in the brain and the neurotransmitter system which involve the catecholamines, cortisol, and the endorphins (Van der Kolk, 1987). Even the immunoresistance of the animal declines so that even casual infections pose a threat to life (Laudenslager, Reite & Harbeck, 1983).

The changes which are found in the brains of animals who have been separated from their mothers tend to persist. They correlate with the behavioral changes which distinguish these animals from animals who were not separated (Kalin & Carnes, 1984). It is thought that when these animals are separated they are immediately overwhelmed by their loss. They cry vigorously and search for the lost mother. After a while, they seem to abandon hope and become quite inconsolable. It may be that the state of anguished hyperarousal is intolerable for the infant animals, and they are forced to curtail their reactivity. In order to do this, they dampen the arousal mechanism in the brain, in effect compromising their capacity to respond emotionally. The animal's baseline state becomes one of diminished arousal from that time on—the price of maintaining a homeostasis in the face of separation.

Without a normal arousal response, infant primates cannot reinstitute their earlier attachment with the mother, nor can they effect a gratifying relationship with any other animal. The expectable social and affectionate learning process does not occur, which means that peer and sexual relationships will inevitably be affected. These animals cannot constructively integrate the arousal response in their behavioral repertoire during development; therefore, they continue to demonstrate an unpredictable and extreme emotional response to stress as they mature (Novak & Harlow, 1979). Such severe decrements make social and emotional adaptation impossible for these animals (Kraemer, 1986). Even the most positive, "therapeutic" experiences can only partially offset the effects of early separation. A traumatic early separation seems to confer a persistent neurobiological vulnerability which has far-reaching effects on the animal's development.

The depression that nonhuman primate infants experience after an early separation is thought to be the animal counterpart of depression in human infants (Kalin & Carnes, 1984; Rosenblum & Paully, 1987). Children who have had a lengthy early separation from the mother or the primary caretaker and who do not have good substitute parenting appear disconsolate, detached, and very empty. First, they are "hungry" for the mother and they protest vigorously; later, they become despondent and they withdraw from the parent when the parent reappears (Bowlby, 1973). In the process, they lose their appetite and refuse to eat or eat listlessly. This suggests that they have deadened their emotional response, perhaps via an increase in endorphins (Van der Kolk, 1987).

This may be an age-old mechanism for diminishing intolerable hunger and emotional pain.

Sugarman, Quinlan and Devenis (1981) suggest that the eating disorders emerge from an anaclitic depression. Yet, in human infants a full-blown anaclitic depression is a distinctly unusual occurrence, whereas the eating disorders are not uncommon at all. There is another possibility: perhaps a lesser degree of separation trauma could produce lesser (but persistent) changes in the brain. There are all degrees of trauma involved in the average expectable separation process; one might say that all such separations are somewhat traumatic. A less than optimal to fairly stressful separation process might be sufficient to create a small but significant change in the neurobiological system. Although infants may not be able to compensate behaviorally for the biologic changes which occur in a very traumatic separation, infants might be able to compensate fairly well for changes which would follow a less traumatic separation. The changes would persist, but the infant would be able to adapt and develop in an age-expectable fashion. In spite of this progress, the alteration in the neurobiological system might predispose the infant to certain problems later in life.

Let us suppose for a moment that a number of individuals in the culture have experienced a difficult separation, perhaps because it occurred before they were developmentally prepared to meet it. They were able to compensate fairly well and they continued to develop and adapt, yet they carried with them a predisposition for certain kinds of problems. These problems might surface if and when these individuals were exposed to stress or an emotional challenge. A construct such as this could explain an increase in certain kinds of conditions, such as the activity disorders, based on changes in child rearing. This concept will be explored further in Chapter 11.

Although research on separation effects in nonhuman primate infants is intriguing and highly suggestive, it may or may not apply to human infants. It does suggest that certain early experiences such as separation can create a permanent, biological predisposition to emotional problems.

HUNGER AND APPETITE

The urge to eat is composed of hunger and appetite. Hunger is the physiologic or visceral response to food deprivation; appetite is the psychological response to a variety of conditions. Eating disordered women and women obligatory runners seem especially prone to an increase in appetite when they are lonely, angry, sad, happy, frustrated, or restless with nothing to do. Some persons are able to differentiate physical hunger from appetite, but many others are not.

Much of the basic research on hunger has not been accomplished: we do not know the interrelationship between physical hunger and appetite, or the extent to which they can be distinguished. We do not know why women experience appetite more acutely than men or if some individuals could be genetically loaded for appetite intensity.

GENDER DIFFERENCES IN APPETITE

There may be sex-linked genetic reasons which contribute to the fact that women are far more likely than men to develop an eating disorder. Eating disordered women, or perhaps women in general, tend to per-sistently confuse appetite with hunger. Among our obligatory runners, the women seem to confuse hunger and appetite while the men seem better able to sort this out. Men and women may experience hunger and appetite differently. Men and women differ dramatically in the circadian rhythm of their hunger and the manner in which they experience appetite and satiation (Di Castro, 1987). Differences between males and females have been demonstrated even in animals: in rats it is the female who is much more likely to voraciously overeat and gain weight after ablation of the hypothalamus (Cox & Sims, 1988).

When women are depressed they are more likely to overeat than men who are depressed; men are less likely than women to gain weight when they are depressed (Frank et al., 1988). When women are depressed they are more likely than men to experience a prodigious increase in appetite. If they become depressed while they are dieting, they are more likely to have episodes of binge eating (Greenberg and Harvey, 1987). Many women experience a dramatic surge in appetite immediately before their menstrual period commences. In women with a premenstrual syn-drome this increase is highly correlated with mood changes, especially depression (Both-Orthman et al., 1988). The association between depres-sion and an increased appetite would place women at a greater risk than men to develop an eating disorder.

STARVATION

When eating disordered women pursue an austere diet or when oblig-atory runners eat less and run more, they become very hungry. Hunger is a painful physical sensation. The gut rumbles and salivation occurs at the thought of food. The person's cognitive world begins to be organized about how to manage these sensations. Keys et al. (1950) conducted the classic experiment on the phenomenon of hunger. These researchers closely monitored young men who volunteered to consume a semi-starvation level diet over a number of months. The men experienced persistent, intense hunger and sometimes felt hungrier after eating than before. They increased their consumption of coffee and tea, smoked cigarettes, and chewed gum in order to control their craving. They became constantly preoccupied with thoughts of food, began to collect recipes, enjoyed cooking and feeding others, and a few wished to become chefs. They developed bizarre food fads and rituals, and would take vivid, vicarious pleasure in watching other people eat. As the weeks dragged on, they became more egocentric and seclusive, somber, serious, and sarcastic. They became involved in many activities: they went on shopping sprees and purchased coffee pots, hot plates, kitchen utensils, secondhand clothes, knickknacks, and other "junk." Later, they wondered why they had bought these things. At other times they appeared listless and disinterested in their surroundings. When food was once again available, the men remained ravenous even when they had gorged themselves; a few developed frank bulimic episodes.

The men in the Keys experiment developed many of the same characteristics that we have observed in starving anorexic women and emaciated obligatory runners. They appear more egocentric and seclusive, somber, serious, and sarcastic. They may engage in a number of unnecessary, seemingly senseless activities such as arranging their food on the plate, counting the number of times they chew before swallowing, or checking their stool to see if it floats. They may report feeling hungrier after eating than before.

Descriptions of individuals who were starved for prolonged periods in labor and concentration camps indicate that these persons become apathetic and inactive. Obligatory runners and eating disordered women who starve themselves do not become apathetic and inactive. On the contrary, they become more energetic and active than they had been before. Yet the percent body fat of many obligatory runners and anorexic women may be less than that found in starvation. One runner, Gary Tuttle, is said to have achieved 1.2 percent body fat; the average for a young, healthy male is 10–15 percent. (Wilmore & Behnke, 1969).

The reason why starving, eating disordered women can remain energetic and obligatory runners can continue to run in the face of exhaustion is far from clear. However, the motivation of the obligatory individuals differs from that of the individuals who were starved naturally or experimentally. Eating disordered women and obligatory runners are consciously attempting to get rid of, rather than conserve, calories and they are aware of the calorie burning effects of exercise. Experimental subjects attempt to conserve calories. The circumstances under which they lose weight are different also: there is no food available to individuals under conditions of natural or experimental starvation, but food is readily available to eating disordered women and obligatory runners. They could have as much food as they could eat if they were willing to yield to their impulses. When individuals experience hunger in the presence of food, perhaps the expectable reaction is for them to become more active. This seems to be the case with animals: they regularly exhibit the greatest activity right before feeding time, when they anticipate being fed.

ACTIVITY AND APPETITE CONTROL

In the Keys experiment the men did not have a choice about eating: they were allowed no more than their meager allotment. They put up with this frustration because they were highly motivated to remain in the program in spite of their discomfort. Meals were structured, they ate and lived in groups, and they had a buddy system when they went out. These external supports, which were so important for the experimental subjects, are not available for most eating disordered women. Eating disordered women must use every available strategy not to eat in the face of their ravenous hunger and readily available food supplies. A common strategy is to stay active and avoid idleness.

Activities which are highly valued, structured, goal directed, and stimulating can effectively distract eating disordered (and non-eating disordered) individuals from their appetite. Involvement in an activity makes the time pass more quickly. In human beings and in other mammals, exercise is an especially effective activity to control appetite (Epling & Pierce, 1988). Individuals who are not dieting will spontaneously cut down their food intake when they embark on an exercise program. Perhaps part of the reason why eating disordered women and obligatory runners exercise is that the physical exertion makes them feel less like eating.

HUNGER AND DIETARY RESTRAINT

We have already learned that most eating disordered women and obligatory runners practice food restriction. This is not especially unusual—in this country more than half the women, and an unknown number of men restrict their food intake (Polivy & Herman, 1987). However, the restriction itself may make dieting more difficult because it increases the tendency to lose control and to binge.

Herman and Polivy (1975) have shown that non-eating disordered dieters ("restrained subjects") will eat more ice cream after being fed one or two milk shakes than after no milk shakes at all. These dieters increase their intake when made to feel depressed or when they are given alcohol to drink (Polivy & Herman, 1976) and they ingest more following the consumption of a preload which they believe to be high in calories (whether or not it actually is high in calories) than they do when they have not been given a preload. Food restriction works against weight loss by predisposing individuals to dietary dyscontrol or binge eating. Yet food restriction, with all of its physiological perversity, has become the norm for women in this culture today.

When dieters binge, they experience the binge as a profound loss of power or control. They become more anxious and they intensify their efforts to control their weight. They may attempt to more rigidly restrict their intake or they may exercise. When obligatory runners overeat, or if they intentionally consume a carbohydrate load, they may use the same strategies: they run an extra mile and/or decrease their intake at the next meal. Many eating disordered women and a few runners employ the additional control tactics of vomiting and diuretic and laxative abuse. Yet, when these individuals place themselves in a deficit state, they intensify their hunger and invite further dyscontrol.

With the exception of the Keys et al. (1950) experiment, the studies on appetite and satiety involve only women. This may be because women are the ones who complain of, and request treatment for, problematic eating behavior. As we have already noted, men seldom complain of their appetite or the need to lose weight. Perhaps, when men are unhappy with their girth, they complain of not being fit instead of being too fat. They might request an exercise program or a trainer rather than a weight loss program or a diet doctor.

FOOD DEPRIVATION AND ACTIVITY

When eating disordered women and obligatory runners combine diet and exercise in an effort to become healthy, thin, or even younger, the pattern of diminished intake and heightened output seems to regenerate and reinforce itself and the system becomes remarkably resistant to change. The animal laboratory provides a clue as to how this process might transpire. Many studies demonstrate that the activity level of animals—especially male animals—increases as a function of food deprivation (Siegel & Steinberg, 1949; Teitelbaum, 1957; Cornish & Morosovsky, 1965). The longer animals are deprived, the more active they become (DeBattista & Bedard, 1987). If these findings can be applied to humans, then when people skip meals or stretch them further apart they would become predictably more active.

Food deprived animals can reach a state in which they seem driven to continue their activity. When rats are fed a single daily meal which is less than what they would need to maintain weight and they are given the opportunity to run on an activity wheel, a strange happening unfolds. The rats begin to restrict their diet even more and they appear compelled to run around and around on the activity wheel. Not only does their body weight decline but if the process is allowed to continue, the animals run until they die of "self-starvation" (Routennberg, 1968). Control animals exposed to the same apparatus and food schedule survive if they are not allowed to run. This experiment has been replicated in a number of species.

Epling and Pierce (1988) suggest that the cultural pressure to diet and exercise sets the stage for individuals to inadvertently develop eating disorders when they combine a strict diet with exercise. They propose that as many as 75 percent of the women who develop anorexia do so because they combine a strict diet with exercise. However, this theory does not explain why some women will develop an eating disorder when they diet and exercise, while many other women will not.

The survival of man may have depended upon his becoming more active when the food supply was scarce. The increase in activity would have been channeled into hunting or gathering. If these endeavors produced food, primitive man would have been likely to gorge himself and go to sleep. If the search for food were not successful, the increase in activity would have persisted—the hunter would have continued to hunt rather than rest.

ATHLETICISM

If the combination of diet and exercise can precipitate an eating disorder, perhaps the combination of diet and exercise can precipitate compulsive athleticism. The principle that diet plus exercise increases activity might operate even if an athlete is not consciously dieting but is expending more calories than he consumes. The athlete who either cuts down on his intake or who increases his distance without increasing his food supply may enter a deficit state of negative nitrogen balance. The deficit state could trigger an increase in the need to run. The athlete would probably assume that he was running more because he enjoyed, or could excel at, the sport, but in actuality he would be running more because he was restricting his diet relative to his energy expenditure. This could lead to a progressive increase in activity to the point that the runner would feel locked into the sport and compelled to continue.

That the combination of diet and exercise is associated with an increase in activity is supported by a study of athletes which was completed by Richert and Hummers (1986). These researchers report that the number of hours that men spend running correlates positively and significantly with the stringency of their diets and with their abnormal attitudes toward food and eating. The more stringently they diet, the more they are involved in various activities (including running) and the more hours they spend involved in these activities. This study not only supports the association between diet and enhanced athleticism in runners but suggests that the involvement in other activities increases along with the athleticism. When they eat less, these men may have an increased tendency to take on many different activities.

Eating disordered women are notable for the number and extent of their activities. Eating disordered women collect recipes, make-up, clothes, etc. They become compulsive exercisers, compulsive shoppers, and sometimes compulsive shoplifters. The increase in these activities is correlated with the severity of the disorder (Kron et al., 1978; Pyle et al., 1983). Obligatory athletes seem to collect running shoes, timing gadgets, running magazines, and sometimes stones and bits of metal scraps along the running route. The overall increase in activities in both groups may be secondary to dietary restriction or, in the case of the runners, insufficient intake relative to output. Alternatively, the dietary restriction and the increase in activity may be secondary to some other factor such as depression.

The subjects who were starved in the Keys experiment (1950) demonstrated an increase in many small activities. They embarked on shopping sprees and purchased coffee pots, hot plates, kitchen utensils, secondhand clothes, knickknacks, and other "junk," which they did not need. Obsessive thoughts accompanied the activities and the increase in activity coincided with the men's increased imaging of, and ruminations about, food. Indeed, eating disordered women and obligatory runners do seem to be involved in many small activities and many small thoughts. The phenomena of "many activities" could be an outgrowth of the frustration of not being able to eat.

STRESS, ACTIVITY, AND EATING BEHAVIOR IN ANIMAL EXPERIMENTS

Rats continue to eat, become "hyperphagic," when their tails are pinched. The pressure on the tail is mild and the rats are only minimally stressed, yet they significantly increase their food intake. If food is not available, they become involved in a variety of other activities. If all stimuli are removed from the cage, the animals will increase their grooming and paw nail pulling activities (Rowland & Antelman, 1976). The hyperphagia in rats is such a predictable occurrence that it has been employed to determine the efficacy of anorexigenic or appetite suppressant medications. The effect of the tail pinch on eating behavior is so strong that it can make animals eat even after their appetite is suppressed by amphetamine or the destruction of the appetite center in the hypothalamus. In fact, when the tail is pinched and the animals are given amphetamine, they will consume significantly more food than do rats that have their tails pinched but are not administered amphetamine.

Bulimic women often respond to stress by binge eating and/or purging. Anxiety serves to aggravate the hunger of most dieting women (Herman et al., 1987), but bulimic women seem to be especially susceptible to stress-induced eating (Abraham & Beumont, 1982). They will binge in response to situations that other people would not view as stressful (Heilbrun & Bloomfield, 1986; Kattanach & Rodin, 1988). If the effect of tail pinching in rats produces stress that is in any way comparable to that which is experienced by bulimic women, it would suggest that stress itself could cause some women to continue to eat or to eat when they are not hungry.

When tail-pinched rats are denied access to food, they increase their interactions with other rats and the environment. The choice of activity is context dependent, i.e., maternal behavior will be displayed in the presence of rat pups, aggression in the presence of a male, etc. If the rats do not have access to food and are placed alone, they direct their activity toward their bodies and they begin to repetitively gnaw or sniff (Antelman & Caggiula, 1977). It is as if the rats need to be active whether the activity involves eating or not.

If this fascinating line of research applies to humans, it would suggest that even mild stress could promote an increase in variety of activities in dieting individuals. Perhaps under stress (and the stress might be hunger), individuals would tend to be more involved in essential activities such as a job or housework; if these activities were not available, they might take on less consequential tasks such as health or fitness related activities; if these activities were not possible, they might groom or otherwise attend to the body. This is one pathway to an understanding of the overall increase in activity in dieters and athletes, eating disordered women and obligatory runners.

An overall increase in activity is described in one further study from the animal laboratory by Falk (1981). He explores the association between food restriction, rigid scheduling, and a variety of seemingly unrelated activities. When rats are placed on a restricted diet where they must earn their pellets by pressing a lever, and regardless how often they press the lever they will receive only one pellet in a given time interval, they always demonstrate a variety of apparently senseless activities. In a curious, compulsive fashion, they repetitively lick the water spout, drinking 10 times the amount they would drink under normal conditions. The drinking of water persists unabated as long as the rats are on the restricted feeding schedule. Other activities increase also: running on the activity wheel, licking at a stream of air, eating non-nutritive wood shavings, attacks on other animals, and generalized running about. The activity appears driven, but character of the activity seems to depend upon the materials which are available in the environment.

In Falk's experiment, the rats become increasingly involved in apparently senseless activities as the interval between pellet droppings increases. The same phenomenon is said to occur in guinea pigs, gerbils, mice, and nonhuman primates. Similar experiments conducted with human subjects (Katchanoff et al., 1973) demonstrate increases in activity level, smoking, drinking, eating, and grooming in response to increasingly restrictive schedules.

Stress seems to interact with diet to foster disturbed eating behaviors in humans as well as in animals. When non-dieting individuals are exposed to stress, they eat less, but dieting women tend to overeat in response to stress even when they are not hungry (Herman et al, 1987). When disordered eating exists, it worsens under conditions of high perceived stress and an increased sense of ineffectiveness (Striegel-Moore et al., 1989). Bulimic women report significantly greater than expectable stress and negative mood prior to their binge episodes (Lingswiler, Crowther & Stephens, 1989). The "new," high-functioning eating disordered women tend to work under competitive, stressful circumstances. At times, these women seem driven by their demanding schedules. When their work increases and their schedules are packed, the eating disorder worsens.

Perhaps stress, rigid scheduling, and food restriction promote pathologic eating behaviors in women and obligatory athleticism in men. The obligatory runners in our study were stressed, achievement-oriented individuals who worked or studied in a competitive environment. They scheduled themselves tightly, squeezing their time for running between their occupational and family responsibilities. They planned every 10 minutes of their day in advance so that they had little or no time to spare. In part, this was due to their desire to spend every free moment running, but it was also the manner in which these individuals were able to succeed in a competitive, demanding environment.

In nature, animal behavior becomes driven and irrelevant when the situation in which the animals find themselves is highly charged and ambiguous (Falk, 1981). A bird who is defending disputed territorial boundaries will "irrationally" feed, preen, or mount instead of fighting or fleeing. When a nesting bird if approached by a predator, she may preen herself instead of defending her brood or taking flight. The function of these apparently senseless activities seems to be to deter the animal from making a premature move when the course of action is dubious. Falk suggests that humans, as well as animals, behave irrationally when they experience a combination of stress (urgency), impeded access to a crucial commodity, and a lack of alternatives or ways to escape from the difficult situation.

Dieting activity in anorexia and the binge/purge cycle in bulimia are seemingly irrational behaviors. Running on stress fractures and continuing to run in spite of deteriorating cartilage in the knee are behaviors that don't make sense. Perhaps these activities are somehow analogous to the irrational behaviors which Falk (1981) describes in highly stressed animals. In the case of obligatory runners and well-functioning eating disordered women, the stress of multiple, often ambiguous demands, the self-imposed restriction of food and/or rest, and the dogged determination to persist in spite of considerable discomfort might combine to promote irrational behaviors.

Perhaps obligatory individuals are especially likely to enter into highly competitive, stressful occupations; to restrict themselves from food and rest in the service of beauty or fitness; and to force themselves to continue because it is the expected or "right" thing to do. In doing so, they would unwittingly set the stage for their behaviors to become driven and irrational.

If the animal experiments outlined above can be applied to humans, then activity may increase and become driven when individuals are stressed, when they restrict their diet, when they combine food restriction and exercise, when they adhere to a rigid, restrictive schedule, and when they are exposed to highly charged, ambiguous circumstances.

SUMMARY

This chapter has presented material from multiple lines of biologic investigation. Some of this material may apply to the eating disorders and compulsive athleticism and some may not. Of the many possibilities that emerge, the most exciting and potentially important are:

- That there are parallel changes in the neuroendocrine status of eating disordered women and long distance runners;
- That an increase in endorphins may allow the anorexic to tolerate starvation and the runner to tolerate pain and exhaustion;
- That certain women could have a biologically based predisposition to amenorrhea, depression, obsessive thoughts, and compulsive or exaggerated behaviors;
- That the manner in which parents separate from their infants could determine the children's vulnerability to certain problems later in life;
- That dieting works against weight loss by predisposing individuals to dietary dyscontrol or binge eating;
- That in animals the combination of food restriction and increased activity can cause the activity to become driven;
- That mildly stressed animals can become hyperphagic. If they are stressed and restricted from food, they will demonstrate an increase in activity;
- That conditions of stress, food restriction, rigid scheduling, and ambiguous circumstance can cause activity to increase and to become senseless and driven.

Although biologic forces must be extremely important in the formation and perpetuation of the activity disorders, biologic forces cannot, by themselves, explain why certain individuals are susceptible to these conditions while others are not.

CHAPTER 7

Psychological Theory

This chapter will review the psychological research on eating disorders, on running, on obligatory running, and on the relationship between obligatory running and the eating disorders.

ASSESSMENT

The reader needs to know something about the tests which are designed to measure eating attitudes and behaviors in order to appreciate current research on the eating disorders. The Eating Attitudes Test (EAT) is a rating scale which tries to distinguish patients with anorexia nervosa from weight preoccupied, but otherwise healthy, female college students (Garner & Garfinkel, 1979). The 26-item questionnaire is broken down into three subscales: dieting, bulimia and food preoccupation, and oral control. Although the EAT measures pathology in underweight girls, its interpretation seems ambiguous for average weight or overweight girls (Wells et al., 1985) and it shows a high false-positive rate in distinguishing eating disorders from disturbed eating behaviors in college women (Carter & Moss, 1984).

Tabulating the number and kinds of symptoms in the eating disorders is simple compared to understanding the woman's psyche. A new generation of questionnaires has been devised to assess the underlying issues in the disorders. The most popular and influential of these is the EDI or Eating Disorder Inventory (Raciti & Norcross, 1987). The Garner group developed the EDI to more thoroughly assess the cognitive and behavioral characteristics of anorexia nervosa (Garner, Olmsted & Polivy, 1983). The eight subscales tap the extent of the drive for thinness, bulimia, body dissatisfaction, ineffectiveness, perfectionism, interpersonal distrust, interoceptive awareness, and fear of maturity. The EDI has been successfully used to predict the emergence of eating disorders in a high risk group of women (Garner, Garfinkel, Rockert & Olmsted, 1987).

Although the EAT and the EDI were developed to assess women who might be eating disordered, these scales have been used with male runners to test the hypothesis that extreme running behavior is analogous to extreme dieting behavior.

EATING DISTURBANCES

Concern about gaining weight is common among women in this culture whether or not they are overweight. The majority of women who are not overweight still consider themselves to be fat (Turnbull et al., 1989). Many women who diet successfully still feel fat. College women who state that they feel fat are not likely to actually be fat, although some of them are. Feeling fat is usually not associated with being fat; it seems to be an index of the women's overall self dissatisfaction.

The women who feel fat when they are slim are a special group of individuals. They perceive more social pressure to be thin, they are highly perfectionistic, and they tend to feel poorly about their bodies (Striegel-Moore, McAvay & Rodin, 1986). They diet repeatedly and they struggle with an intense and persistent desire to eat.

SUBCLINICAL EATING DISORDERS

In colleges and universities a substantial number of male and female students diet, binge, and purge (and exercise compulsively) but they are not sufficiently disturbed to qualify for an eating disorder diagnosis. Individuals who binge and/or purge usually do not meet the DSM criteria for bulimia (Hawkins & Clement, 1980). There are many more persons with disordered eating behavior than there are persons who can be formally diagnosed as eating disordered.

Within a normal college sample, the women who have a greater desire for thinness are the women who are more likely to report disordered eating and weight control behaviors (Lundholm & Littrell, 1986). Between 26 percent and 79 percent of college women binge, a number which may be increasing substantially (Clarke & Palmer, 1983; Pyle et al., 1983; Katzman, Wolchik & Braver, 1984; Moss et al., 1984; Hart & Ollendick, 1985). These women begin to organize their thinking, emotional state, and social lives around their long and exhausting battle with their appetite (Schwartz & Thompson, 1981) and they demonstrate many of the cognitive distortions that are present in the eating disorders. Thinness and scrupulousness about food, eating, and exercise become a way of life (Rothenberg, 1986). In spite of the emotional and physical discomfort they experience, these women do not seek treatment (Hawkins & Clement, 1980).

University women display a range of disturbed eating behavior, although they lean toward the bulimic rather than the anorexic symptomatology (Vanderheyden & Boland, 1987). Average weight college women are consistently dissatisfied with their bodies; their level of dissatisfaction increases after they eat. They feel fat and they overestimate their body size (Wardle & Foley, 1989). The symptoms they present range from occasional binge eating to the full-fledged bulimic syndrome. As college women present more symptoms of an eating disorder, they are apt to exhibit greater anxiety, depression, somatization, interpersonal sensitivity, and obsessive compulsiveness. They are more likely to be socially isolated and concerned with achievement (Vanderheyden, Fekken & Boland, 1988).

Because so many university women are overly preoccupied with weight and because so many of them binge and/or purge, some investigators suggest that most, if not all, women in the culture carry some risk of developing an eating disorder (Schwartz & Thompson, 1981; Thompson, Berg & Shatford, 1987). However, the disturbed eating behavior is characteristic of a very select population composed primarily of high achieving, active, and independent young women. Findings which are based on this population may not apply to all women in the culture.

There are many more individuals with an eating disturbance than there are persons with an eating disorder. Women with an eating disturbance usually do not develop an eating disorder, but they are a great deal more likely to develop an eating disorder than the rest of the population. Their habits and attitudes are the same as those of eating disordered women; the symptoms are simply not as intense or as numerous. A theory which addresses the eating disorders would need to take into consideration the eating disturbances.

THE EATING DISORDERS

Anorexia and bulimia are variations on the theme of weight control; there are many more similarities than there are differences between the two conditions. Forty-seven percent of patients with anorexia nervosa demonstrate bulimic behaviors (Casper et al. 1980; Garfinkel, Moldofsky &

Garner, 1980) and 30–80 percent of patients with bulimia have a history of anorexia nervosa (Mitchell, Pyle & Eckert, 1985). In the past, most of these women became anorexic first and then developed bulimia as a means of coping with the chronic deprivation. At present, relatively more women develop bulimia first and then become anorexic (Kassett et al., 1988). Some women switch back and forth from one condition to the other over the years. The women who are the most disturbed are those women who simultaneously qualify for both disorders (Mickalide & Andersen, 1985).

The following descriptions of anorexia and bulimia are based for the most part on studies of patient populations—women who are sick enough to seek or be forced into treatment. The descriptions are less likely to apply to the "new," well-functioning, eating disordered women who are in outpatient treatment or who are not in treatment at all.

ANOREXIA

There is no personality type that is characteristic of anorexia, but social insecurity, excessive dependency and compliancy, limited spontaneity, perfectionism, and impaired autonomy have been thought to be the earliest warning of a disturbance later on (Strober, 1980, 1985). In childhood, these girls seem too good; they are sensitive to the feelings of others and they try to guess what other people might want of them. They are reserved and they avoid trouble (Crisp, 1965b). When they are with other people they feel as if they might be judged or put to some kind of test. Because of this, they derive very little gratification from relationships.

It is easy to see why anorexic girls become acutely concerned about appearance, as this is an aspect which they can't hide and by which they may be judged. It is as if they have no internal sense of value so they must rely on the reactions of others for their sense of self worth (Russell, 1979; Garfinkel, Moldofsky & Garner, 1980). Through their appearance and their actions, they try to emulate whatever standards of goodness or acceptability they think other people endorse, including independence and achievement. But they are frightened by independence and competition as this means that they will be exposed to many tests, that they could be criticized and could even fail.

Anorexic women are often thought not to be hungry. Because they do not eat, this means that they have no desire for food. This is not the case—even before these women begin to starve themselves, they are constantly aware of an insidious appetite whether or not they have eaten

(Rothenberg, 1986). Anorexic women have a stronger urge to eat, are more preoccupied with food, and more anxious when hungry than control subjects (Garfinkel, 1974). Anorexia could correctly be described as a refusal to eat in the face of a ravenous appetite. Anorexic women who can admit to being hungry, and who deny their illness less, have a more favorable prognosis (Halmi, Goldberg et al., 1979).

The cognitive processes of anorexic patients are marked by selective abstraction, magnifications, overgeneralization, all-or-none dichotomies, and magical thinking (Garner & Bemis, 1982). With starvation, their thinking becomes even more exaggerated, negative and simplistic (Neimeyer & Khouzam, 1985) than it had been before. They feel hopeless and ugly, without the possibility of redemption. Anorexic women use these perceptions in the cognitive strategies which they use to handle the urge to eat. An anorexic woman may sit down to eat with a ravenous appetite. She takes one bite of a potato, and begins to feel anxious. She thinks that potatoes are high calorie foods, and high calorie foods make people fat. If she eats the potato, she will be fat. If she is fat, she will be ugly, and everyone will hate her. Then, she notes her hunger and fears that if she starts eating, she will lose control and be unable to stop. If she can't stop, she will become ugly and fat, and everyone will hate her.

Anorexic women can quickly change their perception of food, their bodies, and their internal state. This comes easily to anorexic women because they lack a stable sense of who they are. The self concept has always fluctuated from moment to moment as they respond to cultural expectations and the attitudes of other people (Scott, 1987). The self assessment depends upon how they perceive others responding to them and what values they think others see as important. Their self assessment influences their mood and their mood influences their self perception. An anorexic woman who has been praised by her superior is apt to feel elated and to be better able to accept her image in the mirror, but the anorexic woman who has been criticized feels angry or depressed and she perceives her image as hideous or disgusting.

Anorexic women's unstable self concept includes a precarious picture of the body (Norris, 1984). They may feel "delectably thin" one moment and "heavy as a horse" the next. At times, they are helpless victims of these shifts, but at other times they orchestrate them. The ease with which they vacillate and the lack of any critical evaluation of their thinking processes is similar to that which has been noted in borderline patients (Kernberg, 1975). However, borderline patients may not be as likely to use the fluctuations in strategies to reinforce their resolve, as do anorexic women.

Regardless of how dependent women are before they develop anorexia, as they become anorexic they deny their dependency and become staunchly independent (Smart, Beumont & George, 1976). As they reject the need for care, they reject the need for food. By the time they self starve to the point of emaciation they present a kind of fierce, embattled autonomy, a proclamation to others that they had best stay away and not try to be of any help. This quality inspired the title of a well-known text: *Anorexia Nervosa—Let Me Be* (Crisp, 1980). They rigorously disavow their desire to eat, perhaps because eating is associated with dependency and loss of control. They control the body by dieting and they control the mind by devoting themselves to duty so that they continue to perform remarkably well in school or on the job even when they have starved themselves almost to death (Schwartz & Thompson, 1981; Swift, 1982).

Anorexic women demonstrate a number of obsessive compulsive personality traits before and after they starve. In fact, obsessive compulsive features are the aspect of the condition which is most frequently reported (Rothenberg, 1988). Pre-anorexic girls are described as hardworking, anxious young women who struggle to achieve (Bruch, 1973). These features intensify as they begin to starve themselves. At the height of the disorder, they are immersed in elaborate food strategies and eating prevention rituals; they can think of little else. They are preoccupied with calorie counting and the mental imaging of food. They resent having to keep thinking about food and wish that they had more control over the process. In spite of their resentment, they seem to derive some unconscious gratification from the mental images of food (Rothenberg, 1986).

Starvation creates or intensifies all of the symptoms of anorexia. As these women continue to fast, they regularly become more seclusive, moody, hostile, distrustful, and depressed. These qualities combine to yield the picture of embattled autonomy which is characteristic of the end stage of anorexia. They begin to appear very much like the starved men in the Keys experiment (1950) which was described in the previous chapter. The embattled autonomy persists well into the weight recovery phase.

Severely compromised anorexics who have regained adequate weight are apt to continue to harbor distorted attitudes toward food, eating, and weight in spite of treatment. These attitudes are quite consistent, although they are somewhat less extreme than they were during the acute phase (Clinton & McKinley, 1986). Several years after hospital treatment, most anorexics continue to restrict their diet and 79 percent consider themselves overweight. They are bedeviled by hunger and beset with obligatory ruminations about calories and food. Forty percent report chronic depression and 22 percent have unsatisfactory social relationships (Nussbaum et al., 1985).

The fact that the outcome in anorexia is not related to the women's success in gaining weight (Kaye, Gwirtsman et al., 1986) suggests that there is a malignant underlying process which surfaces in the guise of an obsession about weight. Whether or not the women are able to gain weight, the process remains intact and resistant to treatment. These women continue to idealize slimness, to struggle against a voracious appetite, and to be angry at themselves and their bodies. Their unstable self representation and the tendency to distort the perception of body and self persists. The process may occasionally become acute, but for most of these women, it remains an ever-present bedfellow.

In the last chapter we described the mechanism by which food restriction leads to an increase in appetite and dietary dyscontrol. Yet food restriction by itself does not explain anorexia. These women are troubled by hunger and dissatisfied with the body whether or not they are practicing food restriction. There must be other mechanisms involved such as stress, biologic factors, or personality variables.

With time, many anorexic women learn to manage their problems with food. The anorexic women in the Garfinkel study (1974) who made good or intermediate adjustments did so by arranging their own structure outside the hospital. They devised a plan by which they would be served three regular meals a day in a restaurant or by an individual such as a relative. They ate the exact amount presented, to the last crumb, and never asked for more. Although they were still troubled, they had managed to contain the disorder. The women who did not do well were the women who attempted to manage meals themselves. They were unable to adhere to a reasonable diet and either sharply restricted their intake, developed food fads, induced vomiting, or abused laxatives.

BULIMIA

Bulimic women are adept at maintaining appearances while they hide their bingeing and purging (Bruch, 1973). Because of this, there are many women who would qualify for a DSM diagnosis of bulimia who have never been identified and who are not in treatment. The true prevalence of bulimia remains a mystery, although the estimates stand at 1.9 percent in the general population (Cooper & Fairburn, 1983) and at about 3–4 percent among college women (Pyle et al., 1983; Katzman, Wolchik & Braver, 1984; Drewnowski, Yee & Krahn, 1988) with estimates as high as 19 percent (Halmi, Falk & Schwartz, 1981).

The incidence of bulimia seems to have increased dramatically over the past 20 years (Jones et al., 1980; Szmulker et al., 1986). The ranks have been swelled by women who are higher functioning, socially adept, and apparently stable—who can appear relatively healthy when they are compared to other psychiatric populations (Johnson, Stuckey, et al., 1982). The bulimic women of today are less likely to act impulsively or to be personality disordered (Turnbull et al., 1989).

Women almost always become bulimic in order not to gain weight. They have usually tried to diet with intermittent success. In the course of dieting they have felt painfully deprived, acutely and constantly hungry. They remain hungry even after they eat (Walsh et al., 1989). Eventually they can no longer resist their hunger and they binge. Then they feel miserable, fat, guilty, and out of control. They may redouble their efforts to restrict or they may try to counter the binge by vomiting, exercise, laxatives, and/or diuretics. Vomiting quickly relieves the misery of having gorged and for some women it becomes a too convenient solution. They can avoid having to tolerate hunger by bingeing and purging (Garner & Garfinkel, 1982; Garner, Olmsted, Polivy & Garfinkel, 1984; Johnson & Connors, 1987).

When bulimic women are dieting they seem to be as consumed with counting calories and planning meals as are anorexic women. When they begin to binge and purge, they can no longer judge their intake with confidence and they tend not to count calories as much. Instead, they become as enveloped in the bingeing and purging as they had been in the dieting. When they are not actually binge eating or purging in their free time, they are planning or gathering food for the next cycle. As bulimic women channel more of their concerns, wishes, and goals into the input/output transaction, they begin to feel controlled by the bulimic activity.

Bulimic women may have always been somewhat limited in their ability to derive gratification from relationships, but they become increasingly isolated after the onset of the disorder. The binge eating and purging seems to be an attempt to satisfy their needs independently of others. It enables them to cope with the various feelings of shame/guilt, anger/rage, and anxiety that result from the emotional isolation and the continued repression of their needs and wishes (Teusch, 1988).

Some bulimic women seem caught between the desire for a totally nurturing relationship and their inability to ask for nurturance or to receive it through a relationship. One of Teusch's subjects said: "I have to put a lot of energy into being with people. I work at being a friend, it is never really relaxing. Bingeing is. . . . absolutely and totally nondemanding. It is time out, just for me." Bulimic women may crave comfort, support, and affiliation (Lazerson, 1984; Swift, 1985) but they are frightened by their neediness, for if they should give in to it they would compromise their independence. Therefore, they attempt to deny their needs and to defend against feeling needy. The binge/purge sequence is a poor substitute for being nurtured, but it may be the only one which these women can accept.

Bulimic women's perceptions of their bodies, food, and the environment become distorted (Garner & Bemis, 1982; Garner, 1985) in the same manner as do the perceptions of anorexic women (Fernandez, 1984). They tend to rigidly categorize food as "good" or "bad," poisonous or health bestowing (Rothenberg, 1986) and they use these perceptions to boost the resolve to rid themselves of food. Bulimic women perceive the environment as more stressful and less controllable, predictable, and desirable than do other women. They binge in response to common events without reflecting, reviewing, or appraising the situation (Heilbrun & Bloomfield, 1986; Kattanach & Rodin, 1988). If they are forced to discontinue the binge eating and purging, they suffer the anxiety, depression, bloatedness, and sense of loss of control which are characteristic of withdrawal in the activity disorders.

ACHIEVEMENT EXPECTATIONS

The families of bulimic women tend to emphasize achievement even more than do the families of anorexic women (Stern et al., 1989). By the time they mature, bulimic women want desperately to succeed. Some investigators suggest that the bulimia is a product of the women's frustration over their ability to achieve. They can be successful in dieting so they focus on dieting instead (Katz, 1985; Johnson & Connors, 1987). Yet, very successful women have bulimia and the bulimia may worsen when they are successful in competition. This has certainly been the case with Jane Fonda and Cathy Rigby. Mintz (1982) describes three bright, achievement-oriented bulimic women who binge when they are faced with a competitive challenge. A more likely explanation than the frustration of not succeeding is the frustration of having unreasonably high self expectations for success. The more that these women expect of themselves, the more likely they are to be frustrated in their performance, regardless of how excellent that performance may be.

Most bulimic women remain bulimic for many years. Some experience a series of remissions but others do not. Although the symptoms wax and wane, there seems to be an overall trend toward improvement in the disordered eating behavior (Mitchell, Pyle, Hatsukami et al., 1986;

Yager, Landsverk & Edelstein, 1987). Even without treatment, some patients revert to eating normally, especially when their circumstances are less stressful or they have separated from a difficult relationship. The bulimia may abate with age along with hunger and the sense of smell.

GENDER ISSUES

MALES WITH EATING DISORDERS

At one time it was thought that only women would develop eating disorders because appearance, weight, and eating were feminine preoccupations (Boskind-Lodahl & White, 1978). We now know that men do become eating disordered, although males comprise only 5–10 percent of all patients with anorexia nervosa (Jones et al., 1980; Anderson & Mickalide, 1983). When men become eating disordered, they appear remarkably like women who are eating disordered. Their social and family history, onset and course of the disorder, and their presentation at initial evaluation are almost identical to that of the eating disordered women (Hall, Delahunt & Ellis, 1985; Crisp, Burns & Bhata, 1986; Fichter & Daser, 1987; Oyebode, Boodhoo & Schapira, 1988). Because the men who become eating disordered are a highly select group, they may differ in some respects from the women. Perhaps they would need to have more unrealistic self expectations, be more compulsive, or have a more ferocious appetite to become eating disordered.

An additional similarity between men and women is that there are many more men with subclinical eating disorders than there are men who qualify as eating disordered. Between 41 and 60 percent of college men binge eat (Clarke & Palmer, 1983; Pyle et al., 1983; Katzman, Wolchik & Braver, 1984). These figures suggest that many men have an unusually robust appetite and that many men are eating disturbed.

The few differences that exist between males and females with eating disorders are intriguing. Compared to women, eating disordered men are more preoccupied in their thoughts about food/weight and they show more hyperactivity, sexual anxiety and a more intense achievement orientation (Fichter, Daser & Postpischil, 1985). Males are more likely to become overly active than are females (Crisp & Burns, 1983) and they often have had a premorbid involvement in athletics. Katz (1986) and Smith (1980) describe males who developed eating disorders after they had become serious athletes. Of the 76 male eating disorder patients studied by Anderson (1984, 1989), 50 percent had been mildly or moderately obese prior to the initiation of a diet. They were more concerned about body shape or muscle definition than about pounds or clothing size. They were more likely to have begun to diet in order to attain better athletic performance or to avoid cardiac disease. Most outcome predictors are the same for males as for females, but the existence of vomiting predicts a good outcome for males and a poor outcome for females (Crisp, Burns & Bhata, 1986).

Kaffman and Sadeh (1989) compare eating disordered men in the kibbutz with eating disordered women. The men begin to diet in order to improve their physical fitness or athletic performance rather than to improve their appearance. They engage in extremely intense physical activity, often long distance running, along with the dieting. Even before they begin to diet, they present an obsessive personality and signs of an obsessive compulsive disorder. These men in the kibbutz seem to closely resemble our male obligatory runners.

Eating disordered men differ from eating disordered women in that they are likely to be intensely athletic and to have begun dieting in order to become fit rather than to lose weight. In this respect, they resemble the obligatory runners. Eating disordered men may assume a position which is intermediate between the eating disorders and compulsive athleticism.

SEXUAL ORIENTATION IN EATING DISORDERED MEN

Dieting and concern about appearance are indeed feminine preoccupations in this culture. Therefore, it is not surprising that male eating disordered patients present with unconventional psychosexual development and orientation (Herzog, Norman et al., 1984; Fichter & Daser, 1987; Schneider & Agras, 1987). There is a statistically significant difference between bulimic men and women in terms of marriage and sexual preference. More women are married and more men report homosexual or bisexual preferences (Schneider & Agras, 1987). Male anorexia nervosa patients are more extroverted than most other men and they score "superfeminine" on the Freiburger Personality Inventory. Male anorexics are said to make excellent chefs (Fichter, Daser & Postpischil, 1985).

Another approach to the relationship between sexual preference and the eating disorders is to study the eating attitudes and behaviors of homosexual males. Yager, Kurtzman et al. (1988) find in homosexual students a higher prevalence of binge eating problems, of feeling terrified of being fat, and of having used diuretics than in other male students.

Homosexual men score higher on the Eating Disorders Inventory scales for drive for thinness, interoceptive awareness, bulimia, body dissatisfaction, maturity fears, and ineffectiveness (Laessle et al., 1988).

SEXUAL ORIENTATION IN WOMEN ATHLETES

If men with eating problems are more likely than other men to present an unconventional sexual orientation, then women distance runners might be expected to be unconventional (homosexual) also. Indeed, women who are serious runners do tend to lose their subcutaneous fat and their secondary sexual characteristics, so that they appear more androgenous or more like men. However, these women are generally heterosexual. The conventional orientation of women athletes may be because in this culture women are permitted or encouraged to act as men do. When women enter a male arena, they are often thought of as courageous, but when men enter a female arena, they are likely to be ridiculed. Masculine appearing women are quite acceptable, while feminine appearing men are subject to criticism and rejection. Therefore, women's sexual orientation does not need to play a large role in their choice of an athletic activity over traditionally "feminine" activities.

Men usually run to enhance their ability or to become fit. Women are more apt to run in order to lose weight and improve their appearance. There is a strong bias against men who run in order to improve their appearance, as these men appear to be "feminine."

Women who diet in order to achieve a more tubular or masculine shape have sometimes been thought to have a deep desire to become a man. This seems not to be the case; women diet because they value certain masculine attributes (leanness, competitiveness, success, etc.) which are prized by the culture, and which are associated with upward mobility (Timko et al., 1987). The same construct seems to hold for women runners who characteristically value speed or endurance, muscularity, and competitiveness. Although these women may be at the androgenous end of the spectrum, this does not mean that they reject their sexual identity or role.

RUNNING

As the regard for health and fitness became commonplace in the 1970s and 1980s, a number of books and magazines began to describe the benefits of vigorous exercise. Physical activity was presented as good for all people—as an energizer, an antidepressant, and a life extender. A person could cultivate the self through developing the body—by paring it, preening it, pumping it up and pounding it down. It was the fantasy about the body, shared by thousands, which gave birth to the running "culture" (Stein, 1982).

The benefits which athletes derive from running have been mentioned in earlier chapters. Running does diminish anxiety (Morgan, 1979) and it does seem to be an effective antidepressant for mild to moderate depressions (Greist et al., 1979). Runners are very likely to have been depressed at some time in their past (Colt et al., 1981). However, running or any vigorous sport can be overdone: very intensive daily practice is associated with an increase in depression (Thirer, Zackheim & Summers, 1987).

It must be a very special runner who chooses to devote all his spare time and most of his energy to running. There are a few studies on the personality characteristics of extreme (but not necessarily obligatory) runners. Gontang, Clitsome and Kostrubala (1977) studied 50 men who had completed marathons in under three hours. The mean number of miles they ran per week was 76.14. These runners tended to be introverted and high achieving persons; 96 percent had completed college. On psychological testing, they appeared to be painstaking, systematic, hardworking individuals who would persevere at any task they undertook. Once committed, they were not easily discouraged or distracted. They quit only when experience made it patently clear that they were wrong. This finding is echoed by another study (Owens & Slade, 1987) in which unselected marathon runners proved to be extremely perfectionistic individuals. They are obligatory persons who characteristically set very high standards for themselves.

Although anxiety and depression are favorably influenced by running, there is no evidence that running per se can change the personality of the individual (Folkins & Sine, 1981). It is more likely that introverted, compulsive, and perfectionistic individuals are attracted to running because of factors such as gender, temperament, current circumstances, and adaptive needs. Once they begin to run, they are likely to feel much better. If they continue to increase their running time and distance, the experience changes: they run at the expense of their health and significant relationships (De Coverly Veale, 1987).

COMPULSIVE ATHLETICISM

A British physician, John Little (1969), was the first to articulate a concern about the adverse psychological effects of extreme exertion. He described the "athlete's neurosis," an affliction of middle aged men who continued to run in spite of injuries and other complications. These runners were high achieving, hard driving individuals such as doctors, lawyers, and other professionals. They tended to make running a compulsive ritual and they often used the running as a magic potion against problems such as growing old. Callen (1983) described a similar group of men who had entered the sport after age 40: compared to other runners they were the hardest running, most competitive group of all. In contrast to other runners who often experienced a runner's high during the last half of their run, these men felt elated only because they had managed to finish the race.

In 1979, Morgan (1979) noted that running can become a "negative addiction." The athlete can become "hooked" into his daily exercise program to the point where he thinks that he cannot exist without it. He continues to run in spite of cogent reasons not to run and he is anxious, irritable, and depressed if he can't run. The overly zealous running can lead to conflicts with the spouse, constriction of interests, dissatisfaction on the job, and pervasive fatigue.

RELATIONSHIP BETWEEN COMPULSIVE EXERCISE AND THE EATING DISORDERS

At the time of the publication of the article *Running: An Analogue of Anorexia?* (Yates, Leehey & Shisslak, 1983), the authors were unaware that Sours (1980) had suggested an association between extreme athleticism and the eating disorders in his book *Starving to Death in a Sea of Objects.* Sours noted the maximization of pain, the minimization of pleasure, and the deadly fear of fat present in both conditions. He remarked on the intense interest in and dissatisfaction about the body, the need to be in total control of body and mind, and the striving toward perfection, all of which could represent a search for the ideal self.

The paper on running and anorexia mentioned above drew attention both from athletes and from the scientific community. A number of researchers began to explore the phenomenon of compulsive athleticism. Many of their projects seemed to be designed to prove that we were wrong. Unfortunately, most of the studies made the mistake of comparing an unselected group of runners to anorexic patients. This design does not consider the uniqueness of the obligatory runner within the running population. These studies produced the expected result: that the anorexic patients were more emotionally disturbed than the population of runners and that they did not resemble the runners in many respects.

Some studies did try to select out obligatory runners, but they employed simplistic measures such as miles run per week or marathon participation. Wheeler et al. (1986) compared runners who averaged more than 40 miles a week to low mileage runners and sedentary controls. The high mileage runners tended to overestimate their waist width. All the runners scored significantly higher on the EAT than the controls, although the scores were below the anorexic range. Owens and Slade (1987) assessed 35 female marathon runners and found that they resembled anorexic women on the perfectionism scale of the SCANS, but not on the dissatisfaction with the body scale.

Several studies devised instruments which addressed some of the complexities of obligatory running. Pasman and Thompson (1988) used an Obligatory Exercise Questionnaire and the EDI to compare runners, weight lifters, and sedentary controls. They found that runners and weight lifters had significantly more eating disturbances than controls, but they scored in a less pathological range than the majority of anorexic patients. A study by Nudelman, Rosen, and Leitenberg (1988) compared "obligatory" male runners to diagnosed bulimic patients and found that the bulimic patients were sicker and more eating disordered than the male runners. Goldfarb and Plante (1984) used a "Zealousness" scale and found that male and female runners who were more zealous also were more assertive, obsessive, perfectionistic, and anxious.

On most psychological test indices, obligatory runners look like healthy, well-functioning individuals. Obligatory runners do not score in the pathological range on the MMPI in our most recent study or in an investigation by Blumenthal, Rose, and Chang (1985). However, obligatory runners do fall in the pathological range when they are unable to run (Chan & Grossman, 1988; Smith et al., 1990). When habituated runners are prevented from running, they experience severe anxiety, depression, anger, confusion, psychic fragmentation, and a feeling of bloatedness (Morgan, 1979; Sachs & Pargman, 1979; Paxton, 1982), symptoms which are similar to those of eating disordered patients who are not allowed to diet, binge, or purge.

The reason obligatory runners appear healthy on psychological tests is because most of them are healthy, well-functioning individuals. Running "works"; it provides an excellent adaptation. When obligatory runners are compared to anorexic and bulimic patients, the patients always appear more pathological. This is because these patients are the most seriously disordered individuals among a rather heterogenous group of women with eating disorders. The patients are restricted from indulging in the activity which provided at least a partial homeostasis, i.e. they are in a state of decompensation. Obligatory runners need to be compared to well-functioning women with eating disorders who are in outpatient treatment or no treatment at all.

Instead of searching for signs of an eating disorder in athletes, other investigators (Touyz, Beumont & Hook, 1987) have assessed the exercise habits of anorexic patients. Fifteen anorexic patients, all but one of whom engaged in strenuous activity for more than two hours a day, were compared to 17 anorexic women who were not overly active. All of the exercisers kept a careful record of the intensity and duration of the activity which "paid" for the food they would consume thereafter. All of these women experienced withdrawal symptoms of irritability, depression, guilt, or anxiety when their activity was curtailed. Most had sustained sports injuries, but continued to exercise in spite of the pain. These women had a history of shifting back and forth between restricting without exercise, restricting with exercise, and bulimia with and without exercise. In short, these women could have qualified as obligatory athletes.

The Touyz study clearly illustrates that when anorexic women exercise, they become obligatory exercisers. This has been our experience also. All of the eating disordered women we could find who ran, did so compulsively. Touyz et al. stressed that anorexic exercisers present with the "pursuit of fitness" rather than with the "pursuit of thinness." In our experience with obligatory runners, the male runners were more likely to run in order to be healthy or fit while female runners were more likely to run in order to lose weight but the basic concern was the same. In compulsive athleticism and the eating disorders the terms "thinness" and "fitness" may well be equivalent.

Another approach to the relationship between obligatory athleticism and the eating disorders is to study how eating attitudes and behaviors covary with the commitment to exercise. Richert and Hummers (1986) surveyed 598 undergraduate students enrolled in required freshmen classes and found that the reported hours of jogging per week correlated positively and significantly with the total EAT scores and with scores on the "Dieting" factor. The "Dieting" factor also correlated significantly with number of activities and total hours of activities. All EAT factor scores showed a significant positive correlation with a preference for exercising alone. It would seem that high achieving college students, male and female, may become involved in a complex which consists of exercise, concern about diet, investment in many independent activities, and self imposed social isolation.

The similarities between compulsive athletes and eating disordered women are intriguing. High self expectations, independence, perfectionism, and persistence are terms which surface again and again in descriptions of both groups of individuals. By exercise and/or diet, these persons gain a sense of control over body and self.

CHAPTER 8

Analytic Theory

Because the theory presented in the last two chapters was based on clinical and laboratory experiments which often produced quantifiable data, the substance may appear "harder" or more reliable than the analytic theory presented in this chapter. However, there are many questions about the eating disorders and compulsive athleticism which are not yet addressable in the research laboratory.

Analytic theory has paid a major share of attention to the eating disorders and very little attention to compulsive athleticism. Theories about the eating disorders will now be presented and some comments provided as to how they may or may not apply to compulsive athleticism.

THE ANALYTIC APPROACH

The need to eat is an expression of (psychologic) appetite as well as (physiologic) hunger. Eating can be used to express the earliest conflicts over loving and being loved, loving and hating, attacking and being attacked, punishing and being punished (Ritvo, 1984). The passion to eat or not to eat revolves about the body (self), food (mother), hunger (neediness), and activity (independence). Anorexic and bulimic women seem pushed and pulled in a sea of their own desire and thwarted need, perhaps recreating scenarios from the first few years of life.

EARLY THEORIES

From the 1930s through the 1960s, theorists described "classic" anorexic women. These women were thought to reject adult femininity due to an arrest in sexual development. Indeed, the girls who developed anorexia did tend to remain immature and did not develop age appropriate social and sexual relationships. Even today a few of the young anorexic girls in the clinic clearly state that they do not wish to mature. As they grow older, these girls tend to remain emotionally dependent on their families, even when their sexual adjustment is reasonably good (Morgan & Russell, 1975; Raboch, 1986). It is not only physical maturation that these girls fear, but maturation in a broader sense. They are frightened of, and ill prepared for, separating emotionally from the parents so that they can become autonomous adults (Crisp, 1980). They are trapped in a dilemma: they wish to please and to do what is expected, but they are paralyzed at the thought of an independent existence.

Hilde Bruch (1973) is the first psychiatrist to delineate early interpersonal factors which might be responsible for the development of an eating disorder later on. Bruch reasons that, for normal development to occur, the mother must confirm the child's existence and internal state by understanding and responding with intuitive accuracy to her bodily needs. If, instead, the mother superimposes her own distorted or inaccurate perceptions on the child, the child will not be able to learn who she is, how she feels, what her body needs, or what it is to be satiated. A situation such as this could occur if the mother feeds the child only when the mother wishes to eat rather than when the infant is hungry.

Bruch suggests that when the interaction between mother and child is defective, the child may suffer an arrest of cognitive development. She will not able to form an awareness of her internal state or assess whether she is empty or full, needy or not. Because of this, she will feel confused, helpless, and dependent on others for direction. Eventually, she adapts by disregarding her own requirements and attending to the needs of others in an overly compliant manner. This pattern of development signals a miscarriage in the individuation process which will have lifelong consequences.

According to Bruch (1973), the family of the prototypic anorexic child is likely to be intact and nuclear. Both parents are ambitious and upwardly mobile. The mother is a homemaker who reads the latest manuals on child rearing and the father is a hard-driving, logical person. Both parents are opinionated and they clearly underwrite cultural values such as study, exercise, eating the proper food, and not gaining too much weight. The child is neither rejected nor neglected.

As the anorexic-to-be enters school, she is apt to be the teacher's favorite pupil because of her need to please others, her interest in learning, and her participation in many worthwhile activities. To the teacher, she seems refreshingly mature and a solid team player. The pre-anorexic student desperately needs the approval of the teacher and other adults, and she expects to earn it through politeness, honest effort, and solid achievements. However, beneath her well-socialized facade she feels hopelessly inadequate and ineffective as if she has no direction of her own. At times she would like to protest—to be mean and nasty—but she is afraid.

The anorexic girl's self worth depends upon pleasing other people. This makes it impossible for her to establish a sense of who she is and what she would like to accomplish in life. In adolescence she is unable to meet the challenge of establishing an identity which is independent of the expectations of her teacher and family. As she wrestles with these issues, a casual event may crystalize her conflict: a friend's comment about her weight, a remark during a shower in the girls' gym, or a B instead of an A. She responds by taking a new and largely opposite direction. She will establish mastery over her body and a sense of self by doing that which is most difficult—in spite of what others may say. She will control her body through diet.

The anorexia is the result of her ever more rigorous attempts to control her body. She builds an internal compendium of black and white rules, rigid prescriptions, and intellectual formulas by which she stringently restricts her intake. In the process, she brainwashes herself into believing that needing to eat is a sign of weakness and that virtue is achieved by not giving in to these urges. Her self worth rests upon pounds lost and calories denied.

Even when the anorexic woman has established near-complete control over her bodily needs, she continues to be uncertain and to feel ineffective in other spheres. She mistrusts her internal experience and is unable to rely on the standards she sets for herself. She may attend college or graduate school because that is what her parents expect. She lacks a sense of what she really wants to become.

Bruch's theory has become basic to the understanding of "classic" anorexia. It explains many facets of this complicated condition. Bruch's view that eating disordered patients are unaware of their internal state does not reveal why these patients are so intensely disturbed by hunger and why they must defend so mightily against it. In addition, Bruch does not explain anorexia's predilection for females or why some families of anorexic patients function very well (Yager & Strober, 1985). Her assertion that a sense of personal ineffectiveness underlies anorexia is supported by the fact that those anorexics who feel more in charge or less vulnerable have a more favorable outcome (Harding & Lachenmeyer, 1986), but this may be so for any disorder.

The anorexic girls that Bruch treated in the 1960s were young, markedly impaired, rather fragile individuals. She accurately portrayed this population. Bruch (1973) also suggested that when social factors are exceptionally strong, anorexia may develop solely on the basis of social pressure without attendant psychopathology. This may have been Bruch's forecast of the "new" eating disordered women of the 1970s and 1980s.

Obligatory runners are very different from the classic anorexics described by Bruch. They are independent, effective persons who have individuated from the family of origin. The chief similarities seem to be that both groups are composed of hardworking individuals from high achieving, rather traditional families who tend to overcontrol the body, disregard bodily cues, and employ rigid formulas and prescriptions to insure their performance. The commitment to the activity does seem to counteract the underlying sense of ineffectiveness in both groups of individuals.

Following Bruch, most authors have continued to emphasize the anorexic patient's intense neediness on which she superimposes her search for identity, separateness, and autonomy. The eating disorder represents both the wish for and the fear of dependency. However, these constructs do differ somewhat according to the theoretical persuasion. The schools of object relations and self psychology have contributed substantially to our understanding of the eating disorders.

OBJECT RELATIONS SCHOOL

The school of object relations believes that object connectedness begins in infancy. The development of object relations is interwoven with the separation individuation process in the first three years of life. The problematic relatedness of the anorexic patient can be traced to phase-specific issues or occurrences during infancy and toddlerhood.

The separation-individuation process is more complex and hazardous for girls than it is for boys. If the eating disorders are related to individuation, this could explain why more women than men suffer from eating disorders. It is more difficult for girls to individuate from the mother because they must identify with the mother as a female, but at the same time must establish an identity as a person separate from the mother. Individuation is an easier task for boys than it is for girls because they don't have to identify with the mother's femininity as girls do. Because girls feel much closer to the mother, they must constantly resist the regressive pull and the wish to merge with her (Tabin, 1985; Beattie, 1988). In order to resolve this dilemma, girls must first repress their anger and sadism toward the mother, whom they view as powerful and controlling. Girls successfully identify with the mother in part by turning their aggression against the self; they become cleaner, neater, and more docile than boys are or would ever wish to be. Because girls must emphasize self control, they are apt to view the body as an enemy rather than as a source of pleasure (Oliner, 1982). Girls are predisposed to develop an eating disorder because they grow up attempting to control a body which seems alien and treacherous.

There are other forces which make the separation from the mother problematic for girls. Compared to the boundaries between mother and son, the boundaries between mother and daughter tend to be blurred so that mothers are less able to see their daughters as distinctively different from themselves. Mothers are more likely to project their hopes and dreams on their daughters, investing in them as narcissistic extensions of themselves (Beattie, 1988) or seeking to bind and control them (Bernstein, 1983). In addition to these compelling forces, girls lack a visible, easily manipulated external genital which they can control and this may cause them to be more anxious about the intactness of the body and their ability to master it. These concerns may draw them closer to the mother as they seek her comfort and reassurance (Bernstein, 1983).

Even in healthy girls, the ambivalent struggle to individuate from the mother persists long past the oedipal phase and it is revived intensely at puberty (Beattie, 1988). If the mother-daughter relationship has been unusually close and hostile-dependent, a variety of psychopathologies may ensue. Depression and eating disorders are among the most common of these. The eating disorder can become a continuing, locked-in conflict which maintains the original, hostile-dependent tie to the mother.

SELVINI-PALAZZOLI

Selvini-Palazzoli (1978) extends Bruch's interactive theory, addressing the eating disorders from an object relations perspective. She suggests that as an infant the anorexic incorporates an image of the evil and overcontrolling mother. Through this process, the girl comes to equate her body with that of the noxious maternal image which she has introjected. She does not become anorexic in childhood because the poisonous image remains split off and unintegrated into her self image. As she enters puberty, she experiences the changing contours of her body as the return of the archaic mother. She starves her body to prevent it from becoming more like her mother's and she tries to master her body to control her mother. This theory does speak to the anorexic woman's hatred of her body.

MASTERSON

Masterson (1977) views anorexia as a symptom complex which can exist in concert with a variety of personality structures. These range from the psychotic through the borderline (which predominates) to the neurotic. The level of organization which the woman achieves depends upon whether she suffered a developmental arrest at the symbiotic, separation-individuation, or "approaching object constancy" phase of development (Mahler, 1972). The predisposition to an eating disorder is formed when the parent rewards dependent, clinging behavior in the child but discourages independence and exploration. The child wishes to investigate the environment, but is terrified of being abandoned by the parent and is left feeling empty, angry, and afraid. In effect, the parent has rejected the child for developing normally. Later in life, this person continues to feel out of control. She begins to pursue thinness; her body is something she can control. This relieves her anxiety, but effectively halts the maturation process as it inhibits her physical and emotional growth. Masterson describes the developmental path of the eating disorders in the same manner as he describes the developmental track of borderline personalities, whether or not these persons become eating disordered. Masterson does not explain why some of these women develop eating disorders while others do not.

A borderline personality organization (Kernberg, 1975) is often found in severely disturbed eating disordered patients (Masterson, 1977; Bram, Eger & Halmi, 1982; Small, 1984). These women seem unable to form stable, gratifying relationships and they are likely to depend upon the primitive defenses of omnipotence, idealization, devaluation, splitting, and projective identification. Development of a more mature defense system is believed to depend upon the balance between the parents' empathy with the needs of the child and their capacity to permit growth through autonomy (Kernberg, 1975). Children may retain a primitive defense structure when their parents are unempathic and overprotective (Steiger et al., 1989). These qualities have often been noted in the parents of severely compromised patients.

The outcome in therapy for eating disordered women with a borderline personality disorder is similar to the outcome for borderline patients without an eating disorder (Kalucy, Gilchrist et al., 1985), which suggests that the borderline characteristics may stand alone and that they can be powerful predictors of outcome. On the other hand, some bulimic patients who qualify for the borderline personality disorder diagnosis may no longer be assessed as borderline after they have been involved in treatment (Pope & Hudson, 1989). This suggests that in some instances the borderline qualities are a function of the disease process or of the associated physical deprivation.

SOURS

Sours (1980) suggests that, in addition to conflicts, eating disordered patients have sustained a defect in early self-object differentiation which leads to a compromised ego and a distorted self. Their quest for a perfect body is an attempt at narcissistic restitution to counteract the feelings of worthlessness and inadequacy which are the legacy of a difficult infancy. A further byproduct of the faulty interaction in infancy is that eating disordered women acquire an abundance of negative introjects and a penchant for turning primitive rage against the self. They must curb bodily sensations and impulses at all cost. In addition they must punish the body and the self for having harbored such evil urges. They experience the body as separate and alien (Rothenberg, 1986) and they may viciously attack it. This concept gains support from studies which link the eating disorders with destructive rage toward the body (Pyle, Mitchell & Eckert, 1981; Johnson, Stuckey et al., 1982; Norman & Herzog, 1983).

Projective tests have not been used extensively to study eating disordered patients; however, the few studies which do exist consistently indicate ego weakness and/or defect (Small, 1984). This lends support to the contention that the anorexic patient is arrested at a stage of tenuous self-other differentiation. Further support is gained through Sours' (1974) study which shows that two of three subgroups of anorexics demonstrate regressive dedifferentiation, possible loss of self-object separation, and self-body-self differentiation.

SUGARMAN

Sugarman, Quinlan, and Devenis (1981) propose a developmental arrest as a basis for the eating disorders. This occurs when the infant is making a transition from the differentiation to the practicing subphase (Mahler, 1972). This occurs because the parents, usually the mother, are over-involved and overcontrolling or are underinvolved in the care of the child. This causes the child to suppress her natural strivings for independence and to remain fixated at the sensorimotor level of self and object representation (Blatt, 1974). At this, the sensorimotor stage, the child can experience satisfaction only by moving toward an object (the caregiver) and the object is represented by the concrete action sequences (Piaget, 1945). The arrest occurs long before the infant has an internal representation of the mother, so she must rely on the actions of her body to evoke a motoric representation of the mother. For the bulimic woman, this means continuing to eat as the act of eating provides the longed for experience of merger with the mother (Sugarman & Kurash, 1982). As she eats, she experiences her body not just as like her mother's body but as if it is her mother's body. It is the act of eating which soothes and satisfies her; the food itself is of little consequence.

The bulimic woman is in the unfortunate position of being able to maintain the soothing maternal image only by continuing to eat. This is because her developmental arrest occurred prior to the time when she could have internalized the representation of her mother and been able, so to speak, to carry her mother with her in her head. Instead, she must continue to reenact the transaction of succorance if she is to experience it; if she is not eating, she feels alone and without comfort. If she cannot continue to eat, she may encounter the desolation of an anaclitic depression (Blatt, 1974). On the other hand, as she continues to eat she becomes frightened by the intensity of her neediness and the state of fusion with her mother. She vomits and thereby forcibly rejects the image of her mother. She uses her body to gain and then to repudiate the mother. By reenacting with her body the ambivalent struggle with her mother she is able to prevent the collapse of her tenuous self-other boundaries (Sugarman, Quinlan & Devenis, 1981).

Sugarman, Quinlan and Devenis (1981) regard the anorexic's restriction of intake as her need to renounce the maternal representation which eating activates. She tries to differentiate herself from her mother by starving herself; when she is emaciated she presents an image which is significantly and concretely different from that of any other person, including the mother. Although this mechanism differs somewhat from that employed by the bulimic woman, both women are differentiating themselves from the internalized mother by a very basic, concrete mechanism.

Sugarman, Quinlan and Devenis (1981) explain the frenetic activity so frequently found among eating disordered women as an ancillary method which these women employ to prevent the collapse of their ego boundaries. The activity brings a sense of independence and therefore they feel less troubled by their neediness.

According to these authors, eating disordered women are likely to present an infantile personality. This is an incapacitating character disorder which is marked by dependency and poor ego strength. Such persons feel helpless, weak, empty, abandoned, and unloved. They suffer from an anaclitic depression, and must constantly seek gratification. In the infantile state, the supplies (food) are indistinguishable from the supplier (mother).

COMMENTS

Sugarman, Quinlan and Devenis (1981) indicate that a concrete action sequence such as eating can help individuals to maintain their internal homeostasis. This mechanism is not limited to eating disordered women; for most people, eating is a soothing, comforting activity. Eating is known to diminish anxiety (Wolpe, 1958) and some anxiety disorders are treated by having persons eat while they are exposed to threatening circumstances (Johnson, Gilmore & Ramakrishnan, 1982). Perhaps, eating disordered women are more dependent on this mechanism or they might have fewer alternative mechanisms which they can use to maintain their equilibrium.

Theorists of the object relations school attribute eating disorder pathology to a specific developmental arrest in the first two years of life, a result of damaging relationships within the family. The binge eating and purging are an attempt to maintain a workable homeostasis in the face of wholesale ego disintegration. Selvini-Palazzoli (1978) and Sours (1980) present the eating disordered woman as fighting to keep herself apart from the malignant introject. Sugarman and Kurash (1982) portray the binge-purge action sequence as a battle to preserve ego boundaries and to merge with, as well as separate from, the maternal image. Object relations theorists view the existence of an eating disorder as indicative of severe character pathology which is rooted in destructive parenting.

SELF PSYCHOLOGY SCHOOL

Object relations theory perceives the eating disordered patient in terms of distorted self and object representations, structural flaws, and early conflicts which are symbolically expressed. Self psychology views these disorders as the product of a miscarriage in the normal development of the self which results in a defect in the cohesiveness of self. The "self," in the broad sense, is what a person means when he uses the term "I." Self psychology is based on the works of Kohut (1971, 1977) although precursors of this theory may be found in the writings of the British psychoanalysts Fairbairn (1952), Balint (1959, 1968), Winnicott (1965a) and Guntrip (1971).

Self psychologists view early normal development as a process in which the infant internalizes regulatory functions, thus becoming able to self soothe, self vitalize, and modulate his or her level of tension and self esteem. Through this, the infant achieves a state of self cohesion and well-being. Before the infant internalizes these self regulatory functions, he is dependent upon his caretaker, usually the mother, who provides these functions through her soothing, empathic ministrations. If the mother has been empathic or "good enough" (Winnicott, 1965a), and there is not a mismatch between mother and infant, this allows the infant to commence the process of internalization. The regulatory functions are first transferred from the mother to a transitional object such as a baby blanket. Eventually, the child internalizes the regulatory functions as part of his mental structure. Through this, the child gains some independence, but he continues to need the empathic response which the parents and others provide.

In order for the internalization of regulatory functions to occur, the infant must be predictably soothed and protected so that he or she will not be overcome by a variety of external and internal stimuli. The "self" emerges from the empathic mirroring and idealizing activities of the parent. The parent's responsiveness confirms the child's grandiosity and promotes a reciprocal idealization. The parent becomes the child's first "selfobject"—perceived as external to the self, but still experienced as merged with the self.

The parent is not the only selfobject which the child will encounter. He will continue to be changed and enriched through connections with various selfobjects throughout life. If the child experiences a failure in a selfobject relationship before about the end of latency, a defect in the cohesiveness of self may still occur. Although the child's vulnerability to the disruption of the self diminishes at the close of childhood, optimal selfobject relationships are important throughout life.

Kohut (1971) describes two separate and largely independent lines of development. The first, which describes normal development, progresses from autoeroticism, to narcissism, to object love. The second line of development does not result in object love, but progresses from autoeroticism to narcissism, to higher forms and transformations of narcissism. In normal development, the grandiose self gradually becomes more realistic and the idealized parent is slowly incorporated into the child's own value system. Because of failures of the environment, this sequence may be disrupted: the child retains the grandiosity and continues to idealize others. This is the basis for the narcissistic personality and, presumably, the eating disorders.

In following the theory of self psychology, Swift and Letven (1984), Goodsitt (1983, 1985), and Geist (1989) suggest that the eating disordered woman suffers from an early defect which is due to poor or inconsistent caretaking. This can be viewed as a "basic fault" (Balint, 1968) in the structure of the personality. Her defect is in the cohesiveness of self; the self remains loosely bound, and is easily fragmented into various body, affective, and cognitive schemas. The eating disordered woman is not able to self soothe, vitalize, or modulate her affect and self esteem. Therefore, she feels incompetent, ineffectual, out of control, and out of touch with inner experience. Her internal state is one of hunger, emptiness, and restless boredom. The symptoms of the eating disorder offer her a framework of organization and self understanding which can stabilize her precarious self. She defends against her underlying symbiotic needs by assuming a pseudo-independent stance.

Self psychology theorists do not clearly distinguish the personality organization of the bulimic from that of the anorexic, although they do speak to the function of the binging and purging. For Goodsitt (1983), the role of the bulimic behavior is to diminish tension, to regulate the self, and to provide the intense stimulation needed to drown out the anguish and emptiness beneath. As such, the binge-purge sequence can become the central, organizing event in the patient's life. In a similar vein, Swift and Letven (1984) view bulimic behavior as a defensive reparatory maneuver which attempts to alleviate tension, bridge the basic fault, and consolidate the self.

Goodsitt's concept of the function of binge eating and purging is similar to that presented by Sugarman and Kurash (1982): binge eating and purging provide the tension modulation and organization which the individual is not able to provide for herself. The object relations school traces the genesis of the eating disorders to an arrest at a finite stage in the development of object relations, while the ego psychologists relate it to deficiencies in the normal course of development.

RELEVANCE

The theoretical approaches just described are not necessarily contradictory; indeed, a broader understanding of the eating disorders can be gained by applying different aspects of various theories to the individual patient. However, problems are soon encountered when these constructs are applied not to the individual patient but across the board to the eating disordered population.

In the current analytic view, the eating disorders arise from a severe, early insult or defect. Although Sours (1974) describes a subgroup of anorectics who are healthier, in general these women are viewed as suffering from a diffusion of ego boundaries, a "special psychosis" (Meyer & Weinroth, 1957), infantile dependency, states of merger with the introject, and fear of fusion or engulfment. They are characterized as emotionally superficial, compliant, dependent women who need to win the approval of others (Bruch, 1973; Boskind-Lodahl & White, 1978; Allerdissen, Florin & Rost, 1981). While this description may fit the sickest patients, it does not fit many well-functioning eating disordered women or the larger population of women with eating disturbances.

Bruch, Selvini Palazzoli, Masterson, Sugarman and Goodsitt all assume that on some level the child's self expression, initiative, and autonomy must have been discouraged for an eating disorder to occur (Garner & Bemis, 1985). The child is unable to develop healthy autonomy because of forces such as parental overcontrol, overprotectiveness, and enmeshment or the threat of abandonment. Masterson states that the parent actively discourages the child's independence and exploratory behavior. Yet well-functioning eating disordered women have achieved a notable degree of autonomy: they live away from home, are married, raise children, and hold down powerful positions in the business or professional world.

Object relations and self psychology theory indicate that food restriction or binge eating and purging are precipitated by stress, tension, and the associated affects of anger, anxiety, depression, and frustration. This is an accurate description. The disordered behavior also may be precipitated by the patient's having nothing to do—when presumably she might be able to enjoy doing nothing. It is at these times that a different function of the bulimia becomes apparent. By gorging—and by making herself miserable—the bulimic patient seems to be defending against an earlier representation of the good mother who would enfold and soothe her while she remains passive and receptive. When she devours everything in sight, she effectively converts the receptive mode into active, acquisitive strivings (Yates, Leehey & Shisslak, 1983), thus warding off her neediness. Theories based on destructive parenting tend to neglect the succorant, healing aspects of the mother-daughter relationship.

Although Kohut's developmental theory describes positive aspects of the parent-child relationship, when Goodsitt and others apply this theory to the eating disorders, what emerges is the same picture of malignant parenting that is presented by object relations theorists. The across-the-board negative view is tempered only by Sugarman, Quinlan & Devenis' (1981) sense that the action of eating provides the woman with an experience of comfort in the form of a reunion with a mother who is perceived (at that moment) as anything but bad. Although the patient must soon reject the mother, the experience of closeness defends against an anaclitic depression.

RELATIONSHIP TO COMPULSIVE ATHLETICISM

The analytic approach to the eating disorders is only partially applicable to obligatory running because of the emphasis on severe pathology. As a group, obligatory runners are healthy, not pathological. However, analytic theory suggests a manner in which the act of running could serve the obligatory athlete. Sugarman, Quinlan & Devenis (1981) suggest that eating disordered women are maintaining their homeostasis through the body-based activity of eating. Perhaps, obligatory runners are maintaining their homeostasis in the same manner through the body-based activity of running. Running and eating are soothing endeavors which provide a sense of comfort and organization. Both of these activities are an end in themselves, i.e., it is the process of dieting, not reaching a certain weight, that the anorexic woman values; it is the act of eating, not the amount consumed, that the bulimic woman appreciates; and it is the movement through space, not the completion of the course, that the obligatory runner savors.

The body has a very special, central position in the mind of eating disordered women. The body assumes a special, central position for obligatory runners. Eating disordered women feel reunited with the mother through the act of eating; the body becomes the bridge through which they derive contentment and a sense of being. As obligatory runners move through space, they describe a sense of comfort, joy, and wholeness. Perhaps the movement of the body can provide a special sense—one which cannot be gained through the use of more "mature" cognitive mechanisms.

PART III

A Theory
of Activity

CHAPTER 9

Intrapsychic Functions of Activity

Most activities are performed in order to accomplish a goal or to complete a task. Sorting out fishing lures or organizing a party are examples of activities which are justified on the basis of the product or service that they provide. Once the goal is attained, the activity ceases. In the eating disorders and obligatory running, the dieting, purging, and exercise are valuable in and of themselves and not because of the product or service they provide. On the surface, these disorders appear like goal-directed activities, but it is the activity rather than the goal which is important. The true purpose is not to reach a certain weight or speed but to be losing weight, ridding oneself of as much food as possible, or becoming able to travel further or faster. The activities stabilize the emotions and they provide a sense of ongoing self improvement, i.e., they have to do with the persons's internal balance or homeostasis. This chapter explores what the functions of diet and exercise may be: in obligatory runners, eating disordered women, and—to a certain extent—in all individuals who diet and exercise.

FUNCTIONS OF DIET AND EXERCISE

Our work with obligatory runners and eating disordered women suggests that their ongoing preoccupation with diet and/or exercise is a major means by which they maintain a homeostasis. The manner in which this occurs is not simple; there seem to be at least five different intrapsychic functions which the activity provides. These functions interrelate with one another and may exist either simultaneously or sequentially. Only one of the five functions can be said to be intrinsically pathological. Non-obligatory individuals employ activity in a manner which is similar but not identical to the way in which obligatory individuals use activity. The following is a description of the five functions.

1. Self regulation. Healthy individuals feel better when they are active. They may engage in diet and exercise or in other activities because this enables them to be soothed, energized, and organized and/or to stabilize the affective state. Obligatory individuals derive similar benefits from activity. For example, a bulimic woman may resolve the frustrations of a hectic daytime schedule by binge eating during the evening hours. An obligatory runner is revitalized and gains perspective on his life as he runs. Self regulation could be viewed as the primary function of activity.

2. Self definition. Individuals may engage in diet and exercise to derive a sense of self or to reinforce a real or ideal self. An obligatory runner becomes a triathlete because he wishes to prove that he is the kind of person who can "climb glass mountains." An eating disordered women begins to lose weight and learns to sew because she wants to be more like a fashion model.

3. Defense against receptive pleasure. Individuals can use their involvement in activities such as diet and exercise as a particularly effective defense against their passive, receptive needs. Activity is, in many ways, the antithesis of receptivity: when individuals don't wish to yield to the impulse to rest or to eat, they can become active and this reestablishes control. Obligatory dieters and athletes are quite uncomfortable with states of rest and relaxation and they tend to commit themselves to many activities. When they are engaged in an activity, they are distracted from, and better able to deny, their need to rest, to eat, or to be cared for. In addition, their tightly packed schedules make the condition of inactivity very unlikely. On closer examination it seems that any circumstance which contains the possibility of receptive pleasure causes them extreme discomfort. They act as if they could be corrupted by the experience.

Activity disordered individuals tend not to admit their discomfort with states of relative inactivity—states which would permit receptive gratification. Instead, they say, "I'd like to do it, but I have to go (pursue an activity)," i.e., their many responsibilities make it impossible for them to relax and enjoy. What they don't say is that they experience a strong and pervasive fear of inactivity. An about-to-be-divorced obligatory runner complained that his wife had only wanted him to lie around the house, talk about nothing, and visit with the neighbors. He had little in common with her anymore. When asked if she had changed, he said, "No, but I have—I found running." Obligatory runners and dieters are able to rationalize their asceticism in terms of needing the time for life's more essential tasks. They rarely mention the fact that they are extremely uncomfortable when they are in a position of taking in or receiving pleasure.

Perhaps everyone uses one activity or another to defend against the receptive state—to interrupt eating or staying in bed too long. This is a reasonable use of the defense. Obligatory individuals may use the defensive function in a reasonable manner also. One runner trained for a triathalon in part to avoid a vacation which he knew would be disappointing. Through his training program he effectively avoided the depressing circumstances and he felt better because he was running (the self regulating function). A rather plump married woman with a history of anorexia became sexually attracted to a neighbor. She threw herself into a fitness program and was able to forget about her infatuation. She worried about gaining weight and, therefore, before sitting down to eat, she would make herself anxious by calculating calories or by thinking of herself as a chubby teen. The cognitive activities enabled her to eat less.

Activity disordered individuals are oriented toward putting out, not taking in; they defend mightily against receptive pleasure. They preempt most of the receptive gratification which is available to them by their concentration on exercise, diet, or the binge/purge cycle. They are engaged in, or thinking about, the activity during most of their free time. The activity begins to exclude all "less essential" pastimes such as going to the movies, playing with their children, and socializing with friends. Many of our eating disordered patients describe having systematically eliminated sources of pleasure such as listening to music, playing games, looking at "soaps," etc., so that they could adhere to a spartan schedule of work, diet or purging.

4. Separation maintenance. When a person gets up from the table to do the dishes or leaves the partner in bed to work on some papers, that person could be said to be using the activity as a means of separating from the other person(s). When individuals wish to interrupt an enjoyable exchange, they are very apt to do so by involving themselves in an activity which draws them apart. If the activity is viewed as important or pressing, this justifies the interruption. High-achieving individuals regularly preempt close relationships so that they may work.

If individuals are to act independently and productively, they must maintain some degree of separateness from other persons. This is the case in all societies, although it may be especially so in a technological society. A bit of separateness may be necessary for emotional health. A certain degree of non-intimacy, of moving away (rather than moving toward), is necessary if individuals are to form a separate identity or sense of self. Individuals commonly use activity to establish or maintain some degree of separation; this is an essentially healthy operation.

Obligatory runners and eating disordered women seem to push an essentially healthy operation to a pathological extreme. They maintain such a pronounced degree of separateness that they appear inordinately independent. Many of them manage to avoid all close relationships through their dogged adherence to exercise or diet. At first glance, several of our obligatory runners seem not to fit this description. They do fall in love and they do vigorously pursue a relationship (with another runner). Yet, on closer inspection, the relationship is predicated on the other person's involvement in the sport and the runner continues to spend as much or more of his free time running.

When a person engages in an activity to the point of seldom being in a receptive position, that person could be said to be using the activity not just to separate but to maintain a state of separateness. This is a fair description of our eating disordered patients and our obligatory runners. One anorexic patient refused to sit at the table to eat with her family because she needed to straighten the kitchen, do the dishes, and calculate the calories that she consumed. Clint, an obligatory runner described in Chapter 3, no longer socialized because he ran during every free moment of the day and was so tired at night that he fell asleep in company.

5. *Self hurt.* This is, by definition, a pathological function of activity. It is the function of activity which most clearly differentiates obligatory runners and eating disordered women from casual runners and dieters. These persons carry dieting or exercise to such an extreme that they experience discomfort, outright pain, and/or injury to the body. The man who runs marathons on deteriorating cartilage in his knee, the woman who "finally" fits in a size 5 dress and now wants to get down to size 3 despite her dizzy spells, and the bulimic who continues to vomit bloody sputum provide examples of the self hurtful use of activity. The self hurtful function of activity always refers to physical stress or damage to the body. Cognitive activity, however persistent, does not harm the body.

Casual runners may cause themselves pain and body damage when they unintentionally overdo the exercise. This is a fortuitous event to which they react by cutting back on the activity. Obligatory runners will respond to the same circumstances by holding onto or increasing their mileage. When these runners are not in pain they may increase their effort until they experience it. Their motto is "No pain, no gain." The function of pain will be discussed in greater detail later on.

RELATIONSHIP BETWEEN FUNCTIONS

The separation maintenance and the defensive functions of activity are closely associated and may be difficult to tease apart. At times they may seem to be the same: when a person maintains a high degree of separateness, he effectively forestalls any gratification which might be forthcoming from a close relationship. Is the eating disordered woman who turns down an invitation to a party doing so because she wishes to be independent of other people or because she wishes to avoid a position in which she might eat and enjoy herself? Does the runner "hit the road" at 5 A.M. to be alone and self reflective or to avoid the pleasures of sleeping late? Indeed, our subjects often cited both reasons interchangeably, as if one were synonymous with the other. Yet these functions are not the same. Obligatory runners and dieters use activity to insulate themselves from other persons when gratification is not an issue: they are almost always alone.

NATURE OF THE DEFENSE

Obligatory runners and eating disordered women begin to run or diet for many of the same reasons that non-obligatory runners and dieters do—for the pleasure of owning an attractive body and the mastery of moving easily through space. In other words, the activity helps them to self regulate: it soothes, enhances, and invigorates them. In effect it provides receptive pleasure. This can pose a problem for activity disordered individuals as they allow themselves very little pleasure.

Activity disordered persons handle activities which are too pleasurable by converting them into work activities: dieting or running become serious endeavors which must be accomplished. Then they must perform these tasks up to their rigorous standards in order to "enjoy" the activity. Instead of pleasure during the activity, they experience relief when the mission has been accomplished. Callen (1983) describes this phenomenon in a group of older male runners who experience elation only when they manage to finish a race. This group is composed of the hardest and most competitive runners of all.

When obligatory runners and dieters convert an enjoyable activity into a serious task, they are effectively defending themselves against receiving pleasure. In effect, they are shifting from the self regulatory function to the defensive function of activity. There is no conflict involved; they simply readjust the internal economy toward issues of performance and self worth rather than pleasure. The external manifestation of this is that they work harder, with less refueling, to perform better—and they enjoy the activity less. The degree to which they must convert pleasurable activity to work activity seems to be correlated with the severity of the disorder.

When activity disordered individuals are faced with a crisis of self worth, such as moving away from home or a divorce, this seems to foster the internal shift away from the self regulatory to the defensive function of activity. They become even harder on themselves and they focus more on self improvement. They expect a finer achievement and they allow themselves even less receptive pleasure. They worry more about their performance and seem deadly serious about the activity. The running and dieting take on the characteristics of a struggle to survive.

Obligatory runners and dieters have a sense of urgency about their exercise or diet; they view the activity as essential and the consequences of inactivity as devastating. They pit themselves against nature in the trail run, narrowly miss being discovered as they vomit, run an extra mile when exhausted, etc. It is as if they must continue to push against the powerful forces of hunger, exhaustion, and circumstance. In their minds not to diet, run, or purge would mean the loss of everything that is valuable. When these persons feel "in extremis," in imminent danger from internal or external forces, the activity becomes an extremely potent defensive strategy. Instead of being nearly overwhelmed by their neediness, they are nearly overwhelmed by forces in the environment. In effect, they project their neediness on the environment so that they experience the threat from without instead of from within.

When eating disordered women place themselves in situations of imminent danger, they have no choice but to attend to the issues at hand. Other frustrations in life seem less significant. In this manner, the activity can function as a complex defense against the dangers of intimacy and the need for care. This concept is suggestive of Goodsitt's (1983) percept that bulimic behavior provides the woman with the intense stimulation which she needs in order to drown out the anguish and emptiness beneath.

The intrapsychic war found in activity disordered individuals is similar in certain respects to Stoller's (1976) description of masochistic conflict. Stoller presents this struggle as a rapid oscillation between fantasied danger, repetition of early trauma, and fantasied triumph. This produces a sexualized excitement which, among other things, serves to defend against anxiety. In the activity disorders, the person oscillates between the dangers of hunger, exhaustion, or external circumstance; the struggle to maintain a separate state; and the fantasy of triumph over the body. The oscillation generates excitement, and the excitement defends against the anxiety of being overwhelmed by neediness.

Activity disordered individuals seem engaged in a life or death battle for greater independence. Although they struggle heroically, they may continue to entertain the ambivalent wish that they will be caught, restrained, and ultimately cared for. The trail runner who forces himself up a treacherous course knows that he could be injured or collapse from exhaustion. The anorexic woman who continues to take off pounds is cognizant of the risk of hospitalization. The bulimic who purges understands that she may be caught, shamed, and restrained. At a deeper level, these persons may wish that they would be apprehended so that they could escape the activity which controls their thoughts and actions. In this manner they could back into receptive pleasure—forced into having their needs fulfilled, though they may continue to resist every inch of the way.

FROM CASUAL TO OBLIGATORY ACTIVITY

Obligatory runners and eating disordered women differ from other individuals in the culture in several respects. They depend more upon body-based activities and they use those activities more to defend against receptive pleasure and to maintain a separate state. They use activity in a self hurtful manner. The history that they provide suggests that this was not always the case, that in childhood and early adolescence they were able to use activity more to self regulate and define and less to defend or maintain a separate state. They were pleasureably involved in a number of activities. They began to use activity more to maintain a separate state when they needed to prove their self worth and establish themselves apart from the family.

The manner in which obligatory runners and dieters describe having used activities in their early years is similar to the manner in which our casual runners or dieters continue to employ activities: primarily to self regulate. The dieting and exercise make them feel more energetic, optimistic, and better about themselves. They continue to make and enjoy close relationships and they do not knowingly push the activity past the point of physical discomfort.

There is a sequence by which certain, presumably at risk, individuals seem to move from casual running or dieting to compulsive athleticism or an eating disorder. The balance of function of the activity seems to change during this process. The sequence begins with an increase in self dissatisfaction, which follows a crisis of self worth. Obligatory individuals may respond by escalating their self expectations, becoming harder on themselves. They utilize the self-regulating function of activity less and they use the activity more and more to defend against the receptive state. They maintain an increasingly high degree of separateness from significant others. As they become locked into the activity, they become more and more likely to push it to the point of discomfort and, eventually, physical damage.

The shift toward the defensive, separation maintenance, and self hurtful functions of activity is most readily observable in those obligatory runners and anorexic women who have become clearly dysphoric and who feel controlled by the activity. The shift probably could have been detected much earlier by these individuals' increasing aloneness, asceticism, and signs of physical discomfort—despite their claim that the weight loss or the exercise was nothing other than an exhilarating experience. When eating disordered women are prevented from dieting (or the binge/purge cycle) and obligatory runners are injured and can no longer run, the extent to which they have depended upon the separation maintenance function of activity is apparent in their loss of boundaries: the sense of confusion, bloatedness, or bodily deterioration.

FUNCTIONS OF ACTIVITY IN THE ACTIVITY DISORDERS

The history that our obligatory runners provide usually enables us to distinguish all five functions of activity. These individuals continue to experience the running, as somewhat soothing, organizing, or invigorating. They may identify with other serious runners or they describe themselves as a breed apart—as fully committed runners. The investment in the sport separates them from spouse, friends, and family. They run alone and have little time or energy left for social events. When they are not out there running, they are thinking about running: time, running route, body fat, diet, shoes, etc. They often experience pain and sometimes they seem to solicit pain. Our eating disordered patients who run tend to use the exercise in the same manner as the male obligatory runners do, with the exception that they are more concerned about appearance, weight, and diet than time, distance, and physical fitness.

Our sedentary anorexic patients seem to rely more upon cognitive than physical activity to maintain control. They exist in a world apart, immersing themselves in calorie calculations, ruminations, and food rituals.

They have little time for, or interest in, friends and family. Their asceticism is greater than that of the bulimic and they cannot allow themselves to be soothed through the act of eating—although they may derive pleasure from imagining food, by noting their weight loss, and by anticipating a perfect figure.

Our bulimic women are more fortunate than our anorexic women in that they are able to self soothe by eating—at least at first. They often describe feeling relieved and pleasured as they begin to eat. At some juncture (precipitated by physical discomfort or discomfort with the self), they switch over to what seems to be a completely different frame of reference. Eating is no longer pleasurable and they dislike what they are doing. They feel compelled to stuff themselves. When they purge, they seem to reregulate and stabilize themselves through the purging activity. When some women purge, they report feeling at peace, one with the self, or as if they had been freed of a terrible burden. Other bulimic women feel ashamed and miserable. In the course of the binge/purge cycle, the function of the bulimic activity shifts back and forth between self regulation and defense/separation maintenance. Binge eating usually causes discomfort, sometimes pain, and the more frequently they purge, the more they are likely to injure the body.

In addition to their binge/purge activity, most bulimics are intent on replenishing the larder for the next binge and on planning the where and how of the next purge. Some bulimic women binge and purge 20 times a day and they spend many hours replenishing and planning. This is an ancillary activity which is sometimes pleasurable and sometimes not. The time spent replenishing and planning effectively insulates the women from social relationships and sociable pleasures.

The extent to which obligatory runners and dieters employ the activity for self definition varies considerably. Some runners are proud to say, "I am a serious runner (élite runner, triathlete, etc)", but other runners are just "out there," pounding away. Some of our eating disordered women identify with models, stewardesses, fashion designers, etc. Other women who develop an eating disorder want to be thinner but they do not wish to be like certain, characteristically thin, individuals.

SUBJECTIVE EXPERIENCE OF ACTIVITY

The subjective experience of engaging in activity seems to vary according to the function(s) which the activity serves. The most pleasant feeling state seems to be derived from the self regulatory function. Obligatory and non-obligatory runners depict a sense of floating as they run and the feel of power as they surge through space. These are the "peak" experiences that they describe. Dieters relate feeling lighter and more energetic, with a sense of efficacy and purpose. They are delighted with the changes in the body and they feel more desirable because they have lost weight. This, the self-regulating function, helps them to maintain a positive mood state.

The self-defining function of activity is usually accompanied by self satisfaction, sometimes with the exhilaration of becoming a special kind of person. To be a runner differs from being merely a jogger; to be a runner is to be singular and in some way superior to other men. A runner may picture himself as godlike and invincible, a person who could conquer the mountain and the world. The successful dieter may come to resemble a fashion model; she may assume that other women respect and admire her exceptional form.

The defensive function of activity tends to be accompanied by less pleasure and more tension, especially if the defense against receptive pleasure is not quite adequate. There is often a forced quality to the activity: "I'm damn well going to enjoy it"—or an anxious, all-or-nothing flavor: "I better get out there if I'm ever going to do it." Marilyn, described in Chapter 3, never missed a day's run because she was fearful that she would quit running altogether and she never ate desserts because she was afraid that if she did, she could not stop eating.

Various mood states seem to accompany the use of activity to maintain separation. When a runner excuses himself from a family reunion to run, he may describe relief at no longer being confined or a certain pride in being physically effective and independent. The same may be said of the dieter who demonstrates the ability to "push away from the table." However, the feeling state is anything but pleasant by the time that obligatory runners feel controlled by the sport. They run because they have no other choice. They feel embattled, forced, or driven to pursue the activity—in spite of hail, pain, or exhaustion. The same may be said of our eating disordered women who "absolutely must" retire after dinner to tabulate calories or who remain at the table, engrossed in their calculations—despite a ravenous appetite.

The self-destructive function of activity is regularly accompanied by a dysphoric mood, be it anger, depression, anxiety, or the anticipation of deterioration. Runners describe a desperate struggle with pain to keep from giving in. Anorexic women report becoming enraged at their bodies for needing something to eat and bulimic women become more anxious when they continue to purge in spite of bloody emesis or eroded tooth enamel.

RECEPTIVE GRATIFICATION

The receptive state is one of readiness to be satisfied, or to have one's needs fulfilled. It implies an abdication of control, a relinquishment of striving in order to receive. Making love or enjoying friends, food, or music are forms of receptive gratification. Conversely, asceticism can be seen as a denial of receptive pleasure: ascetics wear hair shirts, fast, abstain from sex, and stay up all night. Obligatory runners and dieters fall on the ascetic end of the spectrum as they tend to deny themselves most receptive pleasures.

Receptive pleasure is likely—more than other pleasure—to be associated with the sense of being cared for. In early life, the parent soothes, comforts, and feeds the child and the child receives the care with delight. As children become more independent, they must relinquish a large share of the receptive pleasure that the parents have furnished. To be independent of the parents is to resist the gratification that they provide. Adults continue to resist the pull of many, readily available, pleasures: to eat dessert, to sleep late, to make love to the wrong person instead of mowing the lawn, etc. Most persons manage to achieve some kind of balance between the rewards of independent activity and the gratifications of receptivity. They may yearn for more receptive pleasure, but at least they recognize their needs and grant themselves a modicum of satisfaction.

Obligatory runners and/or dieters tend to be self-sufficient persons who are not dependent on their parents or on anyone else. They may schedule business during lunch or read the paper while eating breakfast. They are apt to view mastery, performance, and achievement as meaningful and rewarding, as indeed they are. Although these gratifications are significant, "putting out" is qualitatively distinct from taking in. If obligatory individuals did not strive to be as independent and if they did not demand such high performance of themselves, they would not need to defend themselves as assiduously against receiving pleasure. In other words, if they were easier on themselves, they could be more open to taking in pleasure from family, friends, and the environment. Perhaps the diet or exercise distracts them from their neediness and protects them from the dangers of being close.

This culture provides many rewards for obligatory individuals who are able and willing to forego receptive pleasure in favor of greater accomplishment. There is a strong, overt bias toward independent activity and a weaker, covert bias against receptive pleasure. If a person is late to work, a "good" excuse would be that the car broke down or he was delayed by talking business on the phone; a "bad" excuse would be that he overslept, forgot what time it was, or was chatting with friends. High levels of independent activity are regarded as a good thing and there are no cultural sanctions against increasing the level of activity even when a person is already extremely active. Increased activity is judged as a sign of strength and ability ("If you want something done, ask a busy man to do it"). On the other hand, there is a strong sanction against too much indulgence in relaxation, eating, or making love.

ALONENESS

When individuals edge toward the extremes of activity, they become more and more isolated from other people, as the Vanderheyden et al. (1988) (eating) and the Richert and Hummers (1986) (exercise) studies noted. This does not mean that they are lonely nor does this mean that they feel empty or that their lives are empty. Active women, especially those who run, are less likely than others to rely on group support. A 1989 Woman's Sports Foundation survey (reported in *Tucson Citizen*, 6/6/89) of women who exercise found that they rated friendship/sociability as of only minor importance. What they held as important, and enjoyed doing while running, was self exploration.

Our eating disordered patients and obligatory runners seem to exist in a world apart. The running, dieting, or binge/purge cycle is not something which can be shared. Even when they are not engaged in the activity, they may choose to be by themselves, to be separate, most of the day. They derive little comfort through relationships and the contact that they have with other people may revolve about study, chores, work, or family—responsibilities that are necessary rather than gratifying. The need to be separate often takes the form of wanting to be physically free or unencumbered. They speak of hating the restraints of heavy clothes or seat belts and of having to sit in committee meetings.

The title of Sours' (1980) book on anorexia, *Starving to Death in a Sea of Objects*, would speak to the aloneness of the runner as well as to the self-imposed isolation of the eating disordered woman. Our obligatory runners were attractive and successful persons; there were many other people in their lives who would have liked to be close to them, to share their aspirations and quandaries. The runners often described spouses and friends as frustrated at their emotional, as well as physical, unavailability. The runners recognized that they could, and perhaps should, be more available to their significant others, but they viewed their isolation as a fact of life, immutable and necessary.

An assumption which is often made about eating disordered women—and which could just as well be applied to obligatory runners—is that they choose to be alone because they are angry at, and wish to reject, other people. Although anorexic women become hostile and resentful of others when they starve, and although a few of the obligatory runners (like Max in Chapter 3) devalue and reject other people, these are the exceptions rather than the rule.

The aloneness of the obligatory runner or dieter seems to be related to the extent to which they must envelop themselves in activity because they need to maintain a high degree of separateness or independence. A high degree of separateness means staying apart.

CORE PATHOLOGY IN THE ACTIVITY DISORDER

There are several features which sharply distinguish obligatory runners and dieters from casual runners and dieters. These are the uncompromising, single-minded drivenness with which they pursue the activity, the physical deprivation which follows, and the attack on the body.

DRIVEN ACTIVITY

The spouse of an obligatory runner once said that if anyone attempted to prevent her husband from running, that person soon would feel as if he or she had been run over by a locomotive. Once she had tried to dissuade her husband: he "clamped in," left for the run, and did not return for two days. A bulimic patient was hospitalized and told that she must not vomit. She vomited while taking a shower, but was apprehended. She vomited behind bushes on an outing and in a hole that she scooped out of the sand in the children's playground. She stole plastic bags off the cleaning cart and provoked the staff so that they would send her to her room. Then she vomited into the bag and hid it in the back of the closet. She spent her entire day figuring out how she could rid herself of food. Activity disordered persons fear that if they stop dieting or running they will collapse, lose their resolve, and fold altogether. What they are saying is that they must hold fast against their very basic human needs.

Obligatory athletes and eating disordered women differ from other persons in that they seek absolute control of body and self through independent activity. They have tremendous difficulty in recognizing and accepting their very human needs—including the need for rest and nourishment. As "captains of their ships," they seem always on the move toward bigger and better accomplishments in miles run or weight lost. They are uneasy when they have nothing on the docket. They have no time to attend to the body when it aches or when it yearns to be held or to be fed. They seem to use activity to defend against the receptive state and the possibility of receptive pleasure.

The history that the obligatory runners and eating disordered women provide suggests that before they became locked into the running or dieting they had been in a stage of progressively stringent denial of their basic needs, including the avoidance of receptive pleasure. This condition seems to set the stage for the activity to become driven or obligatory: when they deny their basic requirements, this increases the body's need to receive rest, food, and care. Activity disordered persons characteristically interpret the neediness of the body as a threat to their ability to control the body. They usually react with anxiety and an escalation of the activity to reassert control. Unfortunately, this serves to increase the body's craving for food or rest even further. They redouble the effort to diet, purge, or exercise and then they redouble it again. As the process continues, it begins to look like a life or death struggle to be free—from the part of the self that craves rest and food, closeness and care. The flavor is that of the young child struggling not to be overwhelmed by his neediness when his parents are away. The pattern becomes self-perpetuating, eventually leading to the picture of embattled autonomy which is the hallmark of the activity disorders.

PHYSIOLOGIC COMPONENTS

The study by Herman and Polivy (1975) described in Chapter 6 indicates that there is a self reinforcing feedback loop which operates in the eating disorders. The loop begins with food restriction: women who restrict their food intake become very hungry; they may lose control of their appetite and binge. The loss of control causes them to redouble the efforts to diet. The renewed restriction makes bingeing more likely and the pattern becomes self-perpetuating. The psychodynamic explanation offered above has its counterpart in the physiologic explanation offered by Herman and Polivy; it suggests that exercisers as well as dieters can place themselves in a deficit state by not attending to their bodily needs. This increases their neediness and they must redouble their exercise to maintain control.

In Chapter 6, we learned that when animals are placed on a restricted diet they become much more active than they are when they are fed freely (Siegel & Steinberg, 1949; Teitelbaum, 1957; Cornish & Morosovsky, 1965); the longer animals are deprived, the more active they become (Mohanti & Mishra, 1984; DiBattista & Bedard, 1987). If an exercise wheel is available, animals on a restricted diet will continue to run until they run themselves to death (Routennberg, 1968). Obligatory runners characteristically restrict their diet and they combine diet with stringent exercise. If the animal studies apply to humans, perhaps the rigorous diet in tandem with exercise fosters the process by which the runners become locked into the activity beyond the dictates of reason. Physiologic as well as psychologic factors could contribute to the obligatory quality of the activity disorder.

Obligatory runners (and runners in general) tend to be male. The phenomenon of increased activity in response to food restriction is more pronounced in male animals at all levels of food restriction (Mohanti & Mishra, 1984). If this research should apply to humans, it would suggest one reason why more males than females become locked into exercise.

DEPRIVATION

As obligatory athletes and eating disordered women decrease their food intake and/or increase their exercise, they may enter a state of physical deprivation. When this occurs, the deprivation begins to contribute substantially to the clinical picture. Eating disordered women become far more introverted, depressed, and obsessional (Strober, 1980, 1985). Starvation must have the same effect on obligatory runners. We know that in men starvation produces many of the symptoms of an eating disorder, including the depression, the seclusiveness, the ruminations, and the rituals (Keys et al., 1950). Many of the emotional symptoms of an activity disorder could be the result of physical deprivation.

Most long distance runners are able to reach a balance in their energy expenditure. When they begin to run, they burn a prodigious number of calories, more than what they can replace by eating, but they are able to adjust by increasing the efficiency of their metabolism. The entire body is lean, but they are not physically deprived. If they continue to escalate their running, they begin to metabolize their own muscle. They lose muscle mass from the arms, shoulder girdle, chest, and neck—tissue which is not directly utilized in the running. They enter a state of negative nitrogen balance, i.e., they burn up their own body.

We did not measure the arm and leg girth or body fat of the runners in our study, but some of them appeared painfully gaunt and wasted in the upper extremities. It was our impression that these runners were the ones who were particularly hostile, somber, tightly controlled, and seclusive. These runners may be the ones who most closely approximate anorexic patients.

COGNITIVE EFFECTS OF DEPRIVATION

The format which some religious cults employ to indoctrinate new members (Hassan, 1988) affords a natural experiment in deprivation. The cults select the brightest, most articulate individuals they can find. They want people who can be productive and they value young persons who can work hard on very little food or rest. They know that inquisitive, idealistic, independent youth are particularly vulnerable (Gallup & Poling, 1980). Backpackers are excellent targets. Once they are recruited, cult members work 15–18 hours a day, with more hours spent singing, chanting, or praying. They consume meager rations and are limited in dress and sexual expression. The deprivation seems to contribute to the "brainwashing" process by which the neophytes come to categorically accept the cult ideology. If cult members leave, it may take months before they can extricate themselves from the stereotyped manner of thinking and acting.

When eating disordered women starve themselves, they regress and their thought patterns change in much the same fashion as that which has been described among cult members. The perception of the body and self becomes more negative, rigid, simplistic, and dichotomous (Fairburn & Cooper, 1984; Garner, 1985; Neimeyer & Kouzam, 1985). They do and say things which they would not have said or done before they were deprived. They may state that they have been redeemed through the deprivation, that they have conquered their bodily needs. Their absolute insistence on the rightness of the diet or exercise becomes patently irrational in the face of inanition and exhaustion. They may, in effect, be brainwashing themselves into an absolute adherence to the regimen. Physical deprivation may foster the irrational behavior and the simplistic, dichotomous cognitive style. It is only after several months of refeeding in a sane environment that their thinking begins to revert to normal.

Do activity disordered individuals enjoy depriving themselves? In our study, this did not appear to be the case. Our subjects seemed caught up in a web which was only partly of their own making. At first, they wanted to achieve an important goal and they strove to attain it. Pushing harder toward the goal led them to a position in which they were unable to stop.

ATTACK ON THE BODY

The severity of an eating disorder seems to be reflected in the degree to which the woman hates and attacks her body through relentless starvation, gut distension, purging, alcohol abuse, etc. (Swift, Andrews & Barklage, 1986). The more disturbed these women are, the more they attack the body. Self mutilation is an index of the severity of the disorder (Garner, Garfinkel & O'Shaughnessy, 1982): 8 percent of normal weight bulimic patients, 19 percent of anorexic bulimic patients, and 7 percent of restricting anorexic patients report self mutilation.

The self-hurtful function of activity is always present in anorexia and bulimia, but it may not be apparent in the early stages of the disorder. It becomes obvious if the woman loses weight to the point of starvation. At this juncture, she may lose all objectivity and all moderation: when she is not doing terrible things to her body, she is thinking terrible thoughts about her body and herself. In bulimia, dramatic complications such as rupture of the stomach, parotiditis, and erosion of the enamel are nowhere near as common as indigestion, esophagitis from repeated retching, and the pain of a distended gut.

Obligatory runners damage the body more consistently than do anorexic or bulimic women. They expect to suffer and may court further harm by continuing to run on stress fractures or an Achilles tendinitis. They go one step further than the women do when they glorify the pain and disability. It is a "true athlete" who would die for the sport.

Eating disordered women and obligatory runners provide a premorbid history of dissatisfaction with the body. They may have made numerous attempts to alter or improve the body before they became seriously committed to diet or exercise. The discontent with the body seems to worsen as the intensity of the exercise, diet, or purging increases. In anorexic women—and perhaps in obligatory runners—the dissatisfaction with the body peaks when the element of deprivation enters the equation. The body becomes an object divorced from the self, to be pounded, stretched, starved, and molded.

Any 10K runner may attempt to finish a race in spite of muscle strain and anyone who diets must expect the ache of being hungry. Learning to water-ski means being dumped a time or two. Why should the eating disorders and obligatory athleticism be pathological if other, occasionally painful, activities are not? The eating disorders and obligatory running are qualitatively distinct from other forms of diet and exercise because of the uncompromising, single-minded drivenness of the activity, the physical deprivation which follows, and the vicious, relentless attack on the body.

DEPRESSION AND SUICIDE

There is no good resolution for some obligatory runners and eating dis-ordered women. They continue to be dissatisfied with their performance and they progressively increase their self expectations. They systemati-cally eliminate pleasurable activities and they continue to escalate the attack on the body. If they become ill, suffer a physical injury, or simply cannot proceed, the superstructure of independence collapses and they are at high risk for suicide. A marathon runner decided to compete in triathalons. He wished to improve his self discipline, so he became a vegetarian and cut his sleep to four hours a night. He increased his mileage to 160 miles per week, an endeavor which meant that he rarely saw his family. After he did poorly (by his standards) in the triathalon, he was hospitalized because of depression with suicidal thoughts. Mary Wazeter, described in Chapter 5, continued to increase her exercise while she systematically decreased her calories. When she was exhausted and could no longer continue, she threw herself off a bridge into the frozen Susquehanna river.

When an anorexic woman starves herself to death or when an obligatory athlete runs with an arrythmia and dies, this becomes the final resolution. Yet death is an uncommon ending. Usually, the activity waxes and wanes without a definitive resolution one way or the other. A few individuals seem to maintain their balance by bootlegging nurturance, i.e., they overdo the activity until they are forced to rest or they are hospitalized and made to eat. Someone else cares for them whether they like it or not.

HEALTH VERSUS PATHOLOGY

Perfectly healthy individuals use activity to self regulate, self define, defend, and maintain a separate state. The self-regulating function soothes, organizes, and energizes. The self-defining and separation main-tenance functions serve to delineate the self and the defensive function supports a number of ego functions such as task persistence and the delay of gratification. The emotional state can be modulated through a shift from one function to another. Activity can most appropriately be viewed as a self-strengthening mechanism.

Activity is a self-strengthening mechanism for obligatory runners and dieters. When eating disordered women begin to diet or when obligatory runners take up running, they most often feel as if they are engaged in something valuable, something which gives them a sense of "total being."

They are not referring to merger or loss of self, they are talking about an enhancement of the self. They continue the activity in part because they don't want to forfeit the soothing, stabilizing effects or the sense of independent achievement that come with the loss of weight or the successful completion of a race.

CHAPTER 10

Adapting to Expectations

In our work with obligatory runners and well-functioning eating disordered women, we have been struck by the success of these individuals, their independence, and their involvement in many activities. Their positive adaptation seems to antedate the disorder and even after they have become obligatory, they tend to continue to function very well. Their apparent health is in sharp contrast to the strange, irrational, self-destructive behavior they exhibit around the issues of diet and exercise.

Our first hypothesis in addressing the health of the obligatory runners was that their favorable adaptation masked the severe and pervasive underlying psychopathology. Yet, they continued to appear healthy by the many psychometric indices and other parameters that we employed. They were not very different from their non-obligatory peers—except that they were, if anything, more independent, more active, and more persistently involved in a number of activities.

We began to reexamine obligatory runners from the standpoint of health rather than illness. This lead to our second hypothesis—that they were basically very healthy individuals who had developed a disorder and that the disorder was somehow related to the healthy aspects of their functioning. The most obvious relationship between health and an activity disorder was that these persons were applying their healthy aptitudes to becoming superlative runners. They were not only active, persistent, and perfectionistic in their daily life, they were active, persistent, and perfectionistic in their running. They approached running from several directions simultaneously and they strove for a personal best. They focused their abundant energy on the task and they kept at it until they were fully proficient. The only item that they failed to master was how to stop.

INDEPENDENCE, ACHIEVEMENT, AND EATING ATTITUDES

In addressing the issue of wellness rather than sickness, we asked ourselves why we perceived the runners as healthy. Several elements came to mind: their initiative, resourcefulness, self reliance, ability to push forward in spite of difficulty, and so forth. Most of the concepts were related to independence or to independent achievement. We recalled that when we asked the runners, "How important is it to you to be independent?" they indicated that independence was a crucial, indispensable part of their self concept. We had already noted that their extreme distress when they were disabled or prevented from running had to do with the condition of dependency. They were deeply resentful at being controlled by the disability, at having no choice but to be cared for. They must be unfettered, free, or life was not worth living. As they mustered strength, they quickly reasserted their independence. They refused help and they tried to assume their own care. They resumed the activity as soon as possible, often against medical advice.

The people in the United States score higher than the people of any of a number of other nations in the value they place on independence and personal freedom (National Opinion Research Poll, 1989). We see independence as a virtue, a quality which betokens health and maturity. We closely associate independence with achievement; in fact the term "achievement" tends to be synonymous with "independent achievement." Obligatory runners and dieters are high achieving individuals who are in tune with the cultural system of values. As might be expected, they greatly treasure their independence.

The striving to be independent may play an important role in the genesis of the activity disorders. That this is indeed the case is suggested by several large studies of university women. As a group, university women tend to value independence and achievement more highly than women who have not continued their education. Timko et al. (1987) found that in these women disordered eating attitudes and behaviors correlate with the value they place on certain masculine attributes (leanness, competitiveness, success, etc.), values which are prized by the culture and which are associated with upward mobility and success. In addition, the women who obtained high scores on disordered eating were the ones who listed a number of roles which they saw as central to their self concept. They had become invested in many goals and activities. The researchers concluded that these students wished to become "super-women." In this study, eating disturbance, multiple activities, and an orientation toward independent achievement were closely associated.

In the previous chapter, we noted that the eating disordered patients and obligatory runners seem to exist in a world apart and that they are quite comfortable when they are alone. The preference for being alone could be a function of the striving toward greater independence and greater achievement. High achieving, independent persons might actually prefer to be alone.

DEPENDENCE VERSUS INDEPENDENCE IN THE EATING DISORDERS

Eating disordered women are known to idealize independence and they view social dependency with contempt (Garner & Bemis, 1985). They repudiate the need for nurturance, protection, and affection. They expect themselves to be unrealistically self-reliant. However, issues of independence are different for "classic" eating disordered patients than they are for high-functioning eating disordered women. "Classic" eating disordered patients are overly dependent and ambivalent about becoming more independent (Sours, 1974; Kalucy, Gilchrist et al., 1985; Armstrong & Roth, 1989). The eating disorders often commence when they are away from home for the first time (Zakin, 1989) or when a significant relationship ends (Kalucy, Crisp & Harding, 1977; Ritvo, 1984; Weinstein & Richman, 1984; Van den Brouke & Vandereycken, 1986).

High-functioning eating disordered women are more concerned with achieving or maintaining an advanced degree of independence. They have already proven that they can separate from the parents; the eating disorder may develop long after they move away from home, when they are living alone, or after both parents have died. The eating disorder may emerge around the time of pregnancy and childbirth; while they are in a competitive position such as graduate school; at a time of career indecision; when age becomes an issue; or after retirement (Johnson & Connors, 1987; Hsu & Zimmer, 1988; Yates, 1989).

Well-functioning eating disordered women develop problems in a manner which differs from that described in "classic" patients. The disorder tends to develop when they encounter a situation which challenges their sense of who they are or how valuable they really may be. This could be called a "crisis of self worth." They are unable to live up to their own unrealistically high standards as students, executives, businesswomen, professionals, wives, and mothers. Disappointed in themselves, they attempt greater self control through diet. The high self expectations, the self disappointment, and the need for greater control fuel the eating disorder. The following case illustrates how this can occur:

> Wendy practices pediatrics, is married, and has three children. She grew up as the fourth of six children in a close-knit, affluent family. All of her brothers and sisters became professionals. There was never any question about whether Wendy would attend college, but when she was an adolescent she had wanted to become a violinist instead of a physician.
>
> Wendy stopped eating at age 25 when she was rotating through her internal medicine clerkship. She was on call every third night and slept very little. She tried to do her best, but the resident she was assigned to was very critical of her performance. By the time two months had passed, she had lost 16 pounds. She never regained the weight; she would remain stable on the easier rotations where she was confident about her ability, but would eat little or nothing on the demanding and difficult rotations. She continued to lose weight intermittently during her pediatric residency. She didn't object to the weight loss and rather liked fitting into a smaller dress size.
>
> Shortly after her residency, she entered a group practice and her life became more predictable and somewhat less stressful. She put on 15 pounds, and began to worry about gaining weight. At the time she weighed 112 and stood at 5'4". For the next several years, she dieted more or less successfully, but gained weight whenever she lost her resolve.
>
> After several years had passed, Wendy met and married another physician. Although she had always said that if she had children she intended to stay home with them until they went to school, she returned to work shortly after the birth of each of her three children. It was when she first was juggling childcare, job, and household responsibilities that she began to purge.

Wendy was an independent young woman who achieved well enough in college to be accepted to medical school. Although she felt close to her family, especially several of her siblings, she had no qualms about leaving home to attend school. Her anorexia, and her purging later on, occurred at times of self dissatisfaction, when she was afraid that she couldn't live up to her "superwoman" self expectations. As she attempted to prove herself, she never asked for help from anyone, including her husband.

The "classic" eating disordered patient is a dependent woman, unable to free herself of her ambivalent ties within an enmeshed family. Our experience with obligatory runners and well-functioning eating disordered women suggests that they struggle with independence rather than with dependency. This may seem to be a play on words, but it is indeed an important distinction. Obligatory runners and well-functioning eating disordered women are competent, resourceful, self-reliant individuals who function well under stressful circumstances. The disorder begins with a crisis of self worth and it worsens when their ability to succeed on their own (at what they consider to be an essential task) is challenged. While the "classic" eating disordered women struggle to extricate themselves from dependent, ambivalent relationships, the "new" eating disordered women and obligatory runners struggle with the issue of maintaining a separate state, a state of independence and productivity. The activity disorder is a statement that they can do it, can conquer the glass mountain, can go it on their own.

Perhaps it is the difference between the intensity of the striving to be independent and the strength of the need to depend which increases the risk of developing an eating (or activity) disorder. By this construct, a very dependent person could develop an eating disorder if she rejects her dependency and tries to become somewhat more self sufficient. The disorder would be of the "classic" variety. On the other hand, an extremely independent woman could develop an eating disorder by negating a lesser need to depend. She would present a "new" eating disorder. Both women would develop a disorder because they were striving toward greater independence. They could present with similar symptoms.

PAIN IN THE SERVICE OF SEPARATENESS

Pain is the hallmark of the dedicated athlete (Sheehan, 1979). Obligatory runners know pain as an inconstant companion; they pound and starve their bodies so that they may become better runners. They experience soreness, cramps, and consummate exhaustion in the course of marathons and trail runs. They continue to run on old injuries, deteriorating cartilage, and partly healed fractures. They cite the pain as a requirement of the sport, a badge of commitment, the test of a true athlete. Sometimes they describe the pain as an organizing and invigorating force. The pain has set them free.

Why do obligatory runners run in pain and why do eating disordered women suffer the extremes of hunger and gut distension? There are several possibilities. Pain may reinforce the immediate, concrete sense of self. Pain punishes the body. Pain also distracts from neediness by substituting a stronger, more immediate issue. Pain abolishes physiologic and psychologic hunger by activating the adrenergic and endorphin systems. Goodsitt (1983) suggests that bulimic women starve and gorge themselves to capture the extreme sensations of hunger and fullness so that this will drown out the anguish beneath. The experience of pain "fits" the activity disorders well.

The functions of pain which are described in the literature are: to reestablish a feeling of being real or alive (Panken, 1973); to debase the self in order to aggrandize an illusory object relationship (Socarides, 1958); and to merge with an idealized (hurtful) self object as a source of sustenance and in an attempt to repair an early defect (Kohut, 1971). In the latter instance, the person, when compensated, would be characterized by submissiveness, self denial, and self surrender. By actively provoking pain (instead of simply receiving it), the individual could foster an illusion of magical control and triumphant command. In this manner, he would be able to deny his narcissistic vulnerability (Eidelberg, 1959). Although these constructs do help to explain the active solicitation of pain by some activity disordered individuals, they leave many questions unanswered.

The theory about the function of pain which seems most relevant to the hypothesis presented in this chapter is that of Hermann (1976) and Cooper (1981). They suggest that pain is a regular concomitant of the expectable early separation process and that it functions as the antithesis of the urge to cling by reinforcing the desire to be separate. When the infant's hair is combed or the diaper rash is cleansed, the child attempts to turn away from the parent. Moderately painful sensations are a regular means by which the infant begins to establish self boundaries. Pain may retain this function in adult life: an adult in love but rejected by the partner may feel calmer and more in control after taking a cold shower or hitting the wall with the fist. In this manner, pain continues to enhance the sense of separateness by granting freedom from the urge to cling.

The pain of the anorexic who starves, of the bulimic who retches, or of the runner who struggles up Heartbreak Hill could be viewed as a means by which these persons are able to reinforce their independence and to maintain a separate state. When these individuals experience pain, they are able to regroup and continue in spite of the need for rest and nourishment. The pain sharply defines their boundaries and it bolsters their resolve to continue on their solitary course. The mastery over the task—of finishing the course, or of losing 10 pounds—signifies the conquest of pain and the reaccomplishment of separation.

Eating disordered women and runners who run on injury have been thought to relish discomfort—or why would they continue to invite pain? The obligatory runners in our sample may have courted pain, but they did not seem to savor it. Perhaps, instead of enjoying pain, they were using it to reinforce the sense of separateness: the pain had become a burdensome but valuable companion on a long and arduous journey. As their self denial and neediness increased, they may have welcomed the pain because it reinforced their resolve to continue in spite of hunger and exhaustion.

HEALTH OR PATHOLOGY?

At the present time, the eating disorders are presumed to be the result of severe intrapsychic and family pathology. Yet the rich internal elaboration, respectable ego functions, and capacity for independent achievement which the "new" eating disordered women demonstrate suggest that they have not been completely crippled by insensitive, rejecting, inconsistent, or overly controlling parents. They must have been reared in an environment which was capable of nurturing these vital ego functions. In spite of whatever problems existed in the home, there must have been something healthy about their early life.

The concept presented here—that at risk individuals become disordered because of their overly high self expectations for independence—does not invoke or exclude the more severe forms of psychopathology, but it suggests that there are factors other than severe psychopathology which can contribute to these disorders. The price of independence is at least a partial negation of the need for receptive gratification: those who strive for greater independence must pay a larger price. In other words, the issue is not of boundaries, but of internal homeostasis: of the balance between dependence and independence.

It is the emotional health and ability of the "new" eating disordered women that match them to the obligatory runners. These are productive individuals who organize themselves through activity and who strive for a personal best. They commit themselves to diet or running in the same manner that they commit themselves to vocational and educational activities. They are independent individuals who are locked in a conflict with the self. They have separated from, and have internalized, the parents. Their boundaries are intact, they have an identity of their own, and they appear healthy.

Applying the concept of severe psychopathology to well-functioning individuals poses many difficulties, sometimes to the point of having to stretch the data to fit the theoretical construct. This does not mean that obligatory runners and well-functioning eating disordered women are completely healthy or devoid of problems; this certainly is not the case. However, the dieting, binge eating, and purging can be viewed as their attempt to adapt to the demands that they perceive and the responsibilities that they undertake. This perspective is similar to that of Behrends and Blatt (1985) and of George Vaillant (1977).

THE PATH TO SUCCESS

Obligatory runners and the "new" eating disordered women are impressive persons: valedictorian of the class, president of the student body, magna cum, editor of the law review, boarded in two medical specialties, etc. They seem to have been as caught up by achievement as they are by diet and exercise. Perhaps the persistence, perfectionism, and independence place them at risk for success and for the development of an activity disorder. Once they taste success, it becomes self-reinforcing (Bandura, 1986; Schunk, 1986; Zimmerman, 1986, 1989); they strive even harder and they achieve even more.

Activity disordered individuals have developed a battery of cognitive strategies and self monitoring techniques to enhance their achievement. These strategies closely resemble the strategies they employ to make themselves run farther or eat less. For instance, they may imagine how ugly they would be if they were fat or how weak and flabby they could become if they cut back on their running. They frequently recheck their progress and rate their achievement. They give themselves praise or criticism. They set small, easy-to-attain goals on the way to a supreme goal and they provide themselves with rewards for good performance.

The strategies that obligatory runners and eating disordered women use to insure their attention to diet and exercise happen to be the same strategies that distinguish successful from less successful students in school. Top ranking scholars set stepwise goals, recheck their performance, give themselves consequences, etc. (Schunk, 1989; Zimmerman, 1989). These strategies begin to develop even before they enter school (Wellman, 1988).

Activity disordered individuals may be too well adapted to the demands of the culture. A technological society needs independent, active, achievement oriented individuals who are able to leave home to attend college, settle in a distant city, or move from place to place as they climb up the corporate ladder. Activity disordered individuals are, in a sense, too well geared for success.

CHAPTER 11

Becoming Independent

Separation is the process by which a person draws apart, physically and emotionally, from the parents and others who could or who do care. Separation issues are especially crucial in the first three years of life when children are the most dependent on the parents and in adolescence when individuals strive the most to be independent. The separation process does not end at maturity, as individuals must continue to separate themselves from significant others throughout life, especially as they depart from home and family in order to achieve in the workplace. Individuals must separate in small ways every day of their lives and they must maintain a somewhat separate state if they are to function independently and productively in life. Viewed in this manner, separation is a continuing, dynamic process which commences in infancy and persists throughout the life span.

Activity is very much a part of the separation process, in that individuals leave the comfort of intimate, caring relationships to "do something." In this culture, the "something" is generally an independent activity. Eating disordered women and obligatory runners are individuals who have achieved a high degree of separateness and who need to maintain a high degree of separateness. Their many activities help them to do this. They pursue most of their activities on their own and they rarely seek comfort or ask for help. The running and dieting serve to accentuate their independence and to maintain a high degree of separation.

We would propose that independent activity is both a product and a part of the separation process, and that those persons who maintain a high level of activity are those persons who expect and continue to demand of themselves an extreme degree of separation. Eating disordered women and obligatory runners provide a history of having always been more independent and active than most of their peers. They must have, and have had, an unusually strong desire to be separate.

This chapter will explore the possibility that the increase in the activity disorders is related to changes in child rearing—especially the expectation that children function independently of their parents at a very early age. There has been little research which relates directly to this issue but the studies that do exist will be presented.

SOCIOCULTURAL CHANGE

Over the past several decades, upper SES families have become smaller and upper SES women have become better educated than before. The work of housekeeping is less taxing than it was in the days of the washboard and the wood burning stove. Over these same years, the esteem accorded to the homemaker role has diminished and many families have discovered that they need or desire two incomes to maintain a comfortable or affluent life-style. Because of these and other considerations, more and more women are seeking employment outside of the home. Between 1960 and 1980, the number of women in the work force doubled. At the same time, the divorce rate soared (Fisher, 1989). At present in the United States, 53 percent of married mothers with children age one or under are employed, which is more than double the rate of 24 percent in 1970 (U.S. Bureau of Labor Statistics, 1987). As the children grow, more mothers leave for work: 71 percent of mothers of school aged children are employed outside the home. This trend seems likely to continue in the foreseeable future.

With the diminished value attached to the homemaker role, women who remain at home are more likely to suffer from emotional problems such as stress, depression, and psychosomatic symptoms than are those women who enter the work force (Burke & Weir, 1976; Kessler & McRae, 1982). Employed women feel better and they are healthier, even when they dislike work and would rather be at home (Hock & De Mies, 1990). Employment has its disadvantages for women also. Hochschild (1989) indicates that employed mothers work an average of 13–15 hours a week more than their husbands do, in a combination of job and homemaking duties. Employed women usually continue to rear the children, cook, and keep house for the family. They experience a proliferation of roles rather than a transition from one role to another (Johnson & Johnson, 1980). Career women have problems in delegating responsibility and compartmentalizing roles: i.e., they worry about the children when they are at work. As they cannot work and attend to children at the same time, they must depend upon nannies, babysitters, and child care facilities.

Entwined with the movement of women out of the home comes an increase in the expectations of what a woman should or could achieve in life. At least for upper SES women, the possibilities are legion, but the criteria for success remain ambiguous. Is it possible to be fulfilled as a woman without having children? Is it possible to do both? Will embarking on a "mommy track" prohibit the climb up the corporate ladder? Do the strains placed on a two-career family make divorce the likely outcome? Are children permanently damaged when their parents divorce? These are the dilemmas that well-educated young women face.

As upper SES women grapple with issues of role and self worth, many more women assume the responsibility of continued self development, whether or not they remain at home. In most instances, women choose to evolve via a career—the dual-wage family has been the model family with school age children for the past 20 years (Hoffman, 1989). Women who remain at home are more likely to develop themselves through a variety of civic, craft, sports, educational, or social activities. Although having children (but not too many) and homemaking are still important, they are clearly not enough for most women.

The profound changes in the family and in the role of women must prejudice the manner in which children are raised and the experience of growing up. What kind of influences might there be which would cause a substantial increase in the eating disorders? There are two possibilities that come to mind. The first is that there has been a decline in the ability to parent children. Perhaps, since women are subject to multiple stresses, they are less invested in motherhood or less able to be good mothers. They (together with their spouses and babysitters) may not be providing their children with enough, or good enough, nurturance. This could engender conflict in the children over the issue of dependency ("How am I going to get enough?"). This might place children at risk to develop an eating disorder later on. The second possibility is that there has been an increase in the parents' expectation that children become more independent at an early age, a circumstance which might engender conflicts over dependency of a somewhat different nature ("How am I going to make it on my own?").

A DEFECT IN NURTURANCE?

There are very real impediments to being a good parent today. Mothers and fathers face limitations in time, problems in coordinating schedules, and the pressure of multiple responsibilities in and outside of the home.

Upper SES parents in a nuclear or single parent family may experience exhaustion, frustration, and depression as they attempt to rear children without the support of an extended family. Parenthood can become a stressful experience. These are reasons why parents might be less adequate now than they were in the past.

There are other factors which suggest that although the parenting may be different now, it is no worse than it was several decades ago. Although motherhood may be less of an overall priority in life, most women continue to accord considerable value to it. In an age in which the upper SES is no longer reproducing itself, childbirth can be a very special event—one which is often anticipated with pleasure. For career women, giving birth and caring for an infant may represent an oasis of tenderness, a brief respite from the cutthroat world of business. Through childbirth and infant care, women can gain the luxury of time to create and to nurture—essential experiences which are scarce on the business or professional scene. Women often perceive this period as a unique and precious interlude in an otherwise hectic life.

Career women are able to have children by choice: they have the knowledge and the resources to avoid or to terminate unwanted pregnancies. Some women plan for many years to have a child. They worry that they might not be able to conceive because of age, the possibility of divorce, and the time commitments of becoming trained and educated. They are apt to anticipate the bearing and raising of a child with pleasure.

Although upper SES children are cared for differently now than they would have been 30 years ago, there is no indication that they are less well nurtured. Today's children tend to be properly attended and raised in an environment which is rich with baby equipment, toys, and stimulating activities. The parents are more likely than their own parents were to have attended classes on childbirth, read books on child care, and employed the services of a pediatrician. The parents are generally aware of the dangers inherent in overprotecting children and the importance of facilitating independent growth. They rear children with pacifier and without the constraints of early toilet training or a rigid feeding schedule. Because sex roles have become less traditional (Baruch & Barnett, 1986), fathers tend to be more involved in infant care (Hoffman, 1986). Children in a dual-wage family may see their mothers less, but they play with their fathers more.

If the modal upper SES family of today is child oriented, concerned and able to provide the best for their children, this would suggest that children today would be more likely to experience a joyful, rich early life than children were earlier in this century when there were larger families, less affluence, and less appreciation of child development.

Whether this is the case or not, there is no evidence that upper SES parents now are less invested in their children or that they are not providing their children with enough, or good enough, care. The rise in the eating disorders is not likely to be based on an increase in inadequate or destructive parenting.

ARE PARENTS TOO CLOSE?

From the material presented, it would seem that the level of childcare provided by today's parents is probably as good as or better than the level of care provided by parents in the years prior to the rise of the dual-wage family. Now there are relatively few children in the family and each child can receive a larger share of the parents' attention.

We will take the position of a devil's advocate: perhaps the increase in the eating disorders is associated with a closer and more nurturant parent-child relationship. A close parent-child relationship in the early years would tend to augment both the children's dependency and their identification with the parents. If the parents were independent and achievement oriented, the children would be apt to adopt the same high self expectations. This system could foster children who would enjoy being dependent, but who would, eventually, strive toward greater independence and achievement. The closeness of the relationship would increase the children's need to depend and the striving to be separate; in this manner it might increase the risk of an activity disorder.

That the closeness of the parent-child relationship could predispose children to develop an eating disorder later on is suggested by a study of the Kibbutz in Israel (Kaffman & Sadeh, 1989). There, the incidence of the eating disorders has increased 800 percent over the past 25 years. Until 1965, the eating disorders had been very rare in the Kibbutz, far scarcer than in the non-Kibbutz, urban population. Since that time, the major change which would affect children has been the intensification of the relationships in the family unit (although food also has become more plentiful). In 1965, Kibbutz parents were minimally involved in the care and feeding of their children. Since then, the mothers have become increasingly invested in cooking and child care within the home—although they continue to be occupied outside of the home. The closeness of the relationship has brought about changes in the emotional meaning of food and the role of food in the mother-child relationship. In the Kibbutz, the pattern and intensity of the relationship between parent and child, and the manner in which they separate, is very similar to that which exists in this country.

The association between certain types of eating difficulties and the closeness of the parent/child relationship was noted by Anna Freud and Dorothy Burlingham (1944) in their studies of young children who were separated from their parents during the London blitz. The children who were placed in a residential nursery seemed on the whole to enjoy their food more than did the children who remained in their own homes. Abnormal reactions to food did occur in the residential nursery, but these were in the form of greed and overeating rather than the lack of appetite or refusal of food—reactions that were commonly found in the home.

An association between disordered eating and an overly close relationship to the mother is presented in the Chatoor, Egan et al. (1988) study of children who suffer from a condition called "infantile anorexia." These infants begin to obstinately refuse food during the second six months of life. The mothers of these infants are upper SES women who have high self expectations and seem overly involved in the care of the infants (Chatoor & Egan, 1983). A close mother-child relationship could set the stage for the emergence of an eating disturbance because the intense gratification which the mother provides makes the separation process more difficult for the child. The child resists the closeness of the relationship by refusing the food which the parent offers. The child's refusal causes the mother to become even more involved in the eating behavior.

EXPECTING INDEPENDENCE

Superimposed on the excellent care that children in this culture receive is the strong and pervasive expectation that they should learn to be as independent as possible at an early age. The expectation is communicated to children in many ways, perhaps the clearest of which is the expectation that children adapt to life apart from their parents, with sitters or in day care.

More than half the mothers of infants under age one work outside of the home and in most of these instances the fathers are also employed away from the home. Infants are usually placed with a sitter or in a nursery; less frequently, they remain at home with a relative or nanny. Because of this and because the parents have many responsibilities other than child care when they are at home, the children are encouraged to become as independent as possible. The pattern of early, brief separations and the emphasis on independence would tend to accelerate the early separation process.

Mothers who are not employed outside the home rely upon babysitters also, although they tend to do so less regularly than do women who are employed outside the home. Homemakers often feel constrained by their role and they may wish to develop themselves outside of the home through volunteer work, health clubs, civic organizations, hobbies, etc. The involvement of homemakers outside the home is a relatively recent occurrence. In the first half of this century, it was distinctly unusual for the mothers of young children to become involved in community-based activities. They were more likely to build an identity around child care and homemaking activity.

Generally speaking, when an upper SES parent leaves a young child in order to return to work (or for other reasons), she is sensitive to the fact that this may be difficult for the child. She may do everything possible to minimize the child's pain, including introducing the child to the sitter or child care facility gradually, arranging for additional toys and structured activities, or giving the child extra attention at times when she is at home. The one thing that she does not do is to make herself less attractive to the child so that the child will miss her less.

The separations which the child experiences when the parents return to work are relatively brief; they can be measured in hours rather than in days. The brevity of the separations seems to soften the experience for the child. Infants are less distressed when their mothers have left them for moderate periods of time than when they have been left for slight or prolonged periods of time (Jacobson & Wille, 1984). When the separations reoccur at regular intervals, this may desensitize the child to the parents' departures. The separations become predictable events which the child learns to master, using the many supports which the parents provide.

Children adapt to early separation by becoming more independent. Children of employed mothers demonstrate greater autonomy from a very early age: securely attached 18-month-old youngsters from dual-wage families demonstrate less dependency behavior than do securely attached children of the same age from single-wage families (Weinraub, Yaeger & Hoffman, 1988). Parents in dual-wage families are more likely than parents in single-wage families to encourage children to become independent (Weinraub et al, 1988; Zaslow, 1987). Employed mothers train their children to be independent and they welcome and reward independent functioning, whereas full-time homemakers may view children's independence as a threat to their major role and source of self esteem (Hoffman, 1979). In this culture, independence is equated with health rather than with pathology; therefore, the separated child may appear healthier than the child who has remained with the mother in the home.

There is considerable concern about whether a mother's absence from the home can produce long-term emotional damage in the child. The results of several longitudinal studies are reassuring in that maternal employment per se is but a weak predictor of the subsequent characteristics and behavior of the child. The effects that do exist are mediated through child care arrangements and the impact of the mother's absence on the family environment as a whole. These effects are moderated by family structure, both parents' attitudes, and other variables (Hoffman, 1989). On the basis of these studies, early, brief, repetitive separations from the mother do not seem to be injurious to the child, but they do cause the child to become relatively independent at a very early age (Weinraub et al., 1988).

Perhaps one of the reasons why the children of employed mothers do well is that the women who work outside the home feel more self fulfilled and less depressed. Women who feel fulfilled may be better mothers when they are at home. There is a higher level of satisfaction among the mothers who are employed, especially when the women wish to work and have a good job and stable child care arrangements (Hoffman, 1989). On the other hand, the mothers who stay at home but wish that they were working demonstrate the highest levels of depression and stress (Hock & De Mies, 1990). Behavioral problems are more frequent among the children of depressed mothers (Richman, 1975). Even when employed mothers are depressed, their children may be less affected by their depression than are the children of non-employed, depressed mothers (Ghodsian, Zajicek & Wolkind, 1984). Even the best possible mother may be sorely tested by a temperamentally difficult infant, but the mothers of difficult infants care for the children more effectively if they are employed outside of the home (Dienstag, 1986).

Most of the studies on the effect of early separation measure long-term differences between the children of employed and non-employed mothers. There are very few studies of the immediate physiologic and psychologic effects of relatively brief separations in young children. However, Field and Reite (1984) monitored a series of preschool children separated from their mothers while the mothers were in the hospital giving birth to another child. Because the children visited the mothers repeatedly in the hospital, the model was actually that of a series of repetitive, brief separations. The children were well prepared in advance and were actively cared for by the fathers while the mother was away. In spite of these beneficial circumstances, the children reacted to the mother's absence with a significant increase in activity level, heart rate, fussiness, crying, and aggressive behavior. Once the mother returned home, the children became less active, and their heart rate slowed; their mood appeared flat or depressed. Separation reactions such as these are most pronounced at age two and they diminish by the time children reach age three (Maccoby & Feldman, 1972).

The immediate pain of a separation could be more severe for well-nurtured children than it is for less favored children. Well-nurtured children enjoy their parents; they must face not just the separation, but the loss of a rich and captivating experience. There is one primate study (Wiener, Johnson & Levine, 1987) which bears on this matter. When individually reared infant monkeys are compared to infant monkeys reared in groups, the individually reared monkeys are more distressed and demonstrate higher cortisol and activity levels during separation than the group-reared monkeys. Individually reared monkeys tend to develop a closer, more exclusive relationship with the mother. If the finding can be applied to humans, it would suggest that a close parent-child relationship could increase the child's reaction to separation. Well cared for, happily dependent youngsters may become more distressed and active, and they may need to strive even harder to establish a separate state.

Well-nurtured children may have a difficult time at first when they are separated, but they do adapt. They are fortunate in that the positive relationship with the parents has fostered the development of ego functions and the acquisition of competence. The parents' ongoing concern and support and the adequacy of the carefully selected substitute caregivers are additional factors which facilitate a positive adaptation.

THE MEANING OF ACTIVITY

If separation causes infants to become more active, what does the activity represent? The separation is apt to frighten young children who are used to having the parents close by. This precipitates a vigorous protest and a frantic search for the mother. The fear and the agitation which follow separation have been linked to adrenal catacholamine synthesis and a massive activation of the sympathetic adrenergic system (Breese et al., 1973; Reite et al., 1981). The acute distress of separation is short lived if the mother returns to hold and comfort the child. Monkey experiments indicate that the increase in the infant's activity is specifically down-regulated (diminished) by the warmth of the mother's body. The mother's warmth also down-regulates the activation of the sympathetic adrenergic system (Stone, Bonnet & Hofer, 1976; Hofer, 1984). This suggests that the increase in activity which follows separation does represent the infant's search for the lost mother; when the infant is able to reestablish contact with the warmth of the mother's body, the infant no longer needs to be active.

Human children who are distressed at the time of separation are soothed when they are once again held by the mother. Like monkey infants, they are no longer agitated or active. We do not have human experiments which test the long-term effects of repetitive, brief separations from the mother. Perhaps there would be an overall increase in the level of activity because the children would come to anticipate further separations. If this is the case, then we would expect that most children who have been in day care would demonstrate a higher activity level than most children who have never been in day care. All that we do know is that young children demonstrate a predictable increase in activity when they are separated from their mothers and that the increase in activity will persist for four days, which was the time period specified in the Field and Reite (1984) study. However, we do know that when monkey infants experience a number of brief separations the increase in activity persists even into adolescence and adulthood (Coe et al., 1983; Hennessy, 1986).

If we assume, on the basis of the research available, that infants regularly react to separation with an increase in activity, then activity is apt to become an integral part of the separation reaction. As the child begins to establish independence he might continue to react to the regressive pull, the need to be nurtured, with an increase in activity. He might learn to maintain a separate state by being active outside of the context of the intimate relationship, i.e., in a number of independent exploratory and manipulative activities. This would be the birth of the separation maintenance function of activity.

CASE EXAMPLES

In the therapeutic preschool and the clinic, we have had the opportunity to observe a number of youngsters and to understand something about their families. Many of these children have family problems which may serve to accentuate the striving to be separate. We have noted that the children who are making an unusually strong effort to be independent tend to be the children who seem to be vigorous in play and in exploration of the environment. Michael, for instance, is a four-year-old youngster who was placed in several different foster homes during the second year of his life. Now his life is quite stable as he is living with his mother who is clearly concerned about his well-being. In the preschool, he is constantly active with the tricycle, the blocks, and other play equipment. He never asks for help and is loathe to accept attention from the staff.

At home, Michael will escape from the backyard unless directly super-vised; otherwise, he takes off in whatever direction strikes him, without any concern about what might happen.

Children who are separated from the parents and placed in the hospital for several days may react with a sustained increase in physical activity. A three-year-old girl was hospitalized on pediatrics after a car accident in which her parents were gravely injured. At first she repeatedly in-quired about her mother. As soon as she was up and about, the questions ceased; instead she rode a tricycle ceaselessly, around and around the nurses station. Mahler (1972) describes a year-old child who was hos-pitalized for a week. When the youngster returned from the hospital, his relationship with his mother had become less exclusive and he did not cling or seem anxious about further separations. Instead, his greatest desire was for someone to take him for a walk.

In the previous chapter we suggested that it was not dependency per se which is a basis for the activity disorders but the degree to which the person strives toward greater independence. In the microcosm of these three very young children, we find a clear association between an increase in activity and the striving to be independent in spite of (or because of) an acute need for care. This reaction may be seen in older children and adults. Betsy, the eating disordered woman presented in Chapter 4, was a well-nurtured child who began her pattern of heightened activity when her parents separated and she was trying not to need her mother. She continued the high level of activity into her adult life, and she used it to become successful at work.

From the cases presented, it would seem that the thrust toward activity can be associated with the striving to maintain a separate state. In these children, the need to establish greater independence coexists with an acute need to be more dependent, against which the children must struggle. These children are engaged in an internal struggle to be more independent; their dependency makes a resolution difficult.

The increase in activity may not be prominent in childhood. It may become more apparent in adolescence or early adult life when the person must separate from the family and establish an independent, worthy self. Perhaps, an early, intense struggle to maintain a separate state sets the stage for an increase in activity when a separation occurs later on, but we do not know if this is the case.

If the increase in activity and independence associated with early sep-arations should persist and become part of the personality, an accelerated early separation process could contribute a substantial risk for the emerg-ence of an activity disorder later on. In this line of reasoning, very active, independent adults would be more likely than inactive adults to have experienced an accelerated early separation process; these adults would carry a higher risk for the development of an activity disorder.

ACTIVITY TO RESIST DEPENDENCY

In the cases presented above, the children were involved in an internal struggle to maintain a separate state. These cases must be distinguished from other instances in which the children are using activity to resist the pull of dependency:

Theresa is a four-year-old child who has been raised by her maternal grandmother since birth. She is the center of her grandmother's life, and they are rarely apart. Theresa is developing well, but she exhibits several unusual behaviors: when her grandmother wishes to dress her, she cries for her crayons and coloring book; when her grandmother takes her for a walk, she stops repeatedly to pick up stones and twigs. These behaviors occur only when she is with her grandmother. She does not want to walk alone or to visit away from home.

Theresa is overly involved with her grandmother and she is using independent activity to diminish the intensity of the primary relationship (Rheingold & Eckerman, 1970). In this case, the conflict is more external (with the grandmother) than internal (with the self). The separation process is impeded rather than accelerated.

MULTIPLE INFLUENCES

When a parent sequesters an infant with toys in a crib or playpen, chooses the bottle over the breast, or cautions a toddler not to cling, this could accelerate the separation process in a manner which is not dissimilar to leaving the child with a sitter. The repetitive, brief separations which children experience when their parents go out to work are probably less significant in their development than the overall expectation that it is good for children to become autonomous. When parents role model self-reliance, this fosters independence in the child. In a broader sense, independence is underwritten by customs such as sleeping in separate bedrooms, covering the body, and the scheduling of sleep, eating, and other activities.

A REPETITIVE PATTERN

Upper SES mothers often work outside of the home to augment the family's standard of living or because working is important in their self concept, rather than because their wages are indispensable to the family economy. Even when women feel strongly that mothers should remain at home until their children are old enough to go to school, they are very likely to return to work when the infants are a few months old. A survey of 1000 woman psychiatrists (Wood & Paley, 1988) reveals that although these women thought that it was best for young children if the mothers were to remain at home, 84 percent had returned to work by the time their children were six to nine months old.

The point to be taken from this is that upper SES women are likely to have a significant need to be independent and active, even before they marry or have children. This may be partly determined by growing up in an achievement and activity oriented system and partly a product of their own accelerated separation process, perhaps from mothers who were beginning to be "freed up" and out of the house.

The etiology of the eating disorders remains obscure despite 20 years of research (Stunkard, 1990). The reason for the recent, dramatic increase in the eating disorders (Jones et al., 1980; Szmulker et al., 1986) is not apparent, nor is the reason why so many of these cases occur in college students and in the upper SES. Does this mean that college women are more disturbed or more fragile? Or more likely to have been damaged in early childhood? As we become more affluent, are we less able to rear healthy children? A plausible answer to these questions could lie in the manner in which children are raised. The dramatic increase in the eating disorders in upper SES women may be due to the acceleration of the early separation process. This may explain the apparent, dramatic increase in compulsive athleticism, also.

CHAPTER 12

The Body

Obligatory runners and eating disordered women appear to love and hate the body. They often seem as if they would like to disown the body, or at least to find one that is stronger and more self sufficient. At times, they treat the body as something alien, foreign, threatening (Goodsitt, 1983), yet they go to extraordinary lengths to improve the beauty and strength of the body. The body is too much with them: it functions as a best friend and a worst enemy.

The conventional path to success is through cognitive achievement in non-body-based activities. Why, then, do certain achievement oriented persons invest so heavily in body-based activities such as exercise and diet? There are several possible explanations. One is that body-based activities bear an indirect relationship to success because, even in the competitive world of business, people are judged in part on their appearance or the fitness of the body. A body which functions as a killer on the racquetball court may establish a competitive edge in the place of employment. Another possibility is that these persons need the immediate, tangible rewards of a diet or exercise program to counteract the feelings of frustration and inadequacy generated at work. A final possibility is that the body in motion contributes something to the activity which is unique and which cannot be tapped through non-body-based activities.

THEORIES ABOUT THE BODY

Freud (1923) stated that the ego is first and foremost a body ego and that it is ultimately derived from bodily sensations, especially those which spring from the surface of the body. Freud's concept of the "ego" is similar to a commonly accepted concept of the "self." Sandler and Rosenblatt (1962) follow Freud when they indicate that self representations are first and foremost body representations. The infant is involved in a continual interchange between body and world; the body is projected into the world and the world is projected into the body (Schilder, 1950). The relationship between the mother and the child is built on a series of projections and introjections involving the body (Lax, 1972). As the child grows, he experiences, understands, and explores the world in terms of his body. The body and the ego continue to have an integral, mutual relationship throughout development (Ritvo, 1984).

The body schema is the representation of the body in the mind (Torras De Bea, 1987). Infants are likely to experience many and various body representations. These are complex, mobile constellations which have the characteristics of an internal object. The most significant or valued parts of the body are the ones most strongly represented. During the first year of life, the infant integrates feeling states with the responses of the caregivers, and begins to generate self representations of a higher perceptual and cognitive order (Mahler & McDevitt, 1982).

The internal representations of the body, the schemata, are created by the functioning of the body, the parents' affirmation of the body, and the parents' eroticization of the body through childcare processes such as bathing, holding, and feeding. As the infant gazes at his fingers, moves them, and touches objects, he forms an internal representation of the fingers; this image, in turn, enables the fingers to function more efficiently. The parents affirm the infant's body by noting and reacting to its quality and movement. Winnicott (1965a) describes the mother's response to the infant's body as her mirroring function. This essential response is necessary for the development of the infant's body self and the body image. The parents eroticize the baby's body by the care that they provide (Hoffer, 1949). If the care taken of the baby's body is intimate, pleasurable, and tension relieving, the infant should develop a sense of well-being (Sandler, 1960) and of being alive. The parents' responsiveness and care, and the relationship which they develop with the child, are essential ingredients in the formation of the body image and sense of self (Mahler & McDevitt, 1982).

Before infants acquire representational thought, they recall experiences through the body and by the action of the body. They understand the environment by moving within it; the body contacts the parents and the body mediates the relationship to the parents. Although, as children grow, they become less body based and more cognitively based, the cognitive understanding is superimposed on the earlier, motoric perception of the environment. The cognitive concept does not replace the realization of the world through the action of the body.

From the theory presented here, it would seem that the infant's body plays an especially important role in the relationship to the parents. The body translates the child's neediness to the parents and the neediness is relieved through the body. Understanding the role of the body within the early dependency relationship may provide a clue as to the importance of the body later on, as the individual strives for greater independence.

ROLE OF THE BODY IN DEVELOPMENT

The body has many functions during the child's development: ingestion, activity, presentation or appearance, and sensory contact, to name a few. The body is an agent and an object—one that is hungry or full, exhausted or energized, hot or cold. The body is an object to be adorned, preened, presented and sometimes punished. The body needs the parent and the body receives what the parents provide.

Before the child begins to play, or play with his own body, the parents play with the child's body. They tickle it, lift it high, swoop it low, blow on it, kiss it, rub it. As the mother (or the father) plays with the child's body, the child learns to play with the mother on his body—trying to touch her hand and pushing at the belly where she tickles. The tripartite nature of the body-self-mother relationship is well illustrated by the game parents play with the infant and the infant's body: "Pat it, poke it, mark it with a T—put it in the oven for baby and me."

When the child is a few months older, he gladly supplies the parent with the body when the parent requests it ("Give me your foot" or "Show me your tummy"). Toward the end of the first year of life, the child begins to offer the body to the parent, so that the parent can "make it well." The parent directs the attention toward the body to elicit a reaction from the child and the child may extend a part of the body so that the parent may receive it. Diapering and genital touching are often in the same vein; the infant spreads the legs, grabs at the genitals, smiles, and looks intently at the mother as she attends to his body.

THE BODY AS A TRANSACTIONAL AGENT

In the early transaction with the parent, the child's body becomes a gift. The four-month-old infant cries and stretches toward his mother, but the instant she picks him up, his body melts into hers. In effect, he gives her his body so that she may care for it. She may feed and change him and put him down to rest. The body remains relaxed; it contains the mother's care. The care which the body has received continues to nourish the child.

When the body absorbs comfort through a transaction with the parent, the mother is regulating the child's internal state. The mother owns the child's body more than the mother owns the child's self. At first, the ownership seems almost complete, and the child is wholly dependent upon the parent to modulate the body state. Only very gradually does the child learn to modulate his own sensory input by changing his position, perception, or mood. The parents help the child learn simple self regulation through the body. When the parent plays tickle games with the infant, this encounter enables the child to learn how to self regulate (Stern, 1985). The mother stimulates, the child is delighted. When it is too much, the infant is no longer delighted. He objects, the mother notices and stops.

When the infant's body absorbs comfort through the parent's tender ministrations, the body serves as a receptacle. It does not need to be active in its own behalf. The body tone can best be described as loose or supple, an index of the child's relinquishment of control and his acceptance of the parent's care. Mahler, Pine and Bergman (1975) describe the mother's warmth as reciprocated by the pliability of the infant's body. They note that the infant's body stiffens and distances in the absence of maternal warmth. The softening of the child's body as it receives the warmth of the parent is, so to speak, the original format of the parent-child relationship. In Chapter 11, we noted that when infant animals are separated from their mothers, they become distressed, they cry, and their activity escalates dramatically. This increase in activity is down-regulated specifically by the warmth of the mother's body (Stone, Bonnet & Hofer, 1976; Hofer, 1984). The body and body heat are the currency of care.

From this description, it becomes apparent that the body is not only a basis for the development of the self, but it is a transactional (rather than a transitional) object between the child and the parent. The body represents the self and the parent as well as existing as an object which can be touched, smelled, and felt in its own right (Sugarman & Kurash, 1982). The body links the child with the parent before the child learns to use the body for self regulation. The self-regulating function of the body is derived from the tripartite relationship between self, body, and parent.

AS THE CHILD MATURES

The strength of the body's role as the receptacle of the parent's warmth does not seem to diminish as time passes. For many years, the parent can override the child's struggle to be separate by claiming his body and the child's body continues to provide him access to the parent. As he explores the yard, the toddler falls and hurts his knee; he cries and his mother comes to hold him. The mother continues to interact with the child's body as before: she clothes the child, wraps a warm towel around him after the bath, combs his hair, and ties his shoes.

As the infant continues the process of separation, he differentiates his body from his mother by reaching toward, manipulating, and exploring the environment (Mahler, Pine & Bergman, 1975). These are independent activities, apart from the parent, the parent's body and the parent's warmth. As the child matures, there will be times when he strives to be more separate from the parent. The various ways in which he might do this include avoiding her touch, maintaining significant body tension, focusing on controlling the body and the self, and removing his body from the parent through his involvement in other-than-parent activities.

HOLDING TECHNIQUES

The mother enfolds the child and, with surprising rapidity, the child's body becomes supple and receptive. This key reaction is the basis for the technique of "holding" in which agitated or out-of-control children are soothed by being enclosed in the arms (and sometimes the legs) of the caregiver. Even when the child's most fervent desire is to lash out and break away, the body will fold into the caregiver's arms. As the body continues to be held, the child's thoughts follow the body and he begins to receive through the relationship. Holding is an effective technique for the most combative and resistant youngsters; body contact can override the urge to attack and the striving to be separate. The technique of holding is effective until adolescence, when youths become so powerful that their initial resistance cannot be broached and the struggle can become dangerous for the caregiver.

The principle of holding the body has been applied to disturbed adults, with excellent results. A time-honored technique for soothing agitated hospitalized patients is to wrap them securely in cold, wet sheets (Ross et al., 1988). As the patients' body heat warms the sheets, they relax and are able to receive comfort. Some patients learn to request this treatment when they are becoming agitated.

OWNING THE BODY

Anna Freud (1952) made a crucial observation: that in the youngster's mind, his body belongs to his parents (usually to the mother) until early in adolescence. This means that children assume that their parents "own" their body and are responsible for its health and hygiene. Freud describes children as not to be trusted to care for their own body. She notes that they do with their body as they please: eating with dirty hands, stuffing themselves with the wrong foods, forgetting to change into pajamas or brush their teeth, and so forth. Those children who wash their hands before eating (without being told) are uncommonly obsessional. Even when children are involved in activities away from the home, they continue to use the parent as their point of reference and they assume that the parent is responsible for their care. Even when they seem to be independent, their body remains in the parent's domain.

Anna Freud's concept, that the child's body is owned by the parent, may seem to contradict the concept presented in this chapter: that the child's body is involved in a transaction by which the child "owns" the body and simultaneously presents it as a gift to the parent, i.e., it is only as the recipient of the body as a gift, that the parent comes to own the child's body. Yet Anna Freud was correct in saying that the child does not assume responsibility for the body. Perhaps the reason why children do not seem to own the body is because their most fervent wish is that the parent hold them and minister to their bodily needs. They want the body to be taken by the parent and so they are unwilling to assume the care of the body.

How might the child continue to "give" the body to the parent, even when there is no physical contact? Perhaps the child wishes the body on the parent through the mechanism of projection in its early, more concrete form. According to analytic theory, the mechanism of projection exists prior to the time when the child acquires symbolic or representational thought. Very young children understand the world through body contact, body movement and concrete action sequences. Therefore, the child may project his understanding of the body on the parent, with the wish that the parent will enfold him. The early, concrete form of projection is thought to be an important mechanism by which infants are able to form a separate sense of self (Klein, 1946) and/or establish a primitive form of empathy with the parent (Segal, 1973; Sandler, 1987). In the case presented here, the child would yearn for the parent, want to move toward the parent, and project a much valued part, the body, on the parent, thus reestablishing a primitive bond of empathy with the parent.

Infants seem to value the body highly, in part because of the body's need satisfying transaction with the parent. From age one to three, most youngsters are proud of the body and they may exhibit it to other children and adults. As children grow older and they enter school, they become more ambivalent about the body and the relationship of the body to the parent. There are many reasons for this, not the least of which is the frustration involved in needing the parent and the pressure to become more independent. The increasing ambivalence about the body is especially apparent in the United States, where nearly half of a large sample of grade school children are already dissatisfied with the body (Maloney, McGuire & Daniels, 1988).

When children enter adolescence, they begin to assume the care of their own body instead of expecting that the parent will care for it. They become more independent by selecting their own clothes, learning to blow dry their hair, and fashioning an appearance which is unique and different from the presentation which the parent fostered in the past. Once adolescents begin to care for their body, they are more likely to involve it in intimate transactions with peers, rather than with the parent. However, the body never seems to completely relinquish the need to receive the warmth of the parent.

Some adolescents love the body and they take consistently good care of themselves. This is an indication of healthy narcissism (Dare & Holder, 1981). They may be able to do this because they have internalized the loving aspects of the parents; because the body provides them with pleasure; because the body is used to self regulate; and/or because they do not need to strive inordinately hard to maintain a separate state. Certain circumstances could interfere with the process of assuming the care of the body. Some adolescents may not be ready to withdraw the body from the transaction with the parent; other youths may be constrained by guilt over their sexual or aggressive urges, so that they attempt to inhibit all the needs of the body. Individuals who strive to be especially independent may be threatened by the body's connection to the parent and need to be cared for. They may attempt to control the body and to deny the neediness of the body through various ascetic practices. Anna Freud (1946) and Mogul (1980) describe asceticism in adolescence as a particularly intense struggle for independence and a separate identity.

AMBIVALENCE ABOUT THE BODY IN THE
ACTIVITY DISORDERS

Bruch (1973) asserts that the pre-anorexic child is never able to own her own body because her mother did not respond appropriately to the cues that she initiated and, therefore, she never became aware of her body state. More recent authors suggest that the body of the eating disordered patient continues to be involved in an ongoing relationship with the mother. Woodall (1987) administered the sentence completion test to a large sample of eating disordered women. The responses indicate that, for these women, it is as if the surface of their body is still claimed and controlled by the parent. They hate and reject the body as the parent's possession. In spite of this, they are frenetically preoccupied with the body surface which they seem to love and hate. These findings support the continued tripartite nature of body, self, and parent in the mind of eating disordered women.

The attitude toward the body and the value attached to the body must in some manner reflect the early relationship to the parents and the value of that relationship. In Chapter 11 we suggest that the closeness of the mother-child relationship contributes a risk for the development of an activity disorder in those persons who strive toward greater independence. When the union with the parents is extremely gratifying, they must strive harder in order to disengage themselves. If the attitude toward the body reflects the early relationship with the parents, then these individuals would approach the body in the same, highly ambivalent, manner that they approach the issue of dependency. The ambivalence about the body would represent the ambivalence about dependency.

DISCONNECTION OF BODY AND SELF IN THE
ACTIVITY DISORDERS

One way in which to handle ongoing ambivalence about the body would be to disconnect body and self. In the eating disorders and in compulsive athleticism, body and self have become disconnected to the point that it seems as if the body is headed in one direction and the self is headed in another. The person often acts as if the body were a disobedient child who must be cajoled or forced into a more favorable appearance or performance. The more recalcitrant the body seems, the more it is rejected and the more disconnected from the self it becomes. An obligatory runner once stated that if he could only make his body behave, he would run much further than his accustomed 180 miles a week; some days he had to "fight it" (the body) in order to finish. He related the pain of a chronic Achilles tendinitis to his body's inability to understand how important it was to stay in shape. An anorexic woman refuses food, proclaiming that if her body would take in all those calories, "it" wouldn't be fit to live in.

Individuals who are at odds with the body can express their ambivalence in different ways. "Classic," severely disturbed eating disordered women are likely to utilize a mechanism which is similar to that described by Selvini-Palazzoli (1978). These women are highly ambivalent about dependency. The body is like the mother's body and, because it contains the need for the mother, it represents the dependency on the mother. They disown the body and they try to destroy it through starvation, but they remain immersed in the ambivalent relationship. They continue to involve the mother, to control and wound her, by destroying her body. The dual message is: "You can't control my body," and "Look what you are doing to your body."

Well-functioning eating disordered women and obligatory runners utilize a mechanism which differs somewhat from that which is employed by severely disturbed eating disordered patients. These individuals are ambivalent about dependency not because they are too dependent but because dependency is incompatible with their high self expectations for independence and achievement. The war is with the self, not with the parents. The more independent these individuals expect themselves to be, the more they attempt to perfect and control the body. They disconnect from the body and they hurt the body because the body will not conform to their ideal of beauty or fitness. The body is less than perfect; it represents their vulnerability and the need to be nurtured. In spite of their attempt to make the body autonomous (independent of the need for food or rest), they cannot abolish the neediness. At some level, these persons understand the power of the body—that it can override all of their efforts to be separate.

If the ownership of the body is a major step toward independence and persons who strive exceptionally hard to be independent dissociate themselves from the body, it would seem that these persons are working against themselves. This is simply another way of describing the runner who strives for a personal best by training past the point of exhaustion or the woman who diets down to skin and bones because she wishes to improve her appearance. The court of last resort is marked by an utter disregard for the integrity of the body. If the process is carried to completion and the body collapses, the person may finally realize the unconscious desire to be cared for once again.

Although individuals with an activity disorder seem bent on destroying the body, they also love the body very much. They begin to diet or exercise in order to improve the body, to make it better. It is the body that contains the image of succorance, of rest and replenishment. It is the body which at times supplies a sense of comfort and being, of self worth or efficacy. It is not the body that these persons wish to destroy, but the body as an agent of need. In a concrete sense, the body is the path back to mother.

BABY FAT

Infants are delighted at the opportunity to receive and they do so easily, without the need to censure or control the pleasure or its source. To be an infant is to eat lustily until satiated. To be an infant is to be enjoyed for the vigor of desire and the plumpness of the body. In an age in which six-year-old children are trying to eat less and learn how to play the piano, infancy may be the last bastion of unambivalent receptive pleasure.

The only time in life when it is truly acceptable to be plump is in infancy and early childhood. The chubby cheeks, the dimpled curves, and the rounded tummy are noted with delight by the same adults who are regularly working out in order to stay slim or in shape. Infants and young children are the only ones who are valued for their dependent qualities and who are not expected to achieve. It is no accident that the adults who are most oriented toward independent achievement are the ones who are most concerned about losing weight and staying in shape.

CHAPTER 13

Risk Factors

A disorder "happens" when a number of elements are present in a given individual at a certain time. Heredity, temperament, early life circumstances, family constellation, personality configuration, and current stress are some of the determinants of whether or not a certain person will suffer from a particular emotional disorder. When some of these variables favor the development of a disorder, the person is said to be at risk for that disorder. For instance, if a woman has a family history of depression, lost her parents when she was a child, tends to repress her emotions, and has recently given birth, this places her at considerable risk to develop a depressive disorder. If she is a resilient person with a good social support system, she may not develop a disorder in spite of her high risk status.

Garfinkel, Garner and Goldbloom (1987) and Katz (1985) propose a risk factor model for the eating disorders which includes cultural, family, individual, and biological factors. This model is an important step toward an integrated theory of the eating disorders and perhaps the activity disorders as well.

Table 13.1 lists risk factors for the development of an activity disorder, which follow the Garfinkel, Garner and Goldbloom (1987) format, and it includes many of the risk factors they cite as important for the development of an eating disorder. Table 13.1 also includes factors derived from the material presented in the preceding chapters.

PERPETUATING FACTORS

The risk factors for contracting a disorder are not necessarily the same as the factors which cause the disorder to persist. Garfinkel, Garner and

Table 13.1
Risk Factors

Sociocultural
(*these factors differentially affect members of the upper SES*)
   a. Value placed on independence and achievement
   b. Premium placed on appearance, leanness, fitness, and involvement in multiple activities
   c. Self worth of women defined in terms of appearance; self worth of men defined in terms of strength and efficacy
   d. Stress due to multiple responsibilities, competition, tight schedules, etc.

Family
   a. The degree to which family members endorse cultural values such as independent achievement
   b. The active enhancement of cultural values by family members who diet, exercise, and/or are involved in multiple activities
   c. A childbearing approach which combines abundant nurturance with the expectation that the child will function independently of the parents at an early age

Individual
   a. Task persistence; perfectionism; achievement orientation.
   b. The need to maintain a high level of activity
   c. Striving for greater independence: love and hatred for the body
   d. Capacity for self deprivation; reliance on the defensive function of activity to avoid receptive gratification
   e. Ongoing struggle to maintain a separate state; compromised ability to derive gratification through relationships
   f. Unstable self-representation; perceptual distortions

Biological
   a. Individual differences in hunger, activity, arousal
   b. Gender differences in appetite, aggression, activity
   c. Synergism between food restriction and exercise to generate driven activity
   d. Neurotransmitter balance, set points
   e. Irregular menses (a marker)

Goldbloom (1987) presents a list of perpetuating factors for the eating disorders. The following is an expanded list of perpetuators, based on the material presented in the last several chapters, which could apply to the activity disorders. The elements that perpetuate a disorder also cause the disorder to be resistent to intervention.

1. Cultural support for diet and exercise: "more is better."
2. Pleasure derived from improvements in body functioning and appearance.
3. Persistent ambivalence about independence.
4. Use of activity to control appetite and relieve dysphoria.
5. Increase in appetite secondary to food restriction: leads to greater effort to control intake.
6. Locking in phenomenon.
7. Increase in egocentricity, depression, seclusiveness, and hostility secondary to physical deprivation.
8. Endorphin effects.

MULTIPLE OUTCOMES

Even if every recognized risk factor were present in a given individual, this would not necessarily mean that an activity disorder would develop. There may be a number of other risk factors of which we are not aware. In addition, we know very little about the factors which promote or perpetuate health: some individuals remain resilient under the most adverse circumstances. In addition, risk factors for an activity disorder may be risk factors for other problems or disorders as well. An at-risk individual might develop depression, anxiety, accident proneness, drug/alcohol abuse, or obesity instead of an activity disorder. We do not know all the reasons why a certain person develops a particular problem, just as we do not know why some individuals remain healthy when they are clearly at risk.

EARLY IDENTIFICATION

The risk status of obligatory runners and high-functioning eating disordered women probably would not have been apparent in childhood or in early adolescence. They describe themselves as having been healthy, high achieving youngsters. They were extemely active in adolescence, with high self expectations for independent growth. On close questioning, they reveal unusual eating attitudes and behaviors in adolescence. They often began to expect themselves to do without some creature comforts so that they could work longer, harder and achieve a more perfect product. Perhaps, if these elements are tapped, the risk status of children and adolescents could be identified. A prospective study—using measurements which do not assume that greater independence is necessarily a sign of greater health—might enable us to identify elements which predict the emergence of an activity disorder later on.

There are a number of possible paths to prevention. Educational programs for parents could serve to diminish the family risk factors. School curricula could help students develop a greater awareness of risk factors in their families and themselves. Students could be assessed for risk. There could be less emphasis placed on competition and achievement for those individuals who carry a considerable risk, and perhaps more emphasis placed on competition and achievement for those individuals of less than average risk.

A SPECTRUM OF ACTIVITY

Obligatory athletes and eating disordered women are unusually independent and active individuals who are geared toward success. These are interrelated qualities. Other qualities such as perfectionism and persistence are enlisted as part of the reciprocal feedback loop of greater effort and more success. If we assume that there is a range of variation in these attributes which approximates a normal curve, the activity disorders would fall at one extreme, two or more standard deviations above the mean (see Figure 13.1). The great majority of individuals would fall in the midportion of the curve, within two standard deviations from the mean. Because of their independence, activity, and demands for personal achievement, obligatory individuals would fall on the more active side of the spectrum.

The concept of a spectrum is important because it identifies the need to maintain a high level of activity as a common characteristic of the eating disorders and compulsive athleticism. The high level of activity may be either cognitive and/or physical. Obligatory runners and eating disordered women who exercise present an easily identifiable high level of physical activity; sedentary eating disordered women are characterized by a high level of cognitive activity. Obsessional individuals also demonstrate a high level of cognitive activity and, as we shall see later, share many of the characteristics of an activity disorder.

Obligatory individuals could be pushed toward the activity disordered end of the spectrum by a certain sequence of events. First, they become dissatisfied with themselves or their performance and they decide to

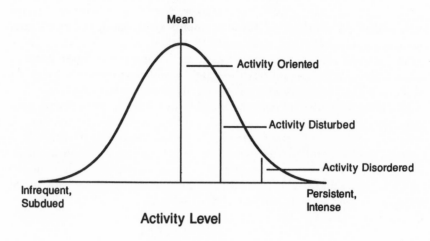

Figure 1: Spectrum of Activity

engage in a diet and/or exercise program to enhance their sense of self worth. They squeeze the diet and/or exercise in between other activities and pursue the program with dogged persistence. At some juncture, they significantly curtail their food intake relative to output (exercise) and this causes them to increase the activity even further. This eventually leads to physical deprivation which, by a physiologic mechanism, causes them to become more seclusive, depressed, distrustful, hostile, and egocentric. Eventually, they assume a position of embattled autonomy and extreme overactivity. In this manner, obligatory individuals may move to the extreme right, or disorder end, of the spectrum.

What about obligatory individuals who exhibit a driven increase in activity but do not enter a state of physical deprivation? The most common instance is that of the normal weight bulimic woman who binges and purges many times a day but manages to digest enough food to maintain an adequate nutritional balance. Her binge/purge activity escalates and appears driven, but she does not enter a state of physical deprivation. In this instance, she would be able to maintain close relationships and would not exhibit the personality changes or embattled autonomy which are secondary to physical deprivation. Individuals such as these would fall on the cusp between the disturbance and disorder sections on the spectrum of activity.

There are a great many more individuals who present distorted eating attitudes and behaviors than there are individuals with an eating disorder. These are persons with an eating disturbance rather than a disorder: they occasionally binge, vomit, or pursue an unreasonably strict diet. Our work with non-obligatory runners suggests that there are individuals with an exercise disturbance also. They present some aspects of an exercise compulsion, but they fall short of compulsive athleticism. In the concept of a spectrum of activity, these persons would fall in the section of the curve between the population mean and the activity disordered end of the spectrum. Activity disturbed individuals might carry a lesser risk, might be more resilient, or might live under less stressful circumstances than individuals with an activity disorder.

CHAPTER 14

Narcissism

Some authors have described contemporary society as a culture of narcissism (Lasch, 1978) where the alienated (but highly successful) man sits in his private theatre as his projectionist and sole audience (Johnson, 1977). Contemporary man is driven by success and wants to be known as a winner, but has developed scant capacity for personal intimacy and social commitment (Macoby, 1977). Other authors note man's shift from the reliance on the strength of institutions and traditions to the reliance on personal ability—to organize, direct and negotiate (Veroff, Douvan & Kulka, 1981). In this view, self definition and self reliance are methods by which the individual copes with increased social complexity and uncertainty about the future (Keniston, 1981).

If the activity disorder is a hyperadaptive state, then activity disordered persons are, by dint of their high achievement, true representatives of contemporary society. Their aloneness, competitiveness, self reliance, and investment in goal rather than person would suggest a narcissistic adaptation in life. Their unrealistically high ego ideal would imply the existence of narcissistic traits and defense mechanisms (Kahn, 1965). Several of the obligatory runners presented in Chapter 3 did display narcissistic traits.

THE EMERGENCE OF NARCISSISTIC TRAITS

In many of the ostensibly narcissistic runners in our sample, the narcissism seemed to arise in conjunction with the overuse of activity. They appeared more and more egotistical as they became enveloped in a cloud of intermingled plans, lists, and actions. As this transpired, they had less and less time for, and interest in, relationships. By the time the activity had reached the point of physical deprivation, they presented many of the features of a narcissistic personality disorder such as a lack of empathy, a sense of self importance, indifference about the feelings of others, and preoccupation with a successful performance. Yet, they often failed to demonstrate the core psychopathology of narcissism, i.e., grandiosity, narcissistic rage, feelings of inner emptiness, loneliness, and inauthenticity.

Narcissistic individuals can become activity disordered; a few of the obligatory and non-obligatory runners in our study could probably have fulfilled the DSM criteria for narcissistic personality disorder before and after they began to run. Yet the persistent overuse of activity seems, by itself, capable of creating narcissistic traits. Perhaps, the overuse of activity fosters a state of *apparent* narcissism, a by-product of the exaggerated striving to be independent. The following cases illustrate the emergence of narcissistic features in the course of an activity disorder.

CASE EXAMPLES

MITCH

Mitch was raised as the third child and only boy among five siblings. Both of his parents were professionals and they raised Mitch to expect that he should become someone important. During high school his grades were good, he excelled in wrestling, and he became an eagle scout. Yet his scores on the Scholastic Aptitude Test were disappointing and he was not accepted in any of the Ivy League schools to which he applied. He entered the state university instead. After "not making the Dean's list" for three consecutive semesters, he abruptly quit college and joined the Armed Forces as an enlisted man, much to his parents' chagrin. During his four-year hitch, he rose to the rank of Sergeant. In the meantime, his next younger sister graduated Magna Cum Laude from Stanford University. After his discharge from the service, Mitch obtained a position with the Post Office and, in the years that followed, received a commendation and several promotions. He married a fellow employee and they had two little girls.

When Mitch's children were eight and 10 years old, his eldest daughter, Nancy, demonstrated a natural talent in gymnastics. Mitch managed to negotiate a transfer to a city where Nancy could be trained by a famous gymnastic coach. His wife and his other daughter resented the move, but agreed to give it a trial. The family's new living quarters were cramped and expensive. Mitch took an extra job and Nancy rode the bus to her gymnastics class. When Nancy failed to place in the State meet, the two girls and their mother decided that they should move back home. Mitch reluctantly agreed.

By the time Mitch was 45 years old, his children had left home for college. He felt depressed and without direction in life. He and his wife had little left in common. After some time had passed, Mitch saw a counselor who referred him to a mid-life crisis group. One of the group members was an avid runner and he persuaded Mitch to give it a try. Mitch found that he was quite good at running and that the running made him feel better. He tried to persuade his wife to run but she said it was a "stupid idea."

By age 49, Mitch had become an extremely committed athlete. A gaunt 130 pounds, he ran 17 miles each day, seven days a week. While running, he enveloped himself in a romantic scenario—the loneliness of the long distance runner. Running was his emotional solace and it was through running that he communed with God. After completing several miles, he would feel a lifting sensation, as if he were floating above the trail and had no need for food or rest—as if he were transcending life itself. He preferred to run alone, through hail, darkness, and in spite of considerable pain in his knees.

Mitch and his wife became increasingly distant from one another. Mitch said she "better learn not to mess with my running." Although he was interested in his elder daughter's progress through college, Mitch did not take time away from running to attend her graduation. He continued to run in spite of an orthopedist's warning that he suffered from deteriorating cartilage in his knees and could become crippled for the rest of his life. He indignantly commented that the physician was not a runner and therefore was not competent to assess the problem. Mitch may not have been to medical school, but he thought he knew more than the doctor did.

ANGELA

Angela was the second-born daughter in an intact family. Her father directed the local Chamber of Commerce and her mother was a part-time librarian who also edited the town newspaper. Angela lived up to her name from the very beginning. She was a compliant, pleasant, and reasonable young lady who loved to read stories. She did well in school and had several friends. When Angela was 12 years old, her 14-year-old sister fell in love with the school janitor and they ran off together. Later, the sister became pregnant and returned home alone. Subsequently, she had an abortion and entered a church sponsored drug treatment program. Angela was often told, "Be thankful that you're a different person than your sister."

When Angela was 16, she was chosen to represent her church at a national youth conference in New York City. During the conference, a boy representative tried to kiss Angela, but she quickly rebuffed him. On the way back from the conference, she began to make serious plans for her future. She decided which college she would attend and mapped out a diet to lose her "baby fat."

At age 18, Angela was 5'8" tall and weighed 88 pounds. She adamantly refused to enter the hospital for the treatment of her eating disorder in spite of the fact that she was spending most of her free time binge eating and vomiting. After her parents forced her into the hospital, she refused to have anything to do with the members of the treatment team. After three days of sullen noncompliance, she made a sudden about face and became a model patient. Although she obeyed all the rules of the program, she remained emotionally detached.

Angela was discharged from the hospital so that she could start her first semester at college on schedule. She was still markedly underweight. Soon after moving in to a dormitory room, Angela began to vomit. When her roommate inquired about her frequent trips to the bathroom, Angela claimed that she suffered from a chronic diarrhea. Several weeks later, she told her roommate that she was trying to lose weight because she yearned for the fragile beauty described in the romantic literature. Once she asked her roommate how she might become infected with the tubercle bacillus as this was said to produce a rosy hue on alabaster skin.

Although Angela initially tried to conform to social expectations, after her habit of purging was discovered she vomited in the wastebasket and once in the roommate's shoes. Eventually, Angela's roommate moved out because of Angela's "disgusting habits." Thereafter, Angela lived alone in a dormitory room designed for two because no one else would room with her. Angela claimed that she didn't want to room with "fatsos" anyway, and that she preferred to be left alone.

Discussion

Although Mitch and Angela are upper SES, achievement oriented individuals, they differ in gender, age, life circumstance, and character structure. Yet, during their illness, they presented narcissistic features which were similar: grandiose fantasies of enormous power or beauty, embattled autonomy, indifference to the feelings of others, entitlement, and the use of primitive defenses such as projective identification, devaluation, and splitting. Before they became activity disordered, they had demonstrated meaningful relationships and the capacity for empathy. With the activity disorder and the physical deprivation, they replaced empathy with a sense of entitlement. In their minds, they "deserved" to run or vomit regardless of the feelings of family or friends. As they developed the disorder, Mitch and Angela turned away from the genuine concern of others and became increasingly disappointed in significant relationships.

Although Mitch and Angela did have problems prior to the emergence of the activity disorder, their problems did not seem to be especially unusual. They functioned well and did not display narcissistic symptomatology. When they began to escalate the activity and to curtail their intake relative to output, they began to exhibit narcissistic traits. The narcissistic symptoms were most apparent when they had become physically deprived.

At nine-month follow-up, Mitch remains essentially the same: a committed runner with joint deterioration (which he continues to deny). At five-year follow-up, Angela was found to have improved during her second, longer hospitalization. After a rocky period post discharge, she settled into long-term therapy. She is now a 24-year-old graduate student in psychology. In addition to her school work, she holds down two part-time jobs and volunteers at a home for the aged. She is described by her professors as sensitive and empathic, but entirely too self-effacing.

Obligatory runners and dieters usually do not qualify for a narcissistic personality disorder diagnosis. Many of them do present narcissistic features as they escalate the activity. The narcissistic symptoms which they display include a lack of empathy, sense of self importance, indifference about the feelings of others, and preoccupation with a successful performance. These symptoms may be viewed as by-products of the exaggerated striving to be independent.

CHAPTER 15

Relationship to Other Conditions

The activity disorders have many features in common with obsessive compulsive disorder (OCD), "workaholism," body dysmorphic disorder, and the sexual dysfunctions or disorders of desire. There may be a family of conditions marked by excessive physical or cognitive activity.

OBSESSIVE COMPULSIVE DISORDER

SIMILARITIES WITH THE ACTIVITY DISORDERS

Similarities between OCD and the activity disorders include the single-minded attention to task; the persistent overactivity; the driven, locked in, serious quality; the ruminations; the need for concrete units of measurement; the tight self-control; and the magical thinking. OCD (Rasmussen, 1984; Perse et al., 1987; Zohar et al., 1988) and anorexia nervosa (Garfinkel & Kaplan, 1985) may be related to a relative deficiency in serotoninergic neurotransmission. Many OCD patients and eating disordered women respond to antidepressants that inhibit serotonin reuptake. They respond whether or not they suffer from a depression (Flament et al., 1985; Walsh et al., 1985).

Activity disordered persons and OCD patients depend upon elaborate cognitive strategies: they set stepwise goals, check and recheck their performance, and give themselves rewards or penalties according to their performance. They protect themselves from upsetting thoughts and impulses by losing themselves in compulsive activity or ruminations. Activity disordered persons worry about deterioration instead of thinking about eating, resting, or being held. OCD patients worry about contamination instead of entertaining sexual and aggressive thoughts and impulses. The mechanism by which one thought protects against another is demonstrated by a study of three women who suffered from posttraumatic stress disorder (PTSD) (McFarlane, McFarlane & Gilchrist, 1988). Each of these women began to experience the intrusive dystonic images, repetitive thoughts, and nightmares which are characteristic of PTSD as well as of OCD. Then each of them contracted an eating disorder. They replaced the terrifying thoughts of fire and assault with a preoccupation with weight and diet.

The ruminations and rituals in OCD serve the same self-regulatory, self-defining, defensive, and separation maintenance functions as do exercise and diet in the activity disorders. These four functions can be identified in the following case vignette:

> A homemaker began to suspect that her husband was having an affair. She had no real basis for her suspicions, but she was enraged at the thought. Shortly thereafter, she began to worry more about germs and became particular about tidying the house. At first, she was soothed and comforted by the routine of going about her duties. She thought that she was performing an essential task in protecting her family from germs. Through her activity, she was able to reassure herself that she was a clean and industrious woman. Yet, as she continued to clean, she became more and more driven to make certain that there was not one speck of dirt left. She would allow no one in the living room and she became so busy cleaning and recleaning that she never left the house. She became increasingly isolated.

DIFFERENCES

Although OCD and the activity disorders have many clinical features in common, there are important differences also. Activity disordered persons tend to be oriented toward success while OCD patients are more socially and emotionally incapacitated. OCD patients may loathe what they do, while obligatory runners and dieters may idealize the activity. OCD patients are driven by their unacceptable thoughts, ideas, and impulses rather than by external events; activity disordered persons are more likely to react to external events. OCD patients rarely damage the body through the activity and they seldom suffer from physical deprivation.

"SUPERNORMAL" YOUNGSTERS

Rapoport (1986) provides what may be a clue to the relationship between OCD and the activity disorders. She studied adolescents who had been identified in an epidemiological study by Flament et al. (1985) as having obsessional characteristics. In spite of their pronounced persistence and perfectionism, some of these youngsters did not prove to have OCD. Instead they appeared to be "supernormal" adolescents: ambitious, energetic, and involved in more academic and extracurricular activities than their classmates. They crammed each day full with sports, clubs, jobs, exercise, extra classes, community volunteer work, etc. They were tightly scheduled and remarkably programmed. They had extremely high self expectations and they worried about not meeting a monstrous list of commitments.

Certain personality traits differentiate "supernormal" adolescents from youngsters with OCD. Members of both groups are persistent and perfectionistic, but the "supernormal" youths seem far more flexible, sociable, and enthusiastic than the youths with OCD. They are oriented toward success and they seem destined to succeed. They appear to be quite similar to the eating disturbed "superwomen" college students described in chapter 6. Although the "supernormal" children have not yet become "supermen" and "superwomen," they seem headed in that direction. They appear like junior editions of the obligatory runners.

OTHER CONDITIONS RELATED TO THE ACTIVITY DISORDERS

If we think of the activity disorders as members of a larger family of "obligatory" conditions, then we might consider body-dysmorphic disorder and workaholism as candidates also.

BODY-DYSMORPHIC DISORDER

Body-dysmorphic disorder is a new diagnostic category first noted in DSM-III-R. Individuals who qualify for this disorder are convinced that some feature of the body is abnormal. They ruminate about an imperfection of the body (usually some facial characteristic), but they are not absolutely convinced that the body part is defective. They are not particularly disturbed by the belief, although they spend considerable time thinking about it. The symptoms are similar to those found in delusional and obsessive compulsive disorders (Hollander et al., 1989), but in those disorders, patients tend to hold onto their fixed beliefs with absolute certainty. Patients with body-dysmorphic disorder are like patients with OCD in that they improve when they are treated with serotonin reuptake inhibitors.

Body-dysmorphic disorder is of interest because it presents many of the features found in OCD and in the activity disorders. The irrational "fixed" quality of the ruminations is like that of the ruminations in OCD. The overconcern with the body, the relatively ego syntonic nature of the ruminations, and the conviction that something about the body is wrong and should be remedied are commonly found in the eating disorders and in compulsive athleticism. The less than absolute certainty of the conviction that these persons hold about the body suggests an unstable body image, a common finding among eating disordered women (Norris, 1984) and in some obligatory runners. In addition, body-dysmorphic disorder has been found in conjunction with anorexia (Sturmey & Slade, 1986) and following recovery from anorexia when the patient's concern about her nose seemed to take the place of the preexisting anorexia (Pantano & Santonastaso, 1989).

WORKAHOLICS

Some high-achieving adults are described in the vernacular as "workaholics." Although workaholism is not a body-based activity, workaholics are overinvolved in many independent (work) activities. They tend to rationalize the extent of their labor and, although they may recognize that they needn't work as hard, they value their work and are quite willing to continue. The involvement in work may be a strategy by which they avoid another, more critical issue. The activity provides the same functions (other than self hurt) that exercise and diet provide in the activity disorders. Work is condoned by the culture and workaholism could be viewed as a hyperadaptive state.

OBLIGATORY CONDITIONS

Perhaps there is a family of obligatory conditions characterized by persistence and perfectionism, a high level of cognitive and/or physical activity, a strong need for self control, and the use of the activity to distract and defend against unacceptable wishes. These conditions may or may not involve the body and may or may not be ego dystonic. Certain individuals seem to be much more susceptible to these conditions than other individuals.

AN ETHOLOGICAL BASE?

Rapoport (1989) and Swedo et al. (1989) propose that compulsive activities resemble certain "fixed" behaviors of animals, behaviors which have been described by Lorenz and Leyhausen (1973). Fixed behaviors are innately determined responses such as picking and grooming or nest building which appear to have been "hard wired" into the brain's circuitry during the course of evolution. Once these behaviors are triggered, they must be executed to completion; in other words, they become driven activities. In OCD patients, the repetitive hand washing, counting, etc. can be viewed as fixed behaviors. Rapoport and Swedo suggest that OCD is a neurological disorder: a disturbance in the brain releases the automatic behaviors and the behaviors continue to recycle. This hypothesis could explain not only the drivenness of compulsive behaviors, but the remarkable similarity in the rituals of children with OCD to the rituals of adult OCD patients, even when the children have never been exposed to adult models of this behavior.

Fixed behaviors are narrowly defined, simple action patterns such as picking and scratching; the behavior follows the same sequence time after time. The checking and sorting rituals found in OCD are the formats which are most like fixed behaviors. The analogy is less precise when applied to the more complex rituals of OCD or the activity disorders. Activity disordered persons do engage in repetitive, apparently senseless (but well rationalized) behaviors, but these behaviors are not as narrowly defined and stereotyped as the checking and sorting rituals in OCD. Eating disordered women may be compelled to weigh calories consumed against calories expended and obligatory runners may measure distance run and calculate the time taken to run it, but these behaviors vary somewhat according to time and circumstance. The concept of fixed behaviors does not quite fit the picture of individuals with an activity disorder and it may not apply to the more elaborate and varied rituals presented by many OCD patients.

There is an alternative physiologic explanation for the repetitive behaviors found in OCD—one which does not presuppose a neurological abnormality. As we saw in Chapter 6, when animals are placed in highly charged, frustrating, or ambiguous circumstances (food restriction with rigid scheduling in the laboratory; threat of attack in the wild) they produce a variety of irrational, driven, repetitive behaviors. The format of the activity seems to depend upon the materials which happen to be available in the environment. The activities vary and they may be quite complex.

Individuals with activity disorders or OCD tend to place themselves in highly charged, frustrating, or ambiguous circumstances. Activity disordered individuals engage in a stressful, competitive environment in order to achieve and they perceive the circumstances as stressful in order to keep themselves motivated. Persons with OCD tend to perceive circumstances as stressful and ambiguous even when they are not. Individuals in both groups are frustrated when they cannot live up to their high self expectations. In this line of thought, certain individuals would tend to expose themselves to highly charged, frustrating, or ambiguous conditions; the circumstances would interact with the personality traits to produce behaviors which are irrational and driven.

Certain individuals seem to have a tendency toward the activity disorders while certain other individuals seem to have a tendency toward OCD, body-dysmorphic disorder, or workaholism. The difference could be largely determined by the personality traits. Individuals in both groups are persistent and perfectionistic, but those persons who are prone to OCD may be more emotionally constricted, with greater self doubt, and initially more rigid and isolated than persons with a tendency toward the other conditions. Whether or not this is the case remains to be determined.

RUMINATIONS

Ruminations have already been defined as the cognitive counterpart of physical activity. Thinking about an activity and engaging in an activity go hand and hand. Ruminations can be agreeable and under the individual's control or they can be dysphoric and driven. An individual may ruminate pleasantly about food or making love as a method of self regulation. On the other hand, a person can "beat on himself" with ruminations in much the same fashion that he can pound his body into the pavement by running long distances.

Ruminations can play a very special role in defending against the wish for receptive pleasure. Ruminations figure prominently in the strategies of eating disordered women and obligatory runners. The hungry anorexic woman may anticipate a meal with pleasure. The food looks delicious and she intends to devour it. Yet even before she feels uncomfortably full or uncomfortable about having eaten, she begins to ruminate about things which have nothing to do with the meal. Or she may read the paper, watch television, or study as she eats. In any event, she directs her concern elsewhere and she no longer pays attention to the food. She is able to sidestep receptive gratification by disconnecting herself from the pleasurable process of eating. The ruminations are ego syntonic: in her mind she needs to plan ahead, avoid certain problems, or figure out her options. However, if she is instructed to simply attend to and enjoy what she eats, she finds that she can maintain her concentration on eating only for a few seconds. The ruminations become more insistent and personal, more invasive and ego dystonic.

The ruminations which occur in the course of eating could easily be ascribed to drive reduction. Once the edge is taken off the appetite, the mind begins to drift. However, this theory does not explain why the mind drifts before the appetite abates or why the ruminations seem to occur more rapidly in very hungry eating disordered women than in their non-restricting sisters. The primary function of the ruminations seems to be to defend against the receptive gratification associated with eating. Eating disordered women need to defend against receptive pleasure more diligently than do most other people.

RUMINATIONS IN THE SEXUAL DYSFUNCTIONS

In the sexual dysfunctions and in the disorders of sexual desire described by Kaplan (1979), ruminations can serve as a major defense against receptive pleasure. In these conditions, the interference with pleasure is similar to that which eating disordered women experience as they eat. Kaplan describes how individuals can "turn off" the sexual response by selectively focusing their attention on extraneous events or by evoking an unpleasant memory which distracts them or causes them to be angry or fearful. As these persons engage in foreplay or intercourse, they are bombarded by irrelevant thoughts and images. They are unable to receive pleasure and the obsessive thoughts keep them from connecting emotionally with the partner. They have no insight into the fact that they are actively evoking negative images and they have no sense of control over the process. The mechanism is unconscious, automatic, and involuntary.

Ruminations are involved in sexual problems as well as in the sexual dysfunctions. Sexual problems are ubiquitous in the upper SES (Frank, Carpenter & Kupfer, 1988); they arise when individuals are able to function but are bored with sex, do not accord it a priority, or are not able to savor it as before. Heimberg and Barlow (1988) provide us with an example of how ruminations feed into this phenomenon: they find that when certain men attempt intercourse, they become locked into thoughts about non-erotic topics (as well as performance fears). Their off-task focusing becomes increasingly "efficient" while their on-task focusing and sexual performance become increasingly impaired.

In the 1940s when Kinsey et al. (1948, 1953) began to ask people about their sexual experiences, they found that a great many persons were sexually dysfunctional. At the time, there were some fairly obvious reasons for this. There was very little information about sex available; sex was a taboo subject. This is no longer the case, but today the estimates of sexual dysfunction are as high as or higher than they were in Kinsey's day and the reasons for the dysfunctions are not as clear.

The need to be very independent could play a role in the disorders of desire. According to the theory presented in this book, the striving to gain or to maintain a separate, independent state often entails some discomfort with receptive gratification. The greater the striving toward independence, the greater that discomfort is likely to be. When a person who wishes to be very independent is placed in a position of receptivity, as in eating or making love, he may quite handily move away from the receptive position by conjuring up negative thoughts or images. The experience of making love is qualitatively different when there are performance anxieties, concern about the appearance of the body, or worry about making an appointment on time.

The disorders of desire are complex and multidetermined conditions, much like the activity disorders. They often affect otherwise well-functioning individuals. In the disorders of desire the ruminations seem to serve the same function that they do in OCD: to protect the individual from unacceptable thoughts or impulses. In the disorders of desire and the activity disorders, the ruminations seem to be protecting the person from the dangers of being close, of being cared for, of receiving pleasure.

CHAPTER 16

Therapy for the Activity Disorders

A chapter on therapy is somewhat premature since, to our knowledge, no therapist has had extensive experience in treating compulsive athletes. Most of us have treated a goodly number of eating disordered women (some of whom are overexercisers) and a few obligatory athletes. The problems do seem to be similar and many of the principles of therapy for high-functioning women with eating disorders do seem to be applicable to compulsive athletes—but the final word will need to rest upon the appropriate experience with a fairly large sample.

This chapter applies some of the treatment principles thought to be effective in the eating disorders to the activity disorders. The approaches are altered somewhat to address the special needs of overly athletic persons. The principles of outpatient intervention, described later in this chapter, can be applied to activity disturbed as well as to activity disordered individuals. Individuals with an activity disturbance are likely to be dealing with the same underlying issues as those with an activity disorder, but since they are not as enmeshed in the activity, they may be more open to examining themselves.

There is no single personality type or problem found among activity disordered adults and there is no characteristic level of disturbance. These people tend to be highly intelligent individuals with considerable internal elaboration. When they are not in a state of deprivation, they have the capacity to build trust. They are responsible and once they are engaged in therapy, they tend to make significant progress. Although the treatment is complex and difficult, they are excellent candidates for therapy.

Persons with an activity disorder are quite various in presentation and motivation. If these persons are to be adequately served, a variety of inpatient and outpatient therapeutic approaches need to be available. The selection of a therapy for a given patient would depend upon the patient's goals, commitment, resources, the availability of the modality, and the therapist's training and orientation. Educational counseling (sports medicine, nutrition, etc.), supportive group, psychodynamic group, psychodrama, behavioral, family, and individual psycho-dynamic and analytic therapies can be useful for many patients. Relax-ation techniques, cognitive restructuring, and assertiveness training have their place in various treatment regimens (Garner, Olmstead et al, 1984). Meditation can be a valuable ancillary method because it directly con-fronts the patient's resistance to the receptive state. The current trend is to employ several approaches concurrently.

A treatment which is geared toward the activity disorders must address one or more of the following: the unreasonable self-expectations, the cognitive and/or physical overactivity, the instability of the body and self image, the ambivalence about independence, psychological hunger, overcontrol of body/self, and the disconnection from the body. A good or excellent resolution may require a reconstructive approach through long-term individual therapy. Many patients are not willing or able to undertake such extensive treatment.

ETHICAL ISSUES

A therapist may become aware of an activity disordered person through a third party, often the significant other. That individual may relate an appalling story: the person they hope to see treated is living on the white meat of chicken, lettuce, and sunflower seeds, but is running 30 miles a day, swimming 80 laps, and lifting weights. Although treatment may be indicated, the chance of treating such a person is slight—unless a catastrophe occurs. In fact, the greater the person's investment in activ-ity, the less willing the person is to enter treatment. The activity is working, more or less, to maintain the person's homeostasis.

Should people be allowed to abuse their bodies in ways which invite permanent damage? The response must be that unless they are causing substantial, life-threatening damage to the body, adults cannot, and should not, be forced into treatment. This conservative approach is based in part upon the course and outcome of the disorder. The outcome in compulsive athleticism has not been systematically studied, but we do have a good deal of information on the course and outcome of the eating disorders (which may or may not apply to compulsive athletes). A few individuals seem to pursue an inexorable downhill path. The mortality rate in anorexia is 6 percent (Schwartz & Thompson, 1981). However, the condition is usually not lethal and it most often waxes and wanes in intensity. The outcome for those individuals who never receive treatment is not known, but there is some indication that in bulimia, at least, there are self correcting forces at work. Many of these women improve without formal therapy (Yager, Landsverk & Edelstein, 1987), perhaps by switching to a less damaging form of activity.

Further issues are raised when there is no adequate treatment available. Many third-party coverages sharply limit payment for inpatient psychiatric hospitalization. With many activity disordered patients, long-term hospitalization (2–4 months) is necessary not only for psychic change, but because an internal reorganization cannot occur until the physical deprivation has been corrected and the ruminations have dissipated. Inadequate treatment can be worse than no treatment at all.

There is no simple answer to the ethical dilemma. A considered decision will depend upon such factors as the extent of the injury to the body, the unfailing nature of the progression, the treatment available, and the psychic status of the individual. When a person who has not caused substantial injury to the body continues to refuse treatment, a supportive, reality-oriented, wait-and-see attitude seems to be the wisest, most humane approach.

INITIAL ASSESSMENT

The first issue to be addressed in the treatment of the activity disorders is whether or not the patient warrants inpatient treatment. Indications for inpatient treatment in anorexia are dangerously low weight, persistent suicidal ideation, or lack of response to outpatient treatment (Anderson, Morris & Santmyer, 1985). In bulimia, patients may be hospitalized because of fluid and electrolyte imbalance, severe depression, the threat of suicide, or resistance to intensive outpatient treatment. Obligatory athletes may be hospitalized because of severe depression and suicidal ideation, which usually follows injury or exhaustion. The initial goal of treatment should be to correct the deprived state by lessening the output (exercise, vomiting) and increasing the input (food, other gratification).

Garner and Garfinkel (1982), Anyan and Schowalter (1983), Hsu (1986), and Yates (1990) review the treatment of the eating disorders. Most activity disordered patients are difficult to treat. They often present with a condition which has already become chronic. Obligatory runners and women with anorexia usually do not wish to be treated. Bulimic women are more likely to seek treatment, but they may expect immediate results and they become easily frustrated with therapy.

The reason why activity disordered patients are taxing to treat is that the central issue for these people is independence. They view therapy as a position of vulnerability where they will be forced to depend upon or to take something from the therapist. If they reluctantly agree to enter therapy, they are apt to choose the modality which is least likely to interfere with their chosen activity—for instance, a therapy group which does not address or monitor activity. One anorexic woman chose psychodrama so that she could understand her early conflicts with her mother and she participated with enthusiasm. This seemed to be an excellent strategy, except that her weight continued to steadily decline.

Activity disordered people are relatively more open to intervention when they reach a point at which the activity is not working for them. This usually occurs after they have been immersed in their endeavors for months or years and they feel burdened and controlled by the activity. This is especially likely to transpire when they have begun to experience some side effects which are an insult to their self concept. For example, one eating disordered woman decided to enter therapy when she was unable to conceive (her menses had ceased and she was no longer ovulating) and a woman runner did so after she suffered a stress fracture due to osteoporosis. These women recognized the connection to diet and exercise.

Activity disordered individuals are more likely to be motivated for treatment when they are in extremis—unable to continue the activity because of physical injury, exhaustion, emaciation, or a forced hospitalization. Occasionally, they enter treatment when they are unable to achieve up to their expectations: a 52-year-old marathon runner was hospitalized with depression after he realized that his running time was steadily increasing. Others request treatment because a significant other is coercing them. They may not have the slightest interest in making a change; they simply wish to continue the activity with less resistance from family members.

Some obligatory individuals request therapy after they reflect upon the driven quality of their daily life. A few of these persons recognize that their lives have become more constricted and that they have lost important areas of gratification. They may note the constant need to maintain a high level of activity and the pattern by which one activity is substituted for another. They wonder what this means and where they are going with their lives.

When activity disordered persons first enter treatment, they are apt to distrust the therapist and to use massive denial. Why should they want to change if the activity feels so right and it works so well? One patient said: "How can anything so good be bad?" In their minds, all they may need is to choose a better diet or change the brand of running shoes. They may be able to accept help only from someone with whom they can identify and who they expect will be sympathetic to their position. This is often a physician in the sports medicine clinic, a trainer, a nurse, or a nutritionist. Ideally, this person would put the patient in contact with a well-trained therapist who can evaluate the severity of the condition and recommend or expedite treatment. Activity disordered persons are not likely to accept help initially from a pudgy, out-of-shape therapist, regardless of his or her professional qualifications.

INPATIENT INTERVENTION

When hospitalization is the only answer, and the facts are presented clearly and firmly, most patients will recognize that inpatient treatment is indicated, although they may continue to present innumerable reasons why it would be foolish. The more quickly the arrangements are made, the better. For activity disordered patients, the hospitalization represents an insult to their intelligence and their maturity. Everything they have struggled to build during their lives begins to crumble as they are forced into a dependent position. The care and concern of the treatment team seems like a poisonous attempt to rob them of all that is precious in life.

When activity disordered patients recuperate a bit, they begin to plan how to wheedle back their independence and activity. The staff is their natural adversary and the strategies they devise would rival Machiavelli's. They are familiar with the input/output equation and they know that output in the form of exercise is exceedingly difficult to monitor. Calisthenics after the lights are out at night, isotonic exercise under the sheets, and walking six flights up from X-ray instead of riding the elevator are but a few examples. Beneath these brilliant, desperate maneuvers is the helpless rage of the independent person who is forced into a position of dependency.

From the beginning, the staff needs to maintain firm behavioral constraints as they support the patients' healthy competencies. The model is that of the parent at hand, who stands nearby and smiles as the child demonstrates a new skill, but is alert to prevent the youngster from toddling into the street. The eating disordered patient may make choices within the limits of her diet and she can participate in setting a specific weight range which she would need to reach before she is ready for discharge. The obligatory athlete may be encouraged to map out a program of graded exercise as his weight increases or as he is able to accomplish therapeutic goals. Patients may be invited to create a picture, a poem, or a story which will enable others to comprehend their predicament better. By noting and supporting these competencies, the treatment team is investing the activities with pleasure and thereby enhancing the self-regulating and self-defining uses of the activity.

Supporting patients' competencies is a delicate task. On one hand the patients may feel as if the staff person is infantilizing them and on the other they may make the task into a driven activity, one which will enable them to be miserable once more. An obligatory athlete was complimented on how well she was able to lead a group; she quickly began to devise therapeutic tasks for every other patient on the ward. Soon she was ruminating about how to make the tasks exactly right and was increasingly resentful when the other patients would not comply.

Activity disordered persons do not accept compliments or encouragement easily. They view hospital activities as childish and demeaning; they think that the staff is condescending, stupid, or out to trick them. This is a defense against metabolizing the pleasurable aspects of relationships, so that they will not be tempted to abandon the separate state. Before hospitalization, they may have handled situations which invited dependence by increasing their chosen activity. They may try to do this in the hospital also. After the staff has been especially kind and supportive, they are at higher risk to act out by purging, by covert exercise, or by eloping. It will be counterproductive if the staff responds as if the patients are disobedient children. If the patients feel infantilized, they will think that they are quite justified in frustrating the staff at every turn. The staff needs to work with these patients so that they may recognize the struggle to maintain a separate state.

The patient's activity and weight must continue to be monitored after the initial period of strict observation. If possible, the staff should employ weight gain, rather than calories or exercise, as the index of physical improvement. This minimizes the patient's struggle over food consumption at mealtimes and it makes hiding food or vomiting and doing push-ups at midnight less likely. Patients should be weighed as infrequently as possible: daily weights only at first, shifting to every three days and then once a week prior to discharge. More frequent weight checks and a focus on weight, calories, and intake can cause patients to think that the staff is attempting to take over their body, the body that they are so desperately trying to control. This increases the patients' need to stay apart and to maintain control at all cost.

A strict behavioral program in an inpatient setting brings out the worst in activity disordered patients. They are apt to become quite infantile, as if this were the intent of the program. Some will obstruct the treatment and some will become exceedingly hopeless and depressed. Others will appear impervious to treatment. Some will comply superficially with the program, as if being hospitalized is a deadly game which they must win. These reactions can be understood by appreciating the extent to which these persons center their lives around being independent. The embattled stance, the driven activity is a defense against the utter helplessness which ensues when the activity is restricted. This is the sense of ineffectiveness which Bruch (1973) describes.

Although the patient's intake and/or output does need to be controlled, the less overt attention paid to control, the better. The proper model is that of the concerned parent who wants to appreciate how healthy and strong the child is becoming. Caring rather than control is the message. The staff is supporting the patients' independent achievement, but the achievement is that of learning to be kind to the body. This approach offers the patients gratification through a relationship but they are not forced to accept it or even to recognize that it is being offered. Patients often disregard or negate the support, as if the staff really doesn't care. This issue needs to be addressed and, if the staff can be tolerant, the patient's position of embattled autonomy may begin to crumble.

The treatment team must meet the patient's regressed and miserable condition by providing staff who are dependable and concerned so as to "hold" (Winnicott, 1965a) the patient while he or she becomes more comfortable with the receptive state. The staff may need to accept the patient in a regressed, infantile state, punctuated with impotent rage. This presentation is far better than the facade of superficial compliance by which some patients dupe the staff into believing they are cured.

The patient's regressed and infantile behavior may seem highly inappropriate to staff. It challenges the reality-based behavioral program. How can the staff "hold" the patient, provide unqualified acceptance, and yet support the behavioral approach? Some therapists are able to do this, but in many instances the team will need to split the treatment into a two-pronged approach. One member of the team functions as the "wicked witch" who administers the behavioral program and another functions as the "good fairy" who provides unqualified attention and support.

There is no way, other than by self report, that the ruminations of the activity disordered patient can be monitored. Yet the cognitive activity is an essential aspect of the disorder and it serves the same intrapsychic function as the physical activity. When the dieting, purging, or obligatory exercise is first restricted, there is an immediate increase in ruminations, which are invariably dysphoric and may contain fantasies of decay, disintegration, or bloatedness. The ruminations subside only when ample time has passed and the internal struggle has abated. The function of the ruminations can be explored only after a therapeutic alliance has been established.

In-hospital modalities which have not been sufficiently utilized in the treatment of activity disordered persons are massage, holding, and bathing in the Hubbard Tank. Before coming to the hospital, the activity disordered patient tortures the body in order to force it on line. The purpose is to annihilate the neediness which resides in the body. The staff must not only model kindness and concern for the body, but they must minister to the body. Nurses need to be nurses, so to speak. Body care tells the patient that the body is good and that its needs can be satisfied without disastrous consequences. Body care goes far to counter the patient's fantasy that the staff wants only to correct the behavior and make an expeditious discharge.

There is no diagnostic entity more trying for the inpatient staff than the activity disorder. On the staff, there is likely to be a single parent struggling to pay the babysitter, a graduate student who works full-time in addition to studying, and an obligatory wage earner with a disabled spouse. In effect, these are persons who are forced to be overly active, whether they like it or not. Because they must forgo their own very human needs, they may understandably become angry at patients who are offered—and who steadfastly refuse—the milk of human kindness. Without support and guidance, the staff may gravitate toward rule enforcement, "whether the patient likes it or not." In effect, this is how they must manage similar issues in their own day-to-day existence: through self control, whether they like it or not.

Body contact is healing for the healer, as well as for the patient. Through guiding a hand in knitting, rubbing a tight muscle until it relaxes, wrapping the body in a warm towel, or pulling the sheets up to protect against the draft, the patient and the caregiver may be able to surrender a bit of the need to control. However, for this to occur, the caregiver must be able to use activity for self regulation. It goes without saying that the persons who are tightly scheduled and under intense pressure are the persons who are more likely to have problems in providing nurturance. Ward staff may become emotionally unavailable when they are overwhelmed by responsibilities on or off the ward. In this case, the care that the staff provides may become indifferent, mechanical, or overly efficient. The staff is experiencing a shift in the balance of function of their activity, due to unfortunate circumstances.

CONTINUED CARE

After some weeks have passed and a nutritional balance has been established, while the patient has survived (and even enjoyed) the receptive state, he or she is typically less hopeless, ritualistic, and distrustful. At this juncture most programs add other treatment modalities such as individual, group, and family. Individual therapy in an in-hospital setting can provide the patient with reassurance, support, and a realistic view of the self (Anderson, Morris & Santmyer, 1985). If there is one therapist, he or she must stand behind the principles of the treatment program, expecting the patient to gain weight and/or to tolerate inactivity. At the same time, the therapist may resonate to the patient's fear of becoming dependent and terror at loss of control. The therapist may need to help the patient identify her feelings (Bruch, 1973) and how they may be reflected in the activity. As the therapist establishes a relationship, he needs to explore the content and extent of the patient's ruminations and mental imaging, so that this dimension can be brought into therapy.

After some weeks of hospitalization when the patients are better nourished, physically and emotionally, they may test the treatment team with inspired, highly manipulative, divisive ploys. They may split staff and therapists into good and bad and manipulate families against the treatment team. It is as if they need to convince themselves that they haven't lost the ability to think, plan, and act on their own. This is an attempt to take back some of the control that was lost when they entered the hospital. Control has been, and is, their major defense against their neediness.

The turning point in therapy often occurs when the patient's strategies are recognized and confronted. This precipitates the second defeat of the improbably independent self during the hospital stay. This stripping of defenses is but slightly less catastrophic than the defeat which occurred on admission. The patient is forced to recognize that he or she cannot command the program and that others are powerful and able to control. Unless this crucial understanding is reached, the patient will not be able to take the next step, which is to begin to depend upon, and to be gratified by, other people. The analogy is that of the child who painstakingly surrounds himself in a world of toys and games when the parents are away. The activities contain him and he no longer feels helpless.

When the parents return, they must be powerful enough to interrupt his activities, to claim his attention so that they may care for him.

Treatment teams need time to meet, open communication, and support from the hospital administration. The staff tends to be disappointed and frustrated when an activity disordered patient shuns their help and prefers to be alone. "It seems like they don't want to get better" is a fairly accurate commentary. Staff may begin to approach eating disordered patients in an obsessive, unbending fashion, simply to protect themselves from being hurt. Ongoing team meetings are a necessity to maintain cooperation between staff and a consistent, empathic attitude toward the patient (Garfinkel, Garner & Kennedy, 1985).

DISCHARGE

Before the activity disordered patients are ready for discharge, they should be comfortable with a level of activity which will not, in and of itself, mediate against receptive pleasure. In addition, they should have shifted the balance of functions of activity strongly in favor of self regulation, so that old and new activities are pleasurable and not driven. They need to be able to allow themselves some gratification through playful or intimate relationships with other people. There should be at least an incipient kindness to, and enjoyment of, the body. These are the goals of the hospitalization; they are not the tasks of the hospitalization. There is no way that these patients can work at these goals and be successful. In order to succeed, they must be able to receive what the hospital has to offer. The hospital offers a holding experience and the comfort of reasonable and predictable expectations.

Some activity disordered patients emerge from the hospital unscathed by the treatment. Yet they have completed to the letter each of the requirements of the program: they stopped the extreme exercise and they gained weight, with little help from the staff. They may have earned points by taking charge of their diet and by becoming a leader in group therapy. They listened carefully to the primary therapist, contributed their thoughts, and seemed to be developing insight. Yet, after they leave the hospital, they drop out of therapy and quickly resume the original activity. This is because they simply substituted the activities of the therapy program for the activity that they had relinquished. The format remained the same. These patients successfully pursue the programmatic tasks in order to become independent of the hospital and the staff. This recapitulates the disorder: once again they have used their excellent ego functions and penchant for self control to strive toward independent achievement.

Patients who have made important progress—real changes—during their hospitalization may slide back into an activity disorder in the weeks and months after discharge. These persons must inevitably encounter forces that are countertherapeutic. Leaving the hospital tells them that they are "ready" for greater independence. They must make pragmatic decisions and confront challenges such as reentering graduate school. They face time pressures and tight schedules. The family's expectations may not have changed. The significant other may still expect to be cared for and parents may continue to ask, "Well, have you given any thought to what you're going to do with your life now?" They may encounter a dearth of structure, social events, and nourishing relationships at home. Under these circumstances, they are apt to experience an extraordinarily powerful internal push toward independent activity.

The current recommendation for therapy in the eating disorders is a multidimensional, flexible approach which includes individual, family, and group therapies according to the needs of the patient (Garner, Garfinkel & Bemis, 1982). This would seem to be the most suitable approach for the activity disorders.

HANDLING THE ISSUE OF ACTIVITY

Regardless of the therapeutic modality employed, the therapist must pay continued attention to the quality and quantity of the patient's activity, both physical and cognitive. If the situation is serious, explicit arrangements can be made for monitoring weight and/or physical exertion but monitoring the ruminations will depend upon the cooperation of the patient. Fortunately, the ruminations are not as self reinforcing as the physical activity and patients are apt to report the cognitive activity in an effort to decrease the amount of time spent ruminating. Initially, the activity can be approached as an index of the patient's need to maintain control within a self-determined, autonomous system.

The activity disordered patient is terrified at the prospect of no longer dieting, vomiting, running, etc. The fear of nothingness, of not having anything to do, inspires fantasies of body deterioration, with loss of integrity and motivation. The terror that the person experiences is similar to the panic and anxiety which can be induced in some individuals by relaxation techniques (Adler, Craske & Barlow, 1987). Without the activity, he may lose control and find himself in a dependent, vulnerable position. The intensity of the reaction is an indication of how great his dependence on activity has been. The fear can be addressed in terms of how much the patient is able to let the self "off the hook" to accept the state of inactivity. The therapist can explore the patient's fantasies about rest and the expectation of rest in the future. The therapist may wish to suggest that there will come a time when the patient will allow himself to rest. As treatment progresses, the therapist can examine the uses of activity in the past and in the present, day-to-day experiences. The patient can learn to identify the associated feeling states, and eventually the underlying issues of need and body state.

FAMILY THERAPY

The most clearly defined and best accepted family approach for the eating disorders is that described by Minuchin (1974). Although this approach was designed for severely disturbed adolescents, some of the principles that Minuchin outlines could be applied to the treatment of the activity disorders. In family therapy for the eating disorders, the therapist attempts to relieve parental guilt, restructure the patient's position in the family, facilitate mutual support, and foster healthy autonomy. "Healthy" autonomy essentially means that the patient pursues whatever it is that she wants for herself rather than reacting against her parents' efforts to bind and direct her.

Although this construct certainly fits the immature anorexic girl, it cannot be applied as well to the career woman bulimic or to the 50-year-old executive who is an obligatory runner. It is true that these people have internalized their parents' values and may be pursuing career goals which would be underwritten by their parents, but they have had considerable latitude in the choice and management of their careers. They grapple with a uniquely personal straightjacket.

In the activity disorders, marital or family therapy usually needs to be directed toward enhancing the patients' dependency gratification rather than their "healthy" autonomy. These patients are oversaturated with "healthy" autonomy. Before these persons can begin to receive pleasure from others, many questions of responsibility, such as the division of labor and the extent of other people's concern for them need to be resolved. Lingering resentments about issues such as chores, child care, vacations, etc. feed into the patients' drive to be active and independent. The unresolved anger prevents them from wanting to take anything from the partner. The activities distract them from their anger and may physically distance them from the issue and from the significant other. Thus, the autonomous system effectively keeps the problems on the shelf.

Once the resentment in the family has ameliorated, a restructuring of dependency relationships may begin. Activity disordered patients are their own worst enemies in that they tend to discount their needs and to take care of duties and other people automatically. They cannot ask for help and they often refuse help when it is offered, sometimes as if it were an affront to their competence. They may think that they are the only ones who are capable enough to do the job. They tend to attract dependent people, and they continue to foster the dependency by assuming the lion's share of responsibility. Other family members become more or less comfortable with the situation and they tend to abdicate their responsibility as if there were not much that they could do about the situation. They usually recognize the enormous power of the person who organizes the house and provides direction for the family.

The families of activity disordered patients may not look that unusual, or that pathological, to the family therapist. This is related to the cultural bias which supports independence and activity. If the therapist follows a tactic of encouraging other family members to become more self-sufficient so that the burden on the shoulders of the activity disordered person will be lightened, the therapy is likely to fail. Although other family members will need to assume more responsibility, the therapy needs to be directed toward the patient becoming less active, more playful, and more receptive. The family will have the responsibility of supplying, and being a part of, more pleasurable transactions.

Because activity disordered people usually have managed their families in much the same manner that they have managed their lives, other family members may find themselves waiting for the patient to define what would be pleasurable and to make plans so that it will happen. This needs to be directly addressed. If the patient, for example, chooses a vacation site, makes the plans, supervises the packing, etc., the vacationing may become as driven an activity as the running or the dieting, and the togetherness will seem oppressive rather than gratifying.

GROUP THERAPY

There are many forms of group therapy—psychoeducational, support, behavioral, and dynamic, to name a few. There are occasional groups specifically designed for compulsive athletes, usually in sports medicine clinics. The largest number of groups that exist are for bulimic women. These groups tend to focus on symptom management and they employ self-monitoring techniques such as asking the patient to maintain an eating behavior diary and expecting her to analyze behavioral antecedents to the bingeing and purging. Specific instructions about symptom management may be provided and the leader often functions as a teacher of dietary principles, of ways to avoid bingeing, of stress management, and of assertiveness training. The patient may be prohibited from purging, instructed to eat three meals a day, and told to avoid foods which might precipitate a binge (Mitchell, Hatsukami et al., 1985; Lacey, 1983; Long & Cordle, 1982). When the binge eating and purging improve, patients report less depression and fewer somatic concerns (Norman, Herzog & Chauncey, 1986) and they exhibit less psychopathology and better social adjustment (Garner, 1985).

Group therapy can be beneficial for eating disordered patients when it encourages them to identify and express feelings (Hedblom, Hubbard & Anderson, 1981). Group therapy can confront intellectualization, teach assertiveness (Grossniklaus, 1980), and support the emergence of competence (Hall, 1985). The most successful group therapies are highly structured, intense, and interactive. The bulimic patients have no choice but to relate to the therapist and be involved if they choose to remain in therapy. Some bulimic women can let the therapist participate in controlling the eating behavior, but other patients are too frightened or too distrustful to relinquish any control; they may refuse therapy or drop out of treatment later on.

Group therapy may be unsuitable for certain bulimic women. In Chapter 11, individuals are described as at risk for an activity disorder when they strive to be more independent than what they actually are. It is not the independence, per se, which contributes to the risk, but the extent to which they try to be different from what they actually are. At least initially, group therapy may be more suitable for individuals who can allow themselves greater dependency; they are less threatened by close relationships and more responsive to group support.

The eating disorders have been compared to alcoholism and drug dependency (Mitchell, Hatsukami et al., 1985) and, indeed, there are many similarities between bulimic behaviors and substance abuse (Hatsukami et al., 1982). Many bulimic women need some form of ongoing support if they are to remain symptom-free. Self-help groups modeled after Alcoholics Anonymous may be able to provide this support. Overeaters Anonymous is an organization which offers treatment groups for compulsive overeaters, including those who gorge and purge. Participants remain in the group indefinitely; although they may be recovered, they are never cured. They are required to eat three meals a day and nothing more. They attend meetings five times a week and call their sponsors daily. A preliminary report of bulimics enrolled in Overeaters Anonymous suggests that the group is salutary when it is combined with other treatments (Malenbaum et al., 1988).

Groups for recurrently injured, obligatory athletes can provide a valuable service in the sports medicine clinic. Physicians in the clinic are frustrated by patients who court further disability by refusing to rest. Obligatory athletes who disregard the physician's advice may accept the wisdom of other athletes.

COGNITIVE-BEHAVIORAL THERAPY

Cognitive-behavioral therapy was developed in Great Britain by Fairburn (1981) and the technique has become increasingly popular in the United States, where it is often used to treat eating disordered patients. This approach is based on principles which were developed by Beck, Rush et al. (1979) to treat depression. It employs a semistructured, problem-oriented approach to change the patient's system of beliefs about the self and the environment. The therapist directs the patient's attention toward the present or the future and away from past events.

When cognitive-behavioral therapy is used to treat the eating disorders, the therapist first focuses on the behavioral control of eating, then upon the modification of dysfunctional perceptions, and finally upon maintaining the improvements. The patients are instructed to keep a detailed account of their eating behavior and to weigh themselves weekly. They are taught to control their negative thoughts and ruminations, strengthen their social and assertiveness skills (Long & Cordle, 1982), improve their problem-solving abilities, and modify their abnormal attitudes toward weight and intake (Fairburn, 1981).

A particular approach to eating disordered behavior is the "exposure plus response-prevention" treatment method of Rosen and Leitenberg (1982). In this technique the patient must eat a series of meals in front of the therapist, composed of the foods which are the most frightening to her and which ordinarily would cause her to purge. During and after the meal, the patient discusses specific concerns about weight gain, appearance, her physical sensations, and the urge to vomit. Cognitive-behavioral techniques are said to produce gratifying results in many patients by effectively interrupting the pernicious cycle of binge eating and purging (Fairburn, 1985), but they have not been systematically evaluated.

Cognitive-behavioral therapy is task-oriented and scheduled; it teaches greater control. Unfortunately, most activity disordered individuals are already acutely task-oriented, scheduled, and controlled. The danger is that the tasks of therapy will simply replace the original activities, leaving the process untouched. The body is not directly involved in the new spate of activities, which makes abuse of the body less likely, but by the same token the new set of activities is less attractive to the patient. Because of this, a relapse is apt to occur once the patient is no longer engaged in the therapy.

Perhaps cognitive-behavioral therapy could be more effective in addressing the underlying issues in the activity disorders. Mavisskalian (1982) treated two anorexic patients who were compulsive exercisers by prescribing an hour of bed rest after meals. The women experienced extreme discomfort which initially lasted the entire time. It was only after a very large number of sessions that the patients were able to adapt. In this format the problem is identified not as an activity but as being without an activity. This directly addresses the patients' discomfort with the receptive state. The rich material produced by an experience such as this can facilitate the women's progress in the more traditional forms of therapy. Other tasks in the same vein would be to ask the patients to meditate, to receive enjoyment from another person, to play with a child, etc. The goal of these exercises is to examine the resistance, not to accomplish a task.

BODY THERAPIES

Psychodrama, bioenergetics, Reichian therapy, dance therapy, body movement therapy, and yoga all make use of the body, but they are not particularly kind to the body. They either use the translation of body tension or movement to understand the unconscious or they attempt to remove the tension, or discipline the body, through certain circumscribed activities. These approaches may be useful for activity disordered individuals, but the benefits tend to be temporary. The activity provided by the therapy never seems to compete with the patient's chosen activity. Perhaps this is because the therapy does not last long enough, is not under the patient's control, or is not sufficiently repetitive and simple. However, in one instance yoga did function as a temporary replacement for running: a disabled obligatory runner gathered a collection of writings on yoga. He read compulsively and methodically began to increase the time he spent holding his body in a most awkward position. As soon as his injuries healed, he dropped the yoga and began to increase his mileage instead.

Although body-based therapies encourage a greater appreciation of the body, the techniques are narrow and they do not allow for the integration of the material in the context of self. While body movement therapy and yoga do attend to the body state, these therapies tend to focus on accomplishment through activity. They do not distinguish between the various functions of the activity.

Should a broader body based intervention be developed? In our opinion, there is a place for a treatment which involves body touch and body movement. The place is in the hospital where body contact is already legitimized and where it can be monitored and integrated with other therapeutic modalities. Any other course would be foolhardy in the current climate of sexual anxiety. Therapy can be effective without body contact. The fundamental task for the patient is to recognize and receive the pleasantness of the body and its original connections with the parents so that tenderness toward the body can emerge. This can be accomplished in the context of a caring, therapeutic relationship.

PHARMACOLOGIC INTERVENTION

There is no medication which will benefit all, or even the majority, of activity disordered individuals. However, medication can produce substantial benefit for some individuals (Yates, 1989). Indicators for antidepressant therapy include a moderate or severe depression which does not remit after a few weeks in the hospital or an adequate trial of outpatient therapy (especially when there is a family history of depression, alcoholism, or bipolar disorder); continued, pronounced resistance to multimodal therapy; and overpowering ruminations and rituals. Fluoxetine (Prozac), a serotonin reuptake inhibitor, is especially promising because of its wide margin of safety, its efficacy in OCD, and its effect in diminishing the appetite. Some patients are helped by fluoxetine but others are not. Some are relieved that they no longer have to battle their appetite and they increase their intake; others diminish their intake even further because they have less desire to eat.

Activity disordered individuals usually dislike the idea of taking medication. Many patients refuse medication or simply forget to fill the prescription. Their resistance is part of their need for self control and their reluctance to receive anything from the therapist. Prescribing medication before a treatment alliance has been established invites noncompliance. These patients need to be enlisted as participants and evaluators in their own treatment program; they can, in conjunction with the therapist, make considered decisions about medication.

INDIVIDUAL OUTPATIENT THERAPY

Some activity disordered persons enter outpatient therapy when they are discharged from the inpatient service, but the majority present themselves directly to outpatient therapy under a variety of circumstances. These individuals usually are functioning quite well in their educational program or their chosen vocation. They may be chronically dissatisfied, but may or may not recognize that they are contributing to the problem. Most of these persons would like to make their lives more gratifying, but only a few of them see the extent of the activity as a problem in itself. Long-term outpatient therapy is the treatment of choice for these individuals and for persons with an activity disturbance who wish to take a closer look at themselves.

Analytic therapy would seem to be especially apt for the activity disordered person, if it is available. The intensity of the relationship, the therapist's position of concern, of fostering growth without giving direction, and the patient's position of recumbency on the couch would tend to draw the therapy toward issues of receptive gratification and the degree of separateness which the person needs to maintain. If analytic therapy is not feasible, these principles may be applied as far as possible in other forms of treatment. Therapy may extend for several years; progress will depend upon the patient's commitment to change, current stress, ego strength, relationship with the therapist, and self-reflective capacity.

At first, long-term psychotherapy appears quite silly to most activity disordered persons. They minimize their problems and would—understandably—prefer an easier answer. Some have tried highly structured treatments but have dropped out as they began to feel controlled by the therapist. Yet, activity disordered persons are profoundly uncomfortable with the concept of engaging in a less structured therapy. In anticipating treatment, they may have gone to considerable length to locate a therapist who will be active in the treatment process. Although this has much to do with their discomfort with inactivity, they have an acute need to know how they appear and how they are doing in therapy. A therapist who provides consistent, nonjudgmental messages about the self helps these patients stabilize their fluctuating self concept. The unstable self and body image is a fundamental aspect of these disorders.

THERAPEUTIC GOALS

The overall goal of therapy is for the patients to strive less valiantly to maintain a separate state. They will need to allow themselves more receptive gratification and they will need to use activity in a self-helpful rather than a self-hurtful manner. Activity should be used more to self regulate and less to defend against receptive pleasure and maintain a separate state. If therapy is successful, they may be somewhat less active than before and they may want to be alone less of the time. If they are to accomplish this, they will need to sort through many preverbal, perceptual defenses as well as the more commonly recognized postverbal defenses.

As activity disordered persons have self expectations which are unreasonably high, therapy might be aimed at the inordinate demands of an overly strict superego. However, since the unrealistic self expectations serve to defend against closeness and receptive pleasure, a more appropriate goal would be for these patients to define and experience what it is that they really need. The therapist's goal in treatment might be for the patient to recognize, accept, and internalize the soothing aspects of the therapist. Therapy can provide comfort within a tender relationship. Over time, this could enable the patient to enjoy sensory experiences such as eating, to maintain a less separate state, and, on occasion, to rest.

FORMING AN ALLIANCE

An obligatory individual is bound within and organized around the chosen activity. The therapist may feel as if he is competing with the activity for the person's attention. As long as the patient is engrossed in the activity, there will be little room for the therapist. Because of the focal nature of the activity and the fact that the activity stands essentially in opposition to the therapeutic process, the activity needs to be brought into the therapy. This means that the therapist must begin by understanding the patient's need to be active and how he or she experiences the activity. The therapist needs to continue to inquire about changes in cognitive activity during the session and physical activity outside the session.

Emaciated patients may need to diminish or cease the exercise, dieting, or binge/purge activity in order to attend to therapy and in order for the physical deprivation, with its attendant alienation, to resolve. In severe cases this means hospitalization. Less severely affected individuals may be encouraged or instructed to modify their activity as a condition of outpatient therapy. Those persons who refuse to modify the activity may decide to do so following a time-limited course of exploration or a confrontation with a significant other during a family session. If specialized group therapy is available, group members may provide effective confrontation. When the patients are ready to curtail their activity, therapy can begin.

Obligatory individuals in therapy feel as if they are on their own in a mysterious land. They try to be "on top of the therapy" by figuring things out before the therapist can. This does not necessarily imply a devaluation of the therapist; it is a method of maintaining control and a position of autonomy. At some level, the patient knows that forming a therapeutic alliance will mean forfeiting the activity in its current form. To forego the activity is to be divested—of power, of control, of protection, of an identity, of a format for life. And for what? To the patient it seems that the result would be a state of vulnerability, aimlessness, and consummate misery.

Obligatory individuals stay "on top of" therapy through a persistent increase in cognitive activity. During the early months of therapy, they may spend many hours each day identifying issues, problem solving, etc. Although they continue to experience this as "getting the hang of therapy," the primary function of the activity is to enable them to maintain a state which is separate from the therapist and to defend against the pleasure which might be contained in a relationship with a person who could care.

When activity disordered individuals happen to lose control over external circumstances, the activity tends to intensify and to become even more driven. A patient was shortchanged 10 dollars in a restaurant and the manager refused to hear his case. He ran five miles home (although he had planned to ride a bus) and dug in his flower bed until his palms were blistered. In his next therapy session, he was preoccupied with thoughts of his garden and he seemed disconnected from the therapist.

RESISTANCE

If there is a stalemate in therapy, the therapist may wish to explore with the patient the possibility of "resting"—of doing nothing for certain periods during the day. This will be very threatening to the patient and, if all goes well, he or she may be able to see how unreasonable is the reaction to the suggestion. Whether or not the patient is able to rest, his or her response to the proposal can contribute substantially to the therapy. If the patient does decide to rest, it is important that the decision to do this be the patient's and not the therapist's.

Patients must be able to "rest" a little in therapy if they are to take anything in from the therapist. Obligatory exercisers prefer not to sit still and they always expect that they should be up doing something. When they aren't doing something they are likely to be considering some pressing issue. They may resist therapy by needing to stretch, go to the bathroom, or cut the session short. They may be involved in so many urgent endeavors outside of therapy that they are often late to sessions. In the session, they may be so busy working on their problems or thinking about their projects that they remain apart in the relationship.

When physical activity is limited during the session, patients may engage in fidgeting, foot tapping, and various patterns of muscular tension. One patient did isometric exercises with his feet. If the couch is utilized, the patient may lie "stiff as a board," controlling the body so that it will not respond to the warmth of the therapist. Unless the therapist calls attention to the body state, the patient may completely disregard it because of the disconnection between body and self. Descriptions of, and reflections on, the body state may be encouraged in any stage of therapy, but interpretations should wait until there is a solid therapeutic alliance.

Eating disordered women and many obligatory runners are bedeviled by their appetite when they rest. The activity guards against appetite and the appetite seems impossible to manage when they are inactive. They may try to distract themselves with a barrage of highly charged thoughts involving various threats and challenges. These deliberations are always accompanied by muscular tension. The thoughts plus the tension effectively abort the resting state. The inability to rest can be brought into therapy; it serves as an example of how activity may be used to defend against the receptive state. Patients who resist the receptive position within the therapy session are likely to be resisting it in other situations as well. They may never sit down to chat or to simply be with another person. The activity protects them against desiring to take in something which another person might supply.

Because of the disconnection between body and mind, activity disordered patients may wish to be close to another but not experience that need in the body. In their minds, they simply do not respond as they would expect. They interpret this as an indication that they are inadequate or that the other person is not as attractive as they had once thought. Because of this, they are often disappointed in themselves or in the quality of their relationships. This is one reason why they may drop out of therapy: they don't really need (want) therapy, the therapy isn't right for them, or it's not the right therapist. The therapist may wish to predict that this problem could arise by pointing out that this has been the pattern in past relationships.

BODY IN THERAPY

Before entering therapy, an activity disordered patient usually recognizes the body only as it is active or only as it is part of the (usually negative) self concept. The patient has little awareness of the body as a sensory entity or its response in the course of a relationship. In therapy, a patient may become aware of the body and changes in the body state within the session. The therapist may wish to comment on the patient's body position and the small motor movements, or to inquire about the tension in the musculature. At first, these patients are apt to either disregard these comments or to think that the therapist is critical or wishes them to correct their behavior.

As activity disordered patients begin to form a relationship with the therapist, the underlying instability of the body concept becomes more apparent. The fluctuations are apt to be negative: to the patients the body seems flabby, weak, fish-belly white, etc. The patients discount any information to the contrary as an attempt to "make it better" and they actively support their negative perceptions with "proof" by odious comparison. They value the pessimism and anxiety which the negative perceptions engender because they augment the resolve to be active. The perception of the body as ugly or imperfect is followed by the urge to do something about it. The ruminations about the body increase and the patients lose contact with the therapist as they search independently for a solution.

As the therapy progresses, the patient may be better able to accept the therapist's concern. The patient may begin to experience the body not just as an object to be pared and primed, but as a part of the self. This may be the first sign that the patient is ready to relinquish some control by reconnecting body and self. He is less on guard, his body relaxes, and it may, at times, become pliable and pleasantly inactive. This indicates a readiness to receive from the therapist and to metabolize the therapy. The body continues to be engaged in a silent transaction with the therapist throughout the treatment process.

TRANSFERENCE ISSUES

In therapy, activity disordered persons recreate the format by which they learned to maintain a separate state. They bury themselves in activity and they work at solving their problems. Therapy is another responsibility, another challenge, another item on an interminable list. This perception of therapy effectively prevents them from receiving the compassion and concern of the therapist and it protects them from being gratified within a close relationship. Although they value the therapist and identify with some aspects of the therapist, they expect very little from the therapist. They operate as if he or she is a good parent, standing behind, approving, but not really part of the activity. They may view the therapist as a gatekeeper or final examiner—someone who is only distantly relevant to the task at hand. They seldom inquire about the therapist, nor do they see such questions as appropriate.

Although activity disordered patients value the therapist, they do not have a sense that the therapist or the relationship could or should be immediately gratifying. It is the completion of the task which is "supposed" to be fulfilling. In this way, these patients can remain emotionally distant from the therapist in spite of the fact that they are in therapy in order to be helped. Because of this style of distant relatedness, the therapist may view these patients as narcissistic: excessively self absorbed, and exhibitionistic. Like the narcissistic patient, they attempt to maintain an illusion of self sufficiency (Modell, 1975). The therapist may feel useless, divorced from the therapy, bored and frustrated.

Although activity disordered patients may appear narcissistic (and some of them are narcissistic), the transference which most activity disordered patients form is quite different from the mirroring or idealizing transferences which Kohut (1977) describes. These patients will deflect or diminish the therapist's positive comments instead of basking in the therapist's approval as in the mirror transference. Although they ascribe power to the therapist, it is a distant power. They do not derive power through their relationship with the therapist and they certainly do not deny that the therapist is a separate person, as in the idealizing transference.

Rather than the non-relatedness of narcissism, activity disordered patients present a compelling self-sufficiency which, as Modell (1975) has indicated, can serve as a defense. These patients assume that the therapist, as the absent parent, wishes them to manage their own problems. They do not dislike it when the therapist interrupts and they may be relieved when this occurs. They do hear the therapist's comments and may integrate them into the understanding of the self. Although these patients guard against a close relationship with the therapist, they do not present the internal deadness or disdainful aloofness which is characteristic of the narcissistic patient.

Activity disordered patients seem content to be alone while they are in therapy just as they often prefer to be alone outside of therapy. The quality of this aloneness seems akin to Winnicott's (1965b) description of "being alone in the presence of another." Under ordinary circumstances, the child develops this capacity through the experience of being well nurtured by the parents. The child introjects this experience and it becomes part of the personality so that the child may be by himself and yet remain content. Stern (1985) presents a similar concept: the child is able to exist apart from the parents by recalling the soothing qualities of the parents as he engages in activities. Activity disordered patients seem to be alone-but-not-alone as they shoulder the therapy by themselves, expecting little or nothing from the therapist.

The apartness of activity disordered patients in therapy could be interpreted as a sign of narcissism, i.e., they are performing on a stage (therapy) and the therapist is their audience. This is not the case with most activity disordered individuals. The therapist is extremely important to these patients and they will describe the importance if asked. The therapist provides the arena in which they strive to comprehend the self and the impetus to do this. The therapist supplies essential, albeit distant, support. This is a vital distinction between narcissistic disorders and activity disorders.

It may be that obligatory individuals, as children, were able to develop especially well the capacity to be "alone-but-not-alone." Perhaps they became able to do this because they were well nurtured by concerned, empathic parents who helped them in the early struggle to exist apart. Yet the parents were the persons who imposed the independent state and the parents were the ones who designated the place in which the children would learn to stay apart. Obligatory adults may recapitulate these circumstances in therapy. They work independently of, but remain connected to, the therapist. They work as they think that the therapist would want them to work, in the place that the therapist designates.

Activity disordered patients avoid making an emotional connection to the therapist in part because of the unconscious fear that if they were closer to the therapist they might enjoy the therapist's concern for them and this would make them more vulnerable and less able to maintain a separate state. It is not until the relationship with the therapist deepens and they use activity less to guard against receptive pleasure that they are able to experience a need for the attention of the therapist.

COUNTERTRANSFERENCE ISSUES

Therapists emerge from the same class and culture as their activity disordered patients and they may have solved corresponding issues in a similar fashion. In order to have climbed the educational ladder to a successful career, they must be independent and activity oriented, i.e., well adapted to the demands of society. Because of this, therapists may overidentify with the patient and covertly or overtly encourage activity.

For instance, they may be impressed by the patient's truly heroic efforts to understand himself. They begin to regard the patient as an "ideal therapy candidate." They may offer support while the patient toils away, but may fail to note the patient's embattled autonomy or continued self deprivation.

The therapist's relationship to his own body will influence his understanding of the patient's relationship with the body. Unless the therapist is closely connected to his body, he may not be able to recognize the significance of the body for the patient or the patient's need to disconnect from the body.

Therapists who have been trained in malignant motherhood, i.e., that rejecting, depriving, and overcontrolling parents are at the root of most serious emotional problems, may unconsciously or consciously encourage the patient's negative perceptions of the parents—perceptions which enhance separateness. While it is true that the parents may be far from ideal and have made many mistakes, it is likely that they care deeply and that the patients' homeostasis depends upon not understanding that they care. These patients are not victims: they need to remain separate from that which was once exceedingly gratifying.

THE COURSE OF THERAPY

Activity disordered persons are experts at maintaining their homeostasis through goal-directed activity. However, when they work exceedingly hard at analyzing themselves but their situation remains essentially unchanged, they become frustrated. This is a welcome moment in therapy, for the affective imbalance can facilitate the formation of a closer relationship with the therapist. The therapist might, at last, be able to assist these patients through clarification and interpretation. In this manner, the therapist attains more of a presence and the patients may begin to achieve insight into the separate state which they are striving to maintain.

Patients may react to the frustration of not being cured in spite of hard work by placing their shoulders to the wheel. Instead of expressing their irritation, they channel it into working at therapy longer and harder than before. Because their ego functions, including frustration tolerance and affect modulation, are so well developed, they are able to continue their solitary struggle indefinitely. The therapy may seem interminable—to the therapist and to the patient.

When patients give therapy their "best shot" but the problems remain, they may leave therapy altogether in favor of some other, presumably more satisfying, activity. They are more likely to blame the ambiguity of therapy or the length of the process than the therapist. How can they be angry at or reject someone who really wasn't responsible for the treatment? Some of these patients will assume the blame themselves: they are not able to solve their problems or they are not "ready" for therapy. Some of them invoke circumstance to usher in an easy exit: the insurance is running out; the company is going to transfer them; they are about to graduate, etc. When they leave therapy, they heave a sigh of relief, as if a burden had been finally lifted.

The way to reach these toiling but disconnected patients is to operate as much as possible within the transference. Patients who have consistently not heard the therapist's comments may quickly pay attention to a discussion about the relationship, the quality of the affective interchange, or the fantasies about the therapy. The therapist may feel as if he is forcing direct contact in the same manner by which he might command the attention of an otherwise occupied child. When this is done in an empathic, open manner, it can serve as a fulcrum for change.

If these patients can be directly engaged by the therapist, the activity, which substitutes and defends against the relationship, becomes irrelevant. As a close relationship begins to form, primitive defenses, such as idealization, devaluation, and projective identification may surface. These may have been present all along but kept in check by the distance which the patient was maintaining. The patients may become furious at the therapist as if the therapist were the parent who had left them in the first place. The therapist may be viewed as controlling, opinionated, stupid, and—most of all—uncaring. The therapist's body may be scrutinized as old, flabby, and fat. When these defenses no longer suffice, the patient may feel empty, depressed, and exceedingly uncomfortable. Analyzing the defenses is not as important as recognizing them—and continuing to support the patient and operate within the transference.

As the patient begins to recognize the therapist and to work within the relationship, he or she may gradually become less separate and less active. He may not need to run as far, work out as rigorously, diet as stringently, or avoid as many social events. His body becomes more relaxed in the therapy session and he is able to take more in from the therapist. Over time, the patient may be able to receive the relationship fully and be gratified by it. This is accompanied by a greater awareness of the body and greater pleasure in taste and smell.

Obligatory individuals have much to work through before they can relate directly to the therapist. The working through involves a sequence which repeats itself again and again. As the patients begin to diminish their control and receive from the therapist, they become distracted by highly charged thoughts—such as concern about their inadequate performance or the imperfection of the body. They attempt to problem solve independently of the therapist, but encounter frustration and identity diffusion. They confront the defense and once again turn to the therapist to rework the issue of independence. Once again they are able to diminish control and once again they become distracted by highly charged thoughts.

The juncture at which patients are able to moderate their striving seems to coincide with their readiness to be nurtured in the context of their relationship with the therapist. This is not an easy process; it often follows years of therapy, years of defending against the pleasure of feeling loved. When patients are able to receive the therapist's concern, they find it easier to remain content rather than driven while they are engaged in their activities and they find it easier to leave the activities in favor of other gratifications. Eating disordered patients become able to enjoy the taste of food and the process of eating; they are able to feel pleasantly satiated. Obligatory runners are able to enjoy the run without increasing their self expectations; they can quit before they are exhausted. The body is reconnected to the self.

If it was the relationship with the parents which enabled the child to derive greater pleasure from activity (Stern, 1985), it may be the relationship with the therapist which ultimately enables the patient to derive greater pleasure from eating and the movement of the body. The pleasure derived from relationships blends with the pleasure of activity.

Some patients are more fragile than others. For some, the need for succorance is acute and the ambivalence about receiving it is excruciating. They wish to relinquish control almost as much as they fear it. These patients are more likely to be severely and chronically impaired with borderline characteristics, much like the "classic" eating disordered patient of yesteryear. The techniques described by Masterson (1977) and Sours (1980) are especially valuable in the treatment of borderline psychopathology.

OUTCOME

The outcome of therapy is determined by the severity and extent of the risk factors, the vigor and appropriateness of the treatment modalities, the skill and patience of the therapist, the flexibility of the family, and the resilience and amenability of the individual patient. The end result of successful therapy is greater comfort with the self, diminished activity coupled with greater enjoyment of the activity, and the ability to receive from others. By internalizing the comforting aspects of the therapist, patients take better care of the body and they no longer harm the body through self hurtful activities such as purging. They remain active and independent, but less so than before. Some become more creative and others simply take vacations.

CHAPTER 17

Toward an
Integrated Theory

"Dear Abby" (*Arizona Daily Star*, 2/14/90) takes the position that a host has the right to rebuff unexpected visitors by claiming to be tired or otherwise occupied. After she is attacked by a proponent of the "Y'all come" school of Southern Hospitality, Dear Abby defends herself with the statement, "Just don't drop in on a busy editor who's fighting a deadline." This statement contains a central theme of this book: that the diminished sociability, the apartness, of so many individuals today has to do with the schedules, the deadlines, and the multiple demands of being a "superman" or "superwoman."

The problems of today could be blamed solely upon the complexity and demands of the culture, but this answer is too easy. The culture interacts with the personality traits of the individual, and the personality traits are influenced in turn by genetic and environmental variables. Personality traits and circumstance combine to determine the individual's area of interest and level of commitment to task. Biologic variables have much to do with the translation of a casual activity into a repetitive, driven activity.

FORMULATION

There is some evidence that high-achieving, persistent, perfectionistic ("obligatory") persons are the ones who plunge themselves into self development activities such as diet and exercise (Folkins & Sine, 1981; Owens & Slade, 1987). They throw themselves into self development just as they throw themselves into study or work. They focus on a goal and they push themselves until they attain it, using an elaborate bank of cognitive strategies to stay on task. When they succeed, they feel good about themselves and they strive even harder. They may work two jobs, study alone all night, juggle three sets of data without assistance, map out a system on their own, take papers and journals home on weekends, and spend three evenings a week at the health club working out. They seem geared for success.

When obligatory individuals strive for excellence in diet and exercise, they may expend many more calories than they ingest. When this happens, they may enter a state of physical deprivation. The deprivation can invoke one or more physiologic mechanisms which tend to intensify and perpetuate the process. Dietary restriction dramatically increases the appetite and the fear of losing control; this can cause an intensification of the diet. The combination of diet and exercise may augment the need to be active to such an extent that the activity begins to appear driven. The combination of diet and a rigid feeding schedule can escalate the activity even further. These physiologic factors may cause the activity to recycle and become resistant to intervention. As this process evolves, it can cause an increase in seclusiveness, hostility, egocentricity, and depression.

This formulation suggests that there is a relatively nonpathological route to the eating disorders and compulsive athleticism. Individuals need not present severe character pathology or a history of having been raised by destructive or neglectful parents to develop these conditions.

FUNCTIONS OF ACTIVITY

Activity disordered men and women derive several intrapsychic functions from the dieting, binge/purge cycle, or exercise. They use the activity to self-regulate, to self-define, to maintain separateness, to defend against receptive pleasure, and to hurt the body. Non-activity disordered persons use activity for many of the same purposes, but they do not intentionally hurt the body. Non-activity disordered individuals do not need to maintain as high a level of activity, nor do they rely as heavily upon the separation maintenance and defensive functions of activity.

Activity disordered persons seem engaged in a love-hate relationship with the body, on the one hand idealizing it and on the other rejecting it, disconnecting from it, and forcing it to conform to a rigid ideal. The need to control the body, to make it function without food, rest, and care, suggests that they strive toward greater self-reliance. On closer examination, they appear to be locked in a struggle with the self over issues of independence. They experience considerable internal and external pressure to be independent. It is when they push themselves toward greater independence and achievement that they become symptomatic.

GENESIS

The problems that activity disordered individuals face may be related to the extent to which this society underscores independence. Early on, infants and young children are encouraged to become more self-sufficient; they are often placed with sitters or in day care so that the parents may return to the workplace. Well-nurtured children tend to adapt to these demands by becoming more active, more independent, and more involved in independent activity. Initially, they may be active because they are acutely distressed and searching for the absent parent, but soon they begin to enjoy the activities. The activities distract them from their neediness. When they engage in activities which they had shared with the parents, they feel soothed and comforted. (Stern, 1985). In this manner, they begin to develop the self-regulating, defensive, and separation maintenance functions of activity.

Infants and young toddlers understand the world through physical activity. When they acquire representational thought in the second year, they are able to substitute cognitive activity for physical activity: thinking about an activity assumes the same self-regulating, defensive, and separation maintenance functions as engaging in the activity. Now, youngsters can lull themselves to sleep in a fantasy about play, daydream instead of tasting the food that they consume, and silently wonder about how to ride a bicycle while walking with the family. These simple cognitive ploys may gradually evolve into sophisticated cognitive strategies.

In the beginning, infants must experience receptive pleasure within the relationship to the parents, through the body gratifications of nursing, being held, playing and snuggling. When children begin to stay apart from their parents, they yearn for the parents' return. They may experience their neediness concretely, as part of the body. If the children are very young, the yearning may be painful. This could cause the children to become angry at the body. They may try to control or reject the body, or disconnect from it. The ambivalence about the body may persist and intensify at times when there is a demand for greater independence. In the activity disorders, the ambivalence about the body and the need to control the body could be a residual of the early struggle to maintain a separate state.

The theory presented above rests on the assumption that, for all individuals, separation is an ongoing, dynamic process. From early in life, activity is used to negotiate and renegotiate a separate state. The manner in which individuals use activity is at once an index of how difficult and how rewarding the separation process has become. Even when separation is a terrible struggle, it continues to contribute to internal growth and elaboration.

LAST WORDS

This is the first time in recorded history that individuals are overdieting and overexercising in the name of self development; the first time that as many infants are experiencing a series of brief, repetitive separations from both parents in the first year of life; the first time that as many adults are consciously choosing to be single or to live alone. Perhaps we should critically examine the equation of independence with health. Perhaps there can be too much of a good thing.

Obligatory runners and high-functioning eating disordered women seem to suffer from too much of a good thing. They try too hard, they adapt too well. They overadapt. Perhaps what we need to do is to help them tone down their health to the point where they can be less demanding of themselves and more accepting of the body. We could recognize their achievements and their promise for the future while we underscore the legitimacy of their very human needs.

References

Abell, T. L., Malagalelada, J. R., Lucas, A. Y., Brown, M. L., Camiller, M., Go, V.L.W., Azpiroz, F., Calloway, C. W., Kad, P. C. & Zinsweis, A. R. (1987), Gastric electromechanical and neurohormonal function in anorexia nervosa. *Gastroenterology, 93:*958–965.

Abraham, S. F. & Beumont, P. J. V. (1982), How patients describe bulimia or binge eating. *Psychol. Med., 12:*628–635.

Adler, C. M., Craske, M. G. & Barlow, D. H. (1987), Relaxation induced panic (RIP): When resting isn't peaceful. *Integrative Psychiat., 5:*84–100.

Alexander, L. (1988), *Six Months Off.* New York: Wm Morrow.

Allerdissen, R., Florin, J. & Rost, M. (1981), Psychological characteristics of women with bulimia nervosa. *Behav. Anal. Modific., 4:*314–317.

Altschul, V. A. (1978), The ego-integrative (and disintegrative) effects of long-distance running. *Current Concepts in Psychiatry.* July/August, 1978.

American Sports Data Inc. Survey, 1988 and 1989. In: *U.S. News and World Report,* May 29, 1989.

American-Statesman, Austin, Texas. 8/10/89.

Anderson, A. E. (1984), Anorexia nervosa and bulimia in adolescent males. *Ped. Annals, 13:*901–907.

Anderson, A. E. (1989), Males with eating disorders. BASH Workshop, April 6–8, St. Louis, MO.

Anderson, A. E. & Mickalide A. E. (1983), Anorexia nervosa in the male: An underdiagnosed disorder. *Psychosom., 24:*1066–1074.

Anderson, A. E., Morris, C. L. & Santmyer, K. S. (1985), Inpatient treatment for anorexia nervosa. In: *Handbook of Psychotherapy for Anorexia Nervosa and Bulimia,* D. M. Garner & P. E. Garfinkel, (eds.). New York: Guilford Press.

Antelman, S. M. & Caggiula, A. R. (1977), Tales of stress related behavior: A neuropharmacological model. In: *Animal Models in Psychiatry and Neurology,* I. Hanin & E. Usdin (eds.). New York: Pergamon Press.

Anyan, W. R. & Showalter, J. E. (1983), A comprehensive approach to anorexia nervosa. *J. Am. Acad. Child Psychiat., 22:*122–127.

Appenzeller, O., Standefer, J., Appenzeller, J. & Atkinson, R. (1980), Neurology of endurance training 5: Endorphins. *Neurology, 30:*418–419.

Armstrong, J. G. & Roth, D. M. (1989), Attachment and separation difficulties in eating disorders: A preliminary investigation. *Int. J. Eat. Dis., 8:*141–155.

Balint, M. (1959), *Thrills and Regressions.* London: Tavistock Publications.

Balint, M. (1968), *The Basic Fault.* London: Tavistock Publications.

Bandura, A. (1986), *Social Foundations of Thought and Action: A Social Cognitive Theory.* Englewood Cliffs, NJ: Prentice-Hall.

Bannister, R. (1973), The meaning of athletic performance. In: *Sports and Society*, J. Talamini & C. H. Page (eds.). Boston: Little, Brown, and Company.

Baruch, G. K. & Barnett, R. C. (1986), Fathers' participation in family work and children's sex role attitudes. *Child Dev.*, 57:1210–1223.

Beattie, H. J. (1988), Eating disorders and the mother-daughter relationship. *Int. J. Eat. Dis.*, 7:453–460.

Beck, J. B., Ward-Hull, C. J. & McLear, P. M. (1976), Variables related to women's somatic preferences of the male and female body. *J. Personality Soc. Psychol.*, 34:1200–1210.

Beck, A. T., Rush, A. J., Shaw, B. F. & Emery, G. (1979), *Cognitive Therapy of Depression*. New York: Guilford Press.

Behrends, R. S. & Blatt, S. J. (1985), Internalization and psychological development throughout the life cycle. *Psychoanal. Study Child 40*:11–39.

Bell, R. (1985), *Holy Anorexia*. Chicago: University of Chicago Press.

Bernstein, D. (1983), The female superego: A different perspective. *Int. J. Psychoanal.*, 64:187–201.

Beumont, P. J. V., Booth, A. L., Abraham, F. F., Griffith, S. D. A. & Turner, T. R. 1983), A temporal sequence of symptoms in patients with anorexia nervosa: A preliminary report. In: *Anorexia Nervosa: Recent Developments in Research*, P. L. Darby, P. E. Garfinkel, D. M. Garner & D. V. Coscina (eds.). New York: Allen R. Liss.

Beumont, P. J. V., George, G. C. W. & Smart, D. E. (1976), "Dieters" and "vomiters and purgers" in anorexia nervosa. *Psychol. Med.*, 6:617–622.

Blatt, S. J. (1974), Levels of object representation in anaclitic and introjective depression. *Psychoanal. Study Child*, 29:107–157.

Blue, A. (1987), *Grace Under Pressure: The Emergence of Women in Sport*. London: Sidgwick & Jackson.

Blumenthal, J. A., Rose, S. & Chang, J. L. (1985) Anorexia nervosa and exercise: Implications from recent findings. *Sports Med.*, 2:237–247.

Bockus, H. L. (Editor) (1974), *Gastroenterology*, Vol. I, pp. 11–13. Philadelphia: W. B. Saunders.

Borgen, J. S. & Corbin, C. B. (1987), Eating disorders among female athletes. *Phys. Sports Med.*, 15:89–95.

Boskind-Lodahl, M. & White, W. C. (1978), The definition and treatment of bulimia in college women—a pilot study. *J. Am. Coll. Health Asso.*, 27:84–86.

Both-Orthman, B., Rubinow, D. R., Hoban, M. C., Malley, J. & Grover, G. N. (1988), Menstrual cycle phase-related changes in appetite in patients with premenstrual syndrome and in control subjects. *Am. J. Psychiat.*, 145:628–631.

Bowlby, J. (1973), *Attachment and Loss, Vol 2: Separation*. New York: Basic Books.

Bram, S., Eger, D. & Halmi, K. A. (1982), Anorexia nervosa and personality type: A preliminary report. *Int. J. Eat. Dis.*, 2:67–74.

Branch, C. H. H. & Eurman, L. J. (1980), Social attitudes toward patients with anorexia nervosa. *Clin. Res. Reports*, 134:631–632.

Breese, G. R., Smith, R. D., Mueller, R. A., Howard. J. L., Prange, Jr., A. J., Lipton, M. A., Young, L. B., McKenney, W. T. & Lewis, J. K. (1973), Induction of adrenal catacholamine synthesizing enzymes following mother-infant separation. *Nature, 246NB:*94–96.

Brooks, S. M., Sanborn, C. F., Albrecht, B. H. & Wagner, W. W., (1984), Diet in athletic amenorrhea. *Lancet, 2:*559–560.

Brown, R. S., Ramirez, D. E. & Taub, J. M. (1978), The prescription of exercise for depression. *Phys. Sports Med., 6:*34–45.

Bruch, H. (1973), *Eating Disorders: Obesity and Anorexia Nervosa.* New York: Basic Books.

Bruch, H. (1975), Obesity and anorexia nervosa: Psychosocial aspects. *Aust. NZ J Psychiat., 9:*159–161.

Burke, R. J. & Weir, T. (1976), Relationships of wives' employment status to husband, wife, and pair satisfaction and performance. *J. Marriage Fam., 38:*279–287.

Calabrese, L. H. (1985), Nutritional and medical aspects of gymnastics. *Clinics in Sports Med., 4:*28.

Callen, K. E. (1983), Mental and emotional aspects of long-distance running. *Psychosom., 24:*133–152.

Carter, P. I. & Moss, R. A. (1984), Screening for anorexia and bulimia nervosa in a college population: Problems and limitations. *Addictive Behav., 9:*417–419.

Cash, T. F. & Janda, C. H. (1984), The eye of the beholder. *Psychol. Today, 18:*46–52.

Casper, R. C., Eckert, E. D., Halmi, K. A., Goldberg, S. C. & Davis, J. M. (1980), Bulimia, its incidence and importance in patients with anorexia nervosa. *Arch. Gen. Psychiat., 37:*1030–1044.

Chan, C. D. & Grossman, H. Y. (1988), Psychological effects of running loss on consistent runners. *Percept. Mot. Skill., 66:*875–883.

Chatoor, I., Egan, J., Getson, P., Menvielle, E. & O'Dannell, R. (1988), Mother-Infant interactions in infantile anorexia nervosa. *J. Am. Acad. Child & Adol. Psychiat., 27:*535–540.

Chatoor, I. & Egan, J. (1983), Nonorganic failure to thrive and dwarfism due to food refusal: A separation disorder. *J. Am. Acad. Child Psychiat., 22:*294–301.

Ching, A. (1963), Primary and secondary anorexia nervosa syndromes. *Br. J. Psychiat., 109:*470–479.

Clarke, M. G. & Palmer, R. L., (1983), Eating attitudes and neurotic symptoms in university students. *Br. J. Psychiat., 142:*299–304.

Clinton, D. M. & McKinley, W. W. (1986), Attitudes to food, eating and weight in acutely ill and recovered anorectics. *Br. J. Clin. Psychol., 25:*61–67.

Clippen, A. V., Gupta, R. K. Eccleston, E. G., Wood, K. M., Wakeling, A. & deSousa, V. F. A. (1976), Plasma tryptophan in anorexia nervosa. *Lancet, 1:*962.

Coe, C. L., Glass, J. C., Wiener, S. G. & Levine, S. (1983), Behavioral but not physiological adaptation to repeated separation in mother and infant primates. *Psychoneuroendocrinol., 8:*401–409.

Colt, E. W. D., Dunner, D. L., Hall, K. & Fieve, R. R. (1981), A high prevalence of affective disorder in runners. In: *The Psychology of Running,* M. H. Sacks (ed). Champaign, Illinois: Human Kinetics Press.

Cooper, A. M. (1981), Masochism and long distance running. In: *Psychology of*

Running, M. H. Sacks & M. L. Sachs (eds.). Champaign, Illinois: Human Kinetics Press.

Cooper, P. J. & Fairburn, C. G. (1983), Binge-eating and self-induced vomiting in the community: A preliminary study. *Br. J. Psychiat.*, *142*:139–144.

Cooper, P. J. & Fairburn, C. G. (1986), The depressive symptoms of bulimia nervosa. *Br. J. Psychiat.*, *148*:268–274.

Coovert, D. L. & Powers, P. S. (1988), Bulimia nervosa with enema abuse: A preliminary analysis based on four case reports. *Int. J. Eat. Dis.*, *7*:697–700.

Cornish, E. R. & Morosovsky, N. (1965), Activity during food deprivation and satiation in six species of rodents. *Animal Behav.*, *13*:242–248.

Cosins, J. M., Frederickx, Y., Yousif, A., Hamoir, M. & Van-den-Eeckhaut, J. (1986), Lé Syndrome du mannequin (Mannequin syndrome). *Acta Otorhinolaryngol. Belg.*, *40*:678–681.

Cox, J. E. & Sims, J. S. (1988), Ventromedial hypothalamic and paraventricular nucleus lesions damage a common system to produce hyperphagia. *Behav. Brain Res.*, *28*:297–308.

Crisp, A. H. (1965a), Clinical and therapeutic aspects of anorexia nervosa: A study of 30 cases. *J. Psychosom. Res.*, *9*:67–78.

Crisp, A. H. (1965b), Some aspects of the evolution, presentation and follow-up of anorexia nervosa. *Proc. Royal Soc. Med.*, *58*:814–820.

Crisp, A. H. (1977), The differential diagnosis of anorexia nervosa. *Proc. R. Soc. Med.*, *70*:686–90.

Crisp, A. H. (1980), *Anorexia Nervosa: Let Me Be*. New York: Grune and Stratton.

Crisp, A. H. & Burns, T. (1983), The clinical presentation of anorexia nervosa in males. *Int. J. Eat. Dis.*, *2*:5–16.

Crisp. A. H. & Burns, T. & Bhata, V. (1986), Primary anorexia nervosa in the male and female: A comparison of clinical features and prognosis. *Br. J. Med. Psychol.*, *59*:123–132.

Crisp, A. H., Hsu, L. K. G., Harding, B. & Hartshorne, J. (1980), Clinical features of anorexia nervosa: A study of a consecutive series of 102 female patients. *J. Psychosom. Res.*, *24*:179–191.

Dally, P. (1969), *Anorexia Nervosa*. London: Heinemann.

Dally, P. (1984), Anorexia tardive—Late onset marital anorexia nervosa. *J. Psychosom. Res.*, *28*:423–428.

Dare, C. & Holder, A. (1981), Developmental aspects of the interaction between narcissim, self esteem, and object relations. *Int. J. Psycho anal.*, *62*:323–337.

De Coverly Veale, D. M. W. (1987), Exercise dependence. *Br. J. Addiction*, *82*:735–740.

Diamond, H. (1985). *Fit for Life*. New York: Warner Books.

DiBattista, D. & Bedard, M. (1987), Effects of food deprivation on hunger motivation in golden hamsters (Mesocriceius auratus). *J. Comp. Psychol.*, *101*:183–189.

Di Castro, J. M. (1987), Circadian rhythms of the spontaneous meal pattern, macronutrient intake, and mood of humans. *Physiol. Behav.*, *40*:437–446.

Dienstag, E. L. (1986), The transition to parenthood in working and non-working pariparous mothers. Presentation at the American Psychological Association August Meeting, Washington, D.C.

Doyne, E. J., Ossip-Klein, D. J., Bowman, E. D. & Osborn, K. M. (1987), Running vs weight lifting in the treatment of depression. *J. Consult. Clin. Psychol.*, 55:748–754.

Drew, F. L. & Stifel, E. N. (1968), Secondary amenorrhea among young women entering religious life. *Obst. Gyne.*, 32:47–51.

Drewnowski, A., Yee, D. K. & Krahn, D. D. (1988), Bulimia in college women: Incidence and recovery rates. *Am. J. Psychiat.*, 145:753–755.

Eidelberg, L. (1959), Humiliation in masochism. *J. Am. Psychoanal. Assoc.*, 7:274–283.

Eisele, J., Hertsgaard, D. & Light, H. K. (1986), Factors related to eating disorders in young adolescent girls. *Adolescence*, 21:283–290.

Epling, W. F. & Pierce, W. D. (1988), Activity based anorexia: A bio-behavioral perspective. *Int. J. Eat. Dis.*, 7:475–485.

Fairbairn, W. R. D. (1952), *Psychoanalytic Studies of the Personality*. London: Tavistock Publications.

Fairburn, C. G. (1981), A cognitive behavioral approach to the management of bulimia. *Psychol. Med.*, 11:707–711.

Fairburn, C. G. (1985), Cognitive-behavioral treatment for bulimia. In: *Handbook of Psychotherapy for Anorexia Nervosa and Bulimia*, D. G. Garner & P. E. Garfinkel (eds.). New York: Guilford Press.

Fairburn, C. G. & Cooper, P. J. (1984), The clinical features of bulimia nervosa. *Br. J. Psychiat.*, 144:238–246.

Falk, J. L. (1981), The environmental generation of excessive behavior. In: *Behavior in Excess*, S. J. Mule (ed.). New York: Free Press.

Feldman, W., Feldman, E. & Goodman, J. T. (1988), Culture versus biology: Children's attitudes toward thinness and fatness. *Pediatrics*, 81:190–194.

Fernandez, R. C. (1984), Disturbances in cognition: Implications for treatment. In: *Current Treatment of Anorexia Nervosa and Bulimia*, P. S. Powers & R. C. Fernandez (eds.). New York: Karger.

Fichter, M. M. (1987), The anorexia nervosa of Franz Kafka. *Int. J. Eat. Dis.*, 6:367–377.

Fichter, M. M. & Daser, C. (1987), Symptomatology, psychosocial development and gender identity in 42 anorexic males. *Psychol. Med.*, 17:409–418.

Fichter, M. M., Daser, C. & Postpischil, F. (1985), Anorexic syndromes in the male, *J. Psychiat. Res.*, 19:305–313.

Field, T. & Reite, M. (1984), Children's responses to separation from mother during the birth of another child. *Child Dev.*, 55:1308–1316.

Fisher, H. (1989), *The Sex Contract: The Evolution of Human Behavior*. New York: William Morrow.

Flament, M. F., Rapoport, J. L., Berg, C. L., Scerry, W., Kilts, C., Melstrom, B., & Linnoila, M. (1985), Clomipramine treatment of childhood obsessive compulsive disorder, a double blind, controlled study. *Arch. Gen. Psychiat.*, 42:977–983.

Folkins, C. H., & Sine, W. E. (1981), Physical fitness training and mental health. *Am. Psychologist*, 36:373–389.

Ford, M. & Dolan, B. M. (1989), Bulimia associated with spontaneous abortion. *Int. J. Eat. Dis.*, 8:243–245.

Frank, E., Carpenter, L. L. & Kupfer, D. J. (1988), Sex differences in recurrent depression: Are there any that are significant? *Am. J. Psychiat.*, 145:41–45.

Freeman, C. P. L., Barry, F., Turnbull, J. D. & Henderson, A. (1988), A controlled trial of psychotherapy for bulimia. *Br. Med., J.*, 296:521–525.

Freud, A. & Burlingham, D. (1944), *Infants Without Families*. New York: International Universities Press.

Freud, A. (1946), *The Ego and the Mechanisms of Defense*. New York: International Universities Press.

Freud, A. (1952), The role of bodily illness in the life of children. *Psychoanal. Study Child*, 7:69–81.

Freud, S. (1923), The ego and the id. *Standard Edition of the Complete Psychological Works of Sigmund Freud, 19*:3–66. London: Hogarth Press.

Fullerton, D. T., Swift, W. J., Getto, C. J., Carlson, I. H. & Gutsmann, L. D. (1988), Differences in plasma beta-endorphin levels of bulimics. *Int. J. Eat. Dis.*, 7:191–200.

Furnham, A. & Alibhai, M. (1983), Cross-cultural differences in the perception of female body shape. *Psychol. Med.*, 13:829–837.

Gadpaille, W. J., Sanborn, C. F. & Wagner, W. W. (1987), Athletic amenorrhea, major affective disorders, and eating disorders. *Am. J. Psychiat.*, 144:939–942.

Gallup, G. & Poling, D. (1980), *Search for America's Faith*. New York: Abington.

Garfinkel, P. E. (1974), Perception of hunger and satiety in anorexia nervosa. *Psychol. Med.*, 4:309–315.

Garfinkel, P. E., Garner, D. M. & Goldbloom, D. S. (1987), Eating disorders: Implications for the 1990's. *Can. J. Psychiat.*, 32:624–631.

Garfinkel, P. E., Garner, D. M., & Kennedy, S. (1985), Special problems of inpatient management. In: *Handbook of Psychotherapy for Anorexia Nervosa and Bulimia*, D. M. Garner & P. E. Garfinkel (eds.). New York: Guilford Press.

Garfinkel, P. E. & Kaplan, A. S. (1985), Starvation based perpetuating mechanisms in anorexia nervosa and bulimia. *Int. J. Eat. Dis.*, 4:651–665.

Garfinkel, P. E., Moldofsky, H. & Garner, D. M. (1980), The heterogeneity of anorexia nervosa: Bulimia as a distinct subgroup. *Arch. Gen. Psychiat.*, 37:1036–1040.

Garner, D. M. (1985), Cognitive therapy for bulimia nervosa. *Annals of Adol. Psychiat.*, 13:358–390.

Garner, D. M. & Bemis, K. M. (1982), A cognitive-behavioral approach to anorexia nervosa. *Cognitive Therapy Res.*, 6:123–150.

Garner, D. M. & Bemis, K. M. (1985), Cognitive therapy for anorexia nervosa. In: *Handbook of Psychotherapy for Anorexia Nervosa and Bulimia*, D. M. Garner & P. E. Garfinkel (eds). New York: Guilford Press.

Garner, D. M. & Garfinkel, P. E. (1979), The Eating Attitudes Test: An index of the symptoms of anorexia nervosa. *Psychol. Med.*, 9:273–279.

Garner, D. M., & Garfinkel, P. E. (1982), *Anorexia Nervosa: A Multidimensional Perspective*. New York: Brunner/Mazel.

Garner, D. M., Garfinkel, P. E. & Bemis, K. M. (1982), A multidimensional psychotherapy for anorexia nervosa. *Int. J. Eat. Dis.*, 1(2):3–46.

Garner, D. M., Garfinkel, P. E., & O'Shaughnessy, M. (1982), Clinical and psychometric comparison between bulimia in anorexia nervosa and bulimia in normal weight women. Report of The Fourth Ross Laboratory Conference on Medical Research, pp. 6–13.

Garner, D. M., Garfinkel, P. E., & O'Shaughnessy, M. (1985), The validity of the distinction of anorexia nervosa with and without bulimia. *Am. J. Psychiat.*, 142:581–587.

Garner, D. M., Garfinkel, P. E., Rockert, W. & Olmstead, M. P. (1987), A prospective study of eating disorders in the ballet. *Psychother. Psychosom.*, 48: 170–175.

Garner, D. M., Garfinkel, P. E., Schwartz, D. & Thompson, M. (1980), Cultural expectations of thinness in women. *Psychol. Reports, 47:*483–491.

Garner, D. M., Olmsted, M. P. & Polivy, J. (1983), Development and validation of a multi-dimensional Eating Disorder Inventory for anorexia nervosa and bulimia. *Int. J. Eating Dis., 2:* 15–34.

Garner, D. M., Olmsted, M. P., Polivy, J. & Garfinkel, P. E. (1984), Comparison between weight preoccupied women and anorexia nervosa. *Psychosom. Med., 46:*255–266.

Geracioti, T. D. & Liddle, R. A. (1988), Impaired cholecystokinin secretion in bulimia nervosa. *N. Eng. J. Med., 319*(11):683–688.

Geist, R. A. (1989), Self psychological reflections on the origins of eating disorders. *J. Am Acad Psychoanal., 17:*5–27.

Ghodsian, M., Zajicek, E., & Wolkind, S. N. (1984), A longitudinal study of maternal depression and child behavior problems. *J. Child Psychol. Psychiat., 25:*91–110.

Gibbon, E. (1900), Origin, progress and effects of the monastic life. In: *Rise and Fall of the Roman Empire, Vol. III*, H. H. Milman, (ed). Philadelphia: Henry T. Coats & Company.

Gibbs, J. & Smith, J. T. (1985), The physiology of hunger and satiety. In: *Am. Psychiat. Assoc. Annual Review No. 4*, R. E. Hales and A. J. Frances (eds.). Washington, D.C.: Am. Psychiatric Press, Inc.

Glassner, B. (1988), *Why We Look the Way We Do (And How We Feel About It)*. New York: Putnam.

Goldfarb, L. A. & Plante, T. G. (1984), Fear of fat in runners: An examination of the connection between anorexia nervosa and distance running. *Psychol. Reports, 55:*296.

Gontang, A., Clitsome, T. & Kostrubala, T. (1977), A psychological study of 50 sub-3-hour marathoners. *Ann. N. Y. Acad. Sci., 301:*1020–1028.

Goodall, J. (1979), Life and death at Gombe. *National Geographic, 155:*592–621.

Goodsitt, A. (1983), Self-regulatory disturbances in eating disorders. *Int. J. Eat. Dis., 2:*51–60.

Goodsitt, A. (1985), Self-psychology and the treatment of anorexia nervosa. In: *Handbook of Psychotherapy for Anorexia Nervosa and Bulimia*, D. M. Garner & P. E. Garfinkel (eds). New York: Guilford Press, pp. 55–82.

Green, H. (1986), *Fit for America: Health, Fitness, Sport, and American Society*. New York: Pantheon Books.

Greenberg, B. R. & Harvey, P. D. (1987), Affective lability versus depression as determinants of binge eating. *Addict. Behav., 12*(4):357–361.

Greist, J. H., Klein, M. H., Eischens, R. R., Faris, J., Gurman, A. S. & Morgan, W. P. (1979), Running as treatment for depression. *Compr. Psychiat.*, 20(1):41–54.

Grossniklaus, D. M. (1980), Nursing interventions in anorexia nervosa. *J. Perspectives in Psychiat. Care*, 18:11–16.

Gull, W. (1874), Anorexia nervosa. *Trans. Clin. Soc. London*, 7:22–28.

Guntrip, H. (1971), *Psychoanalytic Theory, Therapy, and the Self*. London: Hogarth Press.

Habermas, T. (1986), Friderada: A case of miraculous fasting. *Int. J. Eat. Dis.*, 5:555–562.

Hall, A. (1985), Group psychotherapy for anorexia nervosa. In: *Handbook of Psychotherapy for Anorexia Nervosa and Bulimia*, D. M. Garner & P. E. Garfinkel, (eds.). New York: Guilford Press.

Hall, A., Delahunt, J. W. & Ellis, P. M. (1985), Anorexia in the male. *J. Psychiatr. Res.*, 19:315–321.

Halmi, K. A. (1974), Anorexia nervosa: Demographic and clinical features in 94 cases. *Psychosom. Med.*, 36:18–26.

Halmi, K. A. (1987), Anorexia nervosa and bulimia. *Ann. Rev. Med.*, 38:373–380.

Halmi, K. A., Falk, J. R. & Schwartz, E. (1981), Binge eating and vomiting: a survey of a college population. *Psychol. Med.*, 11:697–706.

Halmi, K. A., Goldberg, S. C., Casper, R. C., Eckert, E. D. & Davis, J. M. (1979), Pretreatment predictors of outcome in anorexia nervosa. *Br. J. Psychiat.*, 134:71–78.

Hamilton, L. H., Brooks-Gunn, J. & Warren, M. P. (1985), Sociocultural influences on eating disorders in professional female ballet dancers. *Int. J. Eat. Dis.*, 4:465–477.

Harding, T. P. & Lachenmeyer, J. R. (1986), Family interaction patterns and locus of control as predictors of the presence and severity of anorexia nervosa. *J. Clin. Psychol.*, 42:440–448.

Harlow, H. F. & Harlow, M. K. (1971), Psychopathology in monkeys. In: *Experimental Psychopathology*, H. D. Kimmel (ed.). New York: Academic Press.

Hart, K. J. & Ollendick, T. H. (1985), Prevalence of bulimia in working and university women. *Am. J. Psychiat.*, 142:851–854.

Hassan, S. (1988), *Combating Cult Mind Control*. Rochester, VT: Park Street Press, distributed by Harper & Row.

Hatsukami, D., Owen, P., Pyle, R. & Mitchell, J. (1982), Similarities and differences on the MMPI between women with bulimia and women with alcohol or drug abuse problems. *Addictive Behav.*, 7:435–439.

Hawkins, R. C. & Clement, P. F. (1980), Development and construct validation of a self report measure of binge eating tendencies. *Addictive Behav.*, 5:219–226.

Heavey, A., Parker, Y., Bhat, A. V., Crisp, A. H. & Gowers, G. G. (1989), Anorexia nervosa and marriage. *Int. J. Eat. Dis.*, 8:275–284.

Hedblom, J. E., Hubbard, F. A. & Anderson, A. E. (1981), Anorexia nervosa: A multidisciplinary treatment program for patient and family. *Social Work & Health Care*, 7:67–86.

Heilbrun, A. B. & Bloomfield, D. L. (1986), Cognitive differences between bulimic and anorexic females: Self controlled deficits in bulimia. *Int. J. Eating Dis.*, 5:209–222.

Heimberg, R. G. & Barlow, D. H. (1988), Psychosocial treatments for social phobia. *Psychosom.*, 29:27–36.

Hennessy, M. B. (1986), Maternal separation alters later consumption of novel liquids in the squirrel monkey. *Behav. Neurol. Biol.*, 45:254–260.

Herman, C. P., & Polivy, J. (1975), Anxiety, restraint and eating behavior. *J. Abnormal Psychol.*, 84:666–672.

Herman, C. P., Polivy, J., Lank, C. N. & Heatherton, T. F. (1987), Anxiety, hunger and eating behavior. *J. Abnormal Psychol.*, 96:264–269.

Hermann, I. (1976), Clinging-going-in-search. *Psychoanal. Quart.*, 45:30–62.

Herzog, D. B. & Copeland, P. M. (1985), Eating disorders. *N. Engl. J. Med.*, 313:295–303.

Herzog, D. B., Norman, D. K., Gordon, C. & Pepose, M. (1984), Sexual conflict and eating disorders in 27 males. *Am. J. Psychiat.*, 141:989–990.

Herzog, D. B., Pepose, M., Norman, D. K. & Rigotti, M. A. (1985), Eating disorders and social maladjustment in female medical students. *J. Nervous Mental Dis.*, 173:734–737.

Hewson, G., Leighton, G. E., Hill, R. G. & Hughes, J. (1988), The cholecystokinin receptor antagonist L364,718 increases food intake in the rat by attenuation of the action of endogenous cholecystokinin. *Br. J. Pharmacol.*, 93:79–84.

Hochschild, A. (1989), *The Second Shift*. New York: Viking Press.

Hock, E. & De Mies, D. (in press), Depression in mothers of infants: The role of maternal employment. *Dev. Psychol.* 26:255–291.

Hofer, M. A. (1984), Relationships as regulators: A psychobiologic perspective on bereavement. *Psychosom. Med.*, 46:183–197.

Hoffer, W. (1949), Development of the body-ego. *Psychoanal. Study Child*, 5:18–23.

Hoffman, L. W. (1979), Maternal employment. *Am. Psychol.*, 34:859–865.

Hoffman, L. W. (1986), Work, family and the child. In: *Psychology and Work: Productivity, Change and Employment*, M. S. Pollak & R. O. Terloff (eds.). Washington, D.C.: Am. Psychol. Assoc.

Hoffman, L. W. (1989), Effects of maternal employment in the two-parent family. *Am. Psychol.*, 44(2):283–292.

Hollander, E., Liebowitz, M. R., Winchel, R., Klumker, A. & Klein, D. F. (1989), Treatment of body-dysmorphic disorder with serotonin reuptake blockers. *Am. J. Psychiat.*, 146:768–770.

Hotta, J., Shibasakat, A., Masuda, A., Imaki, T., Demura, H., Ling, N., Shizume, K. (1986), The responses of plasma adrenocorticotropin and cortisol to corticotropin-releasing hormone (CRH) and cerebrospinal fluid immumnoreactive CRH in anorexia nervosa patients. *J. Clin. Endocrinol. Metab.*, 62(2): 319–324.

Hsu, L. K. G. (1986), The treatment of anorexia nervosa. *Am. J. Psychiat.*, 143:573–581.

Hsu, L. K. G. & Zimmer, B. (1988), Eating disorders in old age. *Int. J. Eat. Dis.*, 7:133–138.

Jacobovits, C., Halsted, P., Kelley, L., Roe, D. A. & Young, C. M. (1977), Eating habits and nutrient intakes of college women over a thirty year period. *J. Am. Dietetic Asso.*, 71:405–411.

Jacobson, J. L. & Wille, D. E. (1984), Influence of attachment and separation experience on separation distress at 18 months. *Dev. Psychol.*, 20:477–484.

Janet, P. (1920), *The Major Symptoms of Hysteria*, (2nd Ed). New York: Hafner Publishing Co.

Johnson, C. H., Gilmore, J. D. & Ramakrishnan, S. S. (1982), Use of a feeding procedure in the treatment of a stress related anxiety disorder. *Behav. Ther. & Exp. Psychiat.*, 13:235–237.

Johnson, C. L. & Connors, M. E. (1987), *The Etiology and Treatment of Bulimia Nervosa*. New York: Basic Books.

Johnson, C. L. & Johnson, F. A. (1980), Parenthood, marriage and careers: Situational constraints and role strain. In: *Dual-Career Couples*, F. Pepitone-Rockwell (ed.), Beverly Hills: Sage Publications.

Johnson, C. L., Stuckey, M. K., Lewis, L. D. & Schwartz, E., (1982), Bulimia: A descriptive survey of 316 cases. *Int. J. Eat. Dis.*, 2:3–16.

Johnson, F. A. (1977), Psychotherapy of alienated individuals. In: *The Narcissistic Condition*, M. C. Nelson (ed). New York: Human Sciences Press.

Johnson-Sabine, E. C., Wood, K. H. & Wakeling, A. (1984), Mood changes in bulimia nervosa. *Brit. J. Psychiat.*, 145:512–516.

Jones, D. J., Fox, M. M., Babigian, H. M., & Hutton, H. E., (1980), Epidemiology of anorexia nervosa in Monroe County, New York: 1960–1976. *Psychosom. Med.*, 42:551–558.

Kaffman, M. & Sadeh, T. (1989), Anorexia nervosa in the kibbutz: Factors influencing the development of a monoideistic fixation. *Int. J. Eat. Dis.*, 8:33–53.

Kagan, D. M. (1987), Addictive personality factors. *J. Psychol.*, 121:533–538.

Kagan, D. M. & Squires, R. L. (1984), Eating disorder among adolescents: Patterns and prevalence. *Adolescence*, 19(73):15–29.

Kahn, M. (1965), *The Privacy of the Self*. New York: International Universities Press.

Kalin, N. H. & Carnes, M. (1984), Biologic correlates of attachment bond disruption in humans and nonhuman primates. *Prog. Neuro-Psychopharmacol. & Biol. Psychiat.*, 8:459–469.

Kalucy, R. S., Crisp, A. H. & Harding, B. (1977), A study of 56 families with anorexia nervosa. *Brit. J. Med. Psychol.*, 50:381–395.

Kalucy, R. S., Gilchrist, P. N., McFarlane, C. M. & McFarlane, A. C. (1985), The evolution of a multitherapy orientation. In: *Handbook of Psychotherapy for Anorexia Nervosa and Bulimia*, D. M. Garner & P. E. Garfinkel (eds). New York: Guilford Press.

Kaplan, H. S. (1979), *Disorders of Sexual Desire*. New York: Brunner-Mazel.

Kassett, J. A., Gwirtsman, H. E., Kaye, W. H., Brandt, H. A. & Jimerson, D. C. (1988), Pattern of onset of bulimic symptoms in anorexia nervosa. *Am. J. Psychiat.*, 145(10):1287–1288.

Katchanoff, R., Leveille, R., McLelland, J. P. & Wayner, M. J. (1973), Schedule-induced behavior in humans. *Physiol. Behav.*, 11:395–398.

Kattanach, L. & Rodin, J. (1988), Psychosocial components of the stress process in bulimia. *Int. J. Eat. Dis.*, 7:75–88.

Katz, J. L. (1985), Some reflections on the nature of the eating disorders: On the need for humility. *Int. J. Eat. Dis.*, 4:617–626.

Katz, J. L. (1986), Long distance running, anorexia nervosa, and bulimia: A report of two cases. *Comprehensive Psychiat.*, 27:74–78.

Katzman, M., Wolchik, S. & Braver, T. (1984), The prevalence of frequent binge eating and bulimia in a non-clinical college sample. *Int. J. Eat. Dis.*, 3:53–62.

Kaye, W. M., Ebert, M. J. & Gwirtsman, H. E. (1984), Differences in brain serotoninergic metabolism between bulimic and non-bulimic patients with anorexia nervosa. *Am. J. Psychiat.*, 141:1598–1601.

Kaye, W. H., Gwirtsman, H., George, T., Ebert, M. H. & Petersen, R. (1986), Caloric consumption and activity levels after weight recovery in anorexia nervosa: A prolonged delay in normalization. *Int. J. Eat. Dis.*, 5:489–502.

Kaye, W. H., Picker, D. M., Naber, D. & Ebert, M. H. (1982), Cerebrospinal fluid opioid activity in anorexia nervosa. *Am. J. Psychiat.*, 139:643–645.

Keniston, K. (1981), As quoted in S. J. Blatt (1984), Narcissism and Egocentrism as concepts in individual and cultural development. *Psychoanal. & Contemp. Thought*, 6:291–303.

Kernberg, O. F. (1975), *Borderline Conditions and Pathological Narcissim.* New York: Jason Aronson.

Kessler, R. C. & McRae, J. A. Jr. (1982), The effect of wives' employment on the mental health of married men and women. *Am. Sociol. Rev.*, 47(2):216–227.

Keys, A., Brozek, J., Henschel, A., Mickelsen, O. & Taylor, H. L. (1950), *The Biology of Human Starvation.* Minneapolis: University of Minnesota Press.

Kinsey, A. C., Pomeroy, W. B. & Martin, C. E. (1948), *Sexual Behavior in the Human Male.* Philadelphia: W. B. Saunders.

Kinsey, A. C., Pomeroy, W. B., Martin, C. E. & Gebhard, P. H. (1953), *Sexual Behavior in the Human Female.* Philadelphia: W. B. Saunders.

Kirkpatrick, S. W. & Sanders, D. M. (1978), Body image stereotypes: A developmental comparison. *J. Gene. Psychol.*, 132:87–95.

Klein, A. M. (1985), Pumping iron. *Society*, 22:68–75.

Klein, A. M. (1987), Fear and self-loathing in Southern California: Narcissism and fascism in bodybuilding subculture. *J. Psychoanal. Anthropology*, 10:117–137.

Klein, M. (1946), Notes on some schizoid mechanisms. *Int. J. Psychoanal.*, 27:99–110.

Kleinke, C. L. & Staneski, R. A. (1980), First impressions of female bust size. *J. Social Psychol.*, 110:123–134.

Kohut, H. (1971), *The Analysis of the Self.* New York: International Universities Press.

Kohut, H. (1977), *The Restoration of the Self.* New York: International Universities Press.

Kope, T. M. & Sack, W. H. (1987), Anorexia nervosa in Southeast Asian refugees:

A report on three cases. *J. Am. Acad. Child & Adol. Psychiat.*, 26:795–797.

Kraemer, G. W. (1986), Causes of changes in brain noradrenaline systems and later effects on responses to social stressors in rhesus monkeys: The cascade hypothesis. *Ciba Found. Symp.*, 123:216–233.

Kron, L., Katz, J. L., Gorzynski, G. & Weiner, H. (1978), Hyperactivity in anorexia nervosa: A fundamental clinical feature. *Comprehensive Psychiat.*, 19:433–440.

Lacey, J. H. (1983), Bulimia nervosa, binge eating and psychogenic vomiting: A control treament study and long-term outcome. *Br. Med. J.*, 286:1611–1613.

Lachenmeyer, J. R., Muni-Brander, P. & Belford, S. (1988), Laxative abuse for weight control in adolescents. *Int. J. Eat. Dis.*, 7:849–852.

Laessle, R. G., Kittl, S., Fichter, M. M. & Pirke, K. M. (1988), Cognitive correlates of depression in patients with eating disorders. *Int. J. Eat. Dis.*, 7:681–686.

Lasch, C. (1978), *The Culture of Narcissism.* New York: Norton.

Lasegue, C. (1873), L'anorexie hystérique. *Arch. Gen. Med.*, 21:385–403.

Laudenslager, M. L., Reite, M. & Harbeck, R. (1983), Suppressed immune response in infant monkeys associated with maternal separation. *Behav. Neurol. Biol.*, 36:40–46.

Lax, R. (1972), Some aspects of the interaction between mother and impaired child: Mother's narcisstic trauma. *Int. J. Psychoanal.* 53:339–344.

Lazerson, J. S. (1984), Voices of bulimia: Experiences in integrated psychotherapy. *Psychother.*, 21(4):500–509.

Lerner, R. M., Orlos, J. B. & Knapp, J. R. (1976), Physical attractiveness, physical effectiveness, and self concept in late adolescents. *Adolescence*, 11:313–326.

Lingswiler, V. M., Crowther, J. H. & Stephens, M. A. P. (1989), Affective and cognitive antecedents to eating episodes in bulimia and binge eating. *Int. J. Eat. Dis.*, 8:533–539.

Little, J. C. (1969), The athlete's neurosis—a deprivation crisis. *Acta Psychiatr. Scand.*, 45:187–197.

Long, C. G. & Cordle, C. J. (1982), Psychological treatment of binge-eating and self-induced vomiting. *Brit. J. Med. Psychol.*, 55: 139–145.

Loosli, A. R., Benson, J., Gillian, D. M. & Bourdet, K. (1986), Nutrition habits and knowledge in competitive adolescent female gymnasts. *Phys. Sports Med.*, 14:118–130.

Lorenz, K. & Leyhausen, P. (1973), *Motivation of Humans and Animal Behavior.* Behav. Sci. Series. New York: Van Nostrand Reinhold Company.

Luby, E. D., Marrazzi, M. A. & Kinzie, J. (1987), Treatment of chronic anorexia with opiate blockade. *J. Clin. Psychopharmacol.*, 7:52–53.

Luger, A., Deuster, P. A., Kyle, S. B., Gallucci, W. T., Montgomery, L. C., Gold, P. W., Loriaux, D. L. & Chrousos, G. P. (1987), Acute, hypothalamic-pituitary-adrenal responses to the stress of treadmill exercise. Physiological adaptations to physical training. *N. Engl. J. Med.*, 316:1309–1315.

Lundholm, J. K. & Littrell, J. M. (1986), Desire for thinness among high school cheerleaders: Relationship to disordered eating and weight control behaviors. *Adolescence*, 21:573–579.

Maccoby, E. E. & Feldman, S. S. (1972), Mother attachment and stranger reactions in the third year of life. *Monogr. Soc. Res. Child Dev.*, 37:Serial No. 146.

Macoby, M. (1977), *The Gamesman: The New Corporate Leaders*. New York: Simon and Schuster.

Mahler, M. S. (1972), On the first three subphases of the separation-individuation process. *Int. J. Psychoanal.*, 53:333–338.

Mahler, M. S. & McDevitt, J. B. (1982), Thoughts on the emergence of the sense of self, with particular emphasis on the body self. *J. Am. Psychoanal. Assoc.*, 30:827–849.

Mahler, M. S., Pine, F. & Bergman, A. (1975), *The Psychological Birth of the Human Infant*. New York: Basic Books.

Malenbaum, R., Herzog, D., Eisenthal, S. & Wyshak, G. (1988), Overeaters Anonymous: Impact on bulimia. *Int. J. Eating Dis.*, 7:139–144.

Maloney, M. J., McGuire, J. B. & Daniels, S. R. (1988), Reliability testing of a children's version of the Eating Attitude Test. *J. Am. Acad. Child. & Adol. Psychiat.*, 27:541–543.

Maloney, M. J., McGuire, J., Daniels, S. R. & Specker, B. (1989), Dieting behavior and eating attitudes in children. *Pediatrics*, 84: 482–489.

Markoff, R. A., Ryan, P. & Young, T. (1982), Endorphins and mood changes in long distance running. *Med. Sci. Sports Exer.*, 14:11–15.

Masterson, J. F. (1977), Primary anorexia nervosa in the borderline adolescent: An object relations view. In: *Borderline Personality Disorders*, P. Harticollis, (ed.). New York: International Universities Press.

Mavisskalian, M. (1982), Anorexia nervosa treated with response prevention and prolonged exposure. *Behav. Res. Ther.*, 20:27–31.

McCormick, W. O. (1975), Amenorrhea and other menstrual symptoms in student nurses. *J. Psychosom. Res.*, 19:131–137.

McFarlane, A. C., McFarlane, C. M. & Gilchrist, P. N. (1988), Posttraumatic bulimia and anorexia nervosa. *Int. J. Eat. Dis.*, 7:705–708.

Meyer, B. C. & Weinroth, L. A. (1957), Observations on psychological aspects of anorexia nervosa. *Psychosom. Med.*, 19:389–398.

Mickalide, A. D. & Anderson, A. E. (1985), Subgroups of anorexia nervosa and bulimia: validity and utility. *J. Psychiat. Res.*, 19(2–3):121–128.

Milkman, H. B. & Sunderwirth, S. G. (1987), *Craving for Ecstasy*, p. 77. Lexington, Mass.: D. C. Heath.

Mintz, N. E. (1982), Bulimia: A new perspective in clinical social work. *Clinical Social Work*, 10:289–301.

Minuchin, S. (1974), *Families and Family Therapy*. Cambridge, Massachusetts: Harvard University Press.

Mitchell, J. E. (1987), Pharmacology of anorexia nervosa. In: *Psychopharmacology: The Third Generation of Progress*, H. Y. Meltzer (ed). New York: Raven Press.

Mitchell, J. E., Hatsukami, D., Goff, G., Pyle, R. L., Eckert, E. D. & Davis, L. E. (1985), Intensive outpatient group treatment for bulimia. In: *Handbook of Psychotherapy for Anorexia Nervosa & Bulimia*, D. M. Garner, & P. E. Garfinkel, (eds). New York: Guilford Press.

Mitchell, J. E., Laine, D. E., Morley, J. E. & Levine, A. S. (1986), Naloxone but not CCK-8 may attenuate binge-eating behavior in patients with the bulimia syndrome. *Biol. Psychiat.*, 21:1399–1406.

Mitchell, J. E., Pyle, R. L. & Eckert, E. D. (1985), Bulimia. In: *American Psychiatric Association Annual Review (Vol 4)*, R. E. Hales & A. J. Frances (eds.). Washington: American Psychiatric Press.

Mitchell, J. E., Pyle, R. L., Hatsukami, D. E. & Eckert, E. D. (1986), What are atypical eating disorders? *Psychosomatics, 27:*21–28.

Modell, A. H. (1975), A narcissistic defence against affects and the illusion of self-sufficiency. *Int. J. Psychoanal., 56:*275–282.

Mogul, S. L. (1980), Asceticism in adolescence and anorexia nervosa. *Psychoanal. Study Child, 35:*155–175.

Mohanti, B. & Mishra, P. K. (1984), Hunger drive and spontaneous activity in albino rats. *Psychol. Res. J., 8:*18–25.

Moore, K. (1990), Sons of the wind. *Sports Illustrated, 72(8):*72–84.

Moore, R., Mills, I. H. & Forster, A. (1981), Naloxone in the treatment of anorexia nervosa: Effect of weight gain and lipolysis. *J. Res. Soc. Med., 74:*129–131.

Morgan, W. P. (1979), Negative addiction in runners. *Phys. Sports Med., 7:*57–70.

Morgan, W. P., Brown, D. R., Ragland, J. S., O'Connor, P. J. & Ellickson, K. A. (1987), Monitoring of overtraining and staleness. *Br. J. Sports Med., 21(3):*107–114.

Morgan, W. P. & Costill, D. C. (1972), Psychological characteristics of the marathon runners. *J. Sports Med. & Physical Fitness, 12:*42–46.

Morgan, H. G. & Russell, G. S. M. (1975), Value of family background and clinical features as predictors of long-term outcome in anorexia nervosa: Four year follow-up study of 41 patients. *Psychol. Med., 5:*355–371.

Morton, R. (1714), Phthisologia sev exercitationom de phthisi ulmac: Daniel Bartholomae.

Moss, R. A., Jennings, G., McFarland, J. H., & Carter, P. (1984), Binge-eating, vomiting and weight fear in a female high school population. *J. Family Practice, 18:*313–320.

Neimeyer, G. J. & Khouzam, N. (1985), A repertory grid study of restrained eaters. *Brit. J. Med. Psychol., 58:*365–367.

Newman, J. D., Murphy, M. R., & Harbough, C. R. (1982), Naloxone-reversible suppression of isolation cell production after morphine injections in squirrel monkeys. *Social Neurosci. Abstracts, 8:*940.

Norman, D. K. & Herzog, D. B. (1983), Bulimia, anorexia, and anorexia nervosa with bulimia: A comparative analysis of MMPI profiles. *Int. J. Eat. Dis., 2:*43–52.

Norman, D. K., Herzog, D. B., & Chauncey, S. (1986), A one-year outcome study of bulimia: Psychological and eating symptom changes in treatment and non-treatment group. *Int. J. Eating Dis., 5:*47–57.

Norris, D. L. (1984), The effects of mirror confrontation on self-estimation of body dimensions in anorexia nervosa, bulimia, and two control groups. *Psychol. Med., 14:*835–842.

Novak, M. A. & Harlow, H. F. (1979), Social recovery of monkeys isolated for the first year of life: II. Long term assessment. *Dev. Psychol., 15:*50–61.

Nudelman, S., Rosen, J. D. & Leitenberg, H. (1988), Dissimilarities in eating attitudes, body image distortion, depression, and self-esteem between high-intensity male runners and women with bulimia nervosa. *Int. J. Eat. Dis.,* 7(5):625–634.

Nussbaum, M., Shenker, I. R., Baird, D. & Saravay, S. (1985), Follow-up investigation in patients with anorexia nervosa. *J. Ped., 106:835–840.*

Oliner, M. M. (1982), The anal phase. In: *Early Female Development: Current Psychoanalytic Views,* D. Mendell (ed). New York: Spectrum.

Owens, R. G. & Slade, P. D. (1987), Running and anorexia nervosa: An empirical study. *Int. J. Eat. Dis.,* 6:771–775.

Oyebode, F., Boodhoo, J. A. & Schapira, K. (1988), Anorexia nervosa in males: Clinical features and outcome. *Int. J. Eating Dis.,* 7:121–124.

Panken, S. (1973), *The Joy of Suffering.* New York: Aronson.

Panksepp, J., Sivey, S. M., & Normansell, L. A. (1985), Brain opiates and social emotions. In: *Psychobiology of Attachment and Separation,* M. Reite & T. Fields (eds.). Orlando, FL: Academic Press.

Pantano, M. E. & Santonastaso, P. (1989), A case of dysmorphophobia following recovery from anorexia nervosa. *Int. J. Eat. Dis., 8:701–704.*

Pasman, L. & Thompson, J. K. (1988), Body image and eating disturbance in obligatory runners, obligatory weightlifters, and sedentary individuals. *Int. J. Eat. Dis.,* 7:759–769.

Paxton, L. (1982), Physiological and psychological effects of short term exercise addiction on habitual runners. *J. Sport Psychol.,* 4:73–80.

Perse, T. L., Greist, J. H., Jefferson, J. W., Rosenfeld, R. & Dar, R. (1987), Fluvoxamine treatment of obsessive-compulsive disorder. *Am. J. Psychiat., 144:1543–1548.*

Piaget, J. (1945), *Play, Dreams, and Imitation in Childhood.* New York: Norton.

Pillay, M. & Crisp, A. A. (1977), Some psychological characteristics of patients with anorexia nervosa whose weight has been newly restored. *Br. J. Med. Psychol.,* 50(4):375–380.

Polivy, J. & Herman, C. P. (1976), The effects of alcohol on eating behavior. Disinhibition or sedation? *Addictive Behav., 1:121–125.*

Polivy, J. & Herman, C. P. (1987), Diagnosis and treatment of normal eating. *J. Consulting Clinical Psychology,* 55:635–644.

Pope, H. G. & Hudson, J. I. (1989), Are eating disorders associated with borderline personality disorder? A critical review. *Int. J. Eat. Dis.,* 8:1–9.

Pratt, E. L. (1984), Historical perspectives: Food, feeding, and fancies. *J. Am. College Nutrition,* 3:115–121.

Pumariega, A. J. (1986), Acculturation and eating attitudes in adolescent girls: A comparative and correlational study. *J. Am. Acad. Child & Adol. Psychiat.,* 25:276–279.

Pyle, R. L., Mitchell, J. E. & Eckert, E. D. (1981), Bulimia: A report of 34 cases. *J. Clin. Psychiat., 42:60–64.*

Pyle, R. L., Mitchell, J. E., Eckert, E. D., Halvorson, P. A., Newman, P. A. & Golff, G. M. (1983), The incidence of bulimia in freshman college students. *Int. J. Eating Dis.,* 2:75–85.

Raboch, J. (1986), Sexual development and life of psychiatric female patients. *Arch. Sex. Behav.,* 15(4):341–353.

Raciti, M. C. & Norcross, J. C. (1987), The EAT and EDI: Screening interrelationships, and psychometrics. *Int. J. Eating Dis.*, 6:579–586.

Rapoport, J. L. (1986), Childhood obsessive compulsive disorder. *J. Child Psychol. Psychiat.*, 27:289–295.

Rapoport, J. L. (1989), The biology of obsessions and compulsions. *Sci. Am.*, 260:82–89.

Rasmussen, S. A. (1984), Lithium and tryptophan augmentation in clomipramine-resistant obsessive-compulsive disorder. *Am. J. Psychiat.*, 141:1283–1285.

Reite, M., Short, R., Seiler, C. & Pauley, J. D. (1981), Attachment, loss and separation. *J. Child Psychol. Psychiat.*, 22:141–169.

Rheingold, H. L., & Eckerman, C. O. (1970), The infant separates himself from his mother. *Science, 168:*78–83.

Richert, A. J. & Hummers, J. A. (1986), Patterns of physical activity in college students at possible risk for eating disorders. *Int. J. Eat. Dis.*, 5:757–763.

Richman, N. (1975), Prevalence of behaviour problems in 3-year-old children in a London borough. *J. Child Psychol. Psychiat.*, 16:272–287.

Rippon, C., Nash, J., Myburgh, K. H., & Noakes, T. D. (1988), Abnormal eating attitude test scores predict menstrual dysfunction in lean females. *Int. J. Eating Dis.*, 7:617–624.

Risch, S. C., Ganowsky, D. S., Judd, L. L., Gillin, J. C. & McClure, S. F. (1983), The role of endogenous opioid systems in neuroendocrine regulation. *Psychiatric Clinics of North America, 6:*429–441.

Ritvo, S. (1984), The image and uses of the body in psychic conflict. *Psychoanal. Study Child, 39:*449–469.

Rosen, J. C. & Leitenberg, H. (1982), Bulimia nervosa: Treatment with exposure and response prevention. *Behav. Ther.*, 13:117–124.

Rosen, L. W., McKeag, D. B., Hough, D. O. & Curley, V. (1986), Pathogenic weight control in female athletes. *Phys. Sports Med.*, 14:79–86.

Rosenblum, I. A. & Paully, G. S. (1987), Primate models of separation induced depression. *Psychiatric Clinics of North America, 10:*437–447.

Ross, D. R., Lewin, R., Gold, K., Ghuman, H. S., Rosenblum, B., Salzberg, S. & Brooks, A. M. (1988), The psychiatric uses of cold wet sheet packs. *Am. J. Psychiat.*, 145:242–245.

Rothenberg, A. (1986), Eating disorder as a modern obsessive-compulsive syndrome. *Psychiatry, 49:*45–53.

Rothenberg, A. (1988), Differential diagnosis of anorexia nervosa and depressive illness: A review of 11 studies. *Comp. Psychiat.*, 28:427–432.

Routennberg, A. (1968), Self starvation of rats living in activity wheels: Adaptation effects. *J. Comp. Physiol. Psychol.*, 66:234–238.

Rowland, N. E. & Antelman, S. M. (1976), Stress-induced hyperphagia and obesity in rats: A possible model for understanding human obesity. *Science, 191:*310–312.

Russell, G. F. M. (1970), Anorexia nervosa—its identity as an illness and its treatment. In: *Modern Trends in Psychological Medicine,* J. H. Price (ed). London: Butterworths.

Russell, G. F. M., (1979), Bulimia Nervosa: An ominous variant of anorexia nervosa. *Psychol. Med.*, 9:429–448.

Sachs, M. L. & Pargman, D. (1979), Running addiction: A depth interview examination. *J. Sport Behav.*, 2:143–155.

Sacks, M. H. (1979), A psychodynamic overview of sport. *Psychiatric Ann.*, 9:127–133.

Sacks, M. H. (1981), A psychoanalytic perspective on running. In: *The Psychology of Running*, M. H. Sacks (Ed). Champaign, Illinois: Human Kinetics Press.

Sandler, J. (1960), The background of safety. *Int. J. Psychoanal.*, 41:352–356.

Sandler, J. (1987), The concept of projective identification. *Bull. Anna Freud Centre*, 10:33–49.

Sandler, J. & Rosenblatt, B. (1962), The concept of the representational world. *Psychoanal. Study Child*, 17:128–145.

Sanger, D. J. & McCarthy, P. S. (1980), Differential effects of morphine on food and water intake in food deprived and freely feeding rats. *Psychopharmacology*, 72:103–106.

Schilder, P. (1950), *The Image and Appearance of the Human Body*. New York: International University Press.

Schneider, J. A. & Agras, W. S. (1987), Bulimia in males: A matched comparison with females. *Int. J. Eating Dis.*,6:235–242.

Schunk, D. H. (1986), Verbalization and children's self-regulated learning. *Contemp. Ed. Psychol.*, 11:34.

Schunk, D. H. (1989), Social Cognitive Theory and Self-Regulated Learning. In: *Self-Regulated Learning and Academic Achievement: Theory, Research, and Practice*, B. J. Zimmerman & D. H. Schunk (eds.). New York: Springer-Verlag.

Schwartz, D. M. & Thompson, M. G. (1981), Do anorectics get well? Current research and future needs. *Am. J. Psychiat.*, 138:319–323.

Schwartz, D. M., Thompson, M. G., & Johnson, C. L. (1982), Anorexia nervosa and bulimia: The socio-cultural context. *Int. J. Eating Dis.*, 1:20–36.

Schwartzenegger, A. & Hall, D. K. (1982), *Arnold: The Education of a Bodybuilder*. New York: Pocket Books.

Scott, J. T. (1974), Effects of psychotropic drugs on separation and distress in dogs: *Neuropsychopharmacology*. Proceedings of the IX Congress of the Collegium Internationale Neuropharmacologicum (Paris). J. R. Boissier, H. Hippius, & P. Pichot (eds.). New York: American Elsevier Publishing Company, 359:735–745.

Scott, D. W. (1987), The involvement of psychosexual factors in the causation of eating disorders: Time for a reappraisal. *Int. J. Eating Dis.*, 6:199–213.

Segal, H. (1973), *Introduction to the Work of Melanie Klein*. London: Hogarth.

Selvini-Palazzoli, M. (1978), *Self Starvation: From Individual to Family Therapy in the Treatment of Anorexia Nervosa*. New York: Jason Aronson.

Shanan, J., Brzezins, A., Sulman, F. & Sharon, M. (1965), Active coping behavior, anxiety, and cortical steroid excretion in the prediction of transient amenorrhea. *Behav. Sci.*, 10:461–465.

Sheehan, G. (1979), Negative addiction: A runner's perspective. *Phys. Sports Med.*, 7:49.

Siegel, P. S. & Steinberg, M. (1949), Activity level as a function of hunger. *J. Comp. Physiol. Psychol., 42:*412–426.

Silber, T. J. (1986), Anorexia nervosa in Blacks and Hispanics. *Int. J. Eat. Dis., 5:*121–128.

Silverstein, B., Peterson, B. & Perdue, L. (1986), Some correlates of the thin standard of attractiveness in women. *Int. J. Eating Dis., 5:*145–159.

Small, A. C. (1984), The contributions of psychodiagnostic test results towards understanding anorexia nervosa. *Int. J. Eat. Dis., 3:*47–59.

Smart, D. E., Beumont, P. J. V. & George, G. C. W. (1976), Some personality characteristics of patients with anorexia nervosa. *Br. J. Psychiat., 128:*57–60.

Smith, A. M., Scott, S. G., O'Fallon, W. M. & Young, M. L. (1990), Emotional responses of athletes to injury. *Mayo Clin. Proc., 65:*38–50.

Smith, N. J. (1980), Excessive weight loss and food aversion in athletes simulating anorexia nervosa. *Pediatrics, 66:*139–142.

Sobal, J. & Stunkard, A. J. (1989), Socioeconomic status and obesity: A review of the literature. *Psychol. Bull., 105:*260–275.

Socarides, C. (1958), The function of moral masochism: With special reference to the defence processes. *Int. J. Psychoanal., 39:*587–597.

Sours, J. A. (1974), The anorexia nervosa syndrome. *Int. J. Psychoanal., 55:*567–576.

Sours, J. A. (1980), *Starving to Death in a Sea of Objects: The Anorexia Nervosa Syndrome.* New York: Jason Aronson.

Speroff, L. & Redwine, D. B. (1980), Exercise and menstrual function. *Physician Sports Medicine, 8:*42.

Steiger, H., Van der Feen, J., Goldstein, C., & Leichner, P. (1989), Defense styles and parental bonding in eating-disordered women. *Int. J. Eating Dis., 8:*131–140.

Stein, H. F. (1982), Neo-Darwinism and survival through fitness in Reagan's America. *J. Psychohistory, 10:*163–182.

Stern, D. N. (1985), *The Interpersonal World of the Infant.* New York: Basic Books.

Stern, S. L., Dixon, K. N., Jones, D., Lake, M., Nemzer, E., & Sansone, R. (1989), Family environment in anorexia nervosa and bulimia. *Int. J. Eat. Dis., 8:*25–31.

Sternbach, H. A., Annitto, W., Pottash, A. L. C. & Gold, M. (1982), Anorexic effects of naltrexone in man. *Lancet,1:*388–389.

Stoller, R. J. (1976), Sexual excitement. *Arch. Gen. Psychiat., 33:*899–909.

Stone, E., Bonnet, K. & Hofer, M. A. (1976), Survival and development of maternally deprived rats: Role of body temperature. *Psychosom. Med., 38:*242–249.

Stonehill, E. & Crisp, A. H. (1977), Psychoneurotic characteristics of patients with anorexia nervosa before and after treatment and at follow-up 4–7 years later. *J. Psychosom. Res., 21*(3):187–193.

Striegel-Moore, R. S., McAvay, G., Rodin, J. (1986), Psychological and behavioral correlates of feeling fat in women. *Int. J. Eat. Dis., 5:*935–947.

Striegel-Moore, R. H., Silberstein, L. R., Frensch, P., & Rodin, J. (1989), A prospective study of disordered eating among college students. *Int. J. Eat. Dis., 8:*499–509.

Strober, M. (1980), Personality and symptomatological features in young, nonchronic anorexia nervosa patients. *J. Psychosom. Res., 24:*353–359.

Strober, M. (1985), Personality factors in anorexia nervosa. *Pediatrics, 2:*134–138.

Strober, M. & Katz, J. L. (1987). Do eating disorders and affective disorders share a common etiology? A dissenting opinion. *Int. J. Eat. Dis., 6:*171–180.

Stunkard, A. (1990), A description of eating disorders in 1932. *Am. J. Psychiat., 147*(3):263–268.

Sturmey, P. & Slade, P. D. (1986), Anorexia nervosa and dysmorphophobia. *Br. J. Psychiat., 149:*780–782.

Sugarman, A., Quinlan, D. M. & Devenis, L. (1981), Anorexia nervosa as a defense against anaclitic depression. *Int. J. Eat. Dis., 1*(1):44–61.

Sugarman, A. & Kurash, C. (1982), The body as a transitional object in bulimia. *Int. J. Eat. Dis., 1*(4):57–67.

Swedo, S. E., Rapoport, J. L., Leonard, H., Lenane, M. & Cheslow, D. (1989), Obsessive-compulsive disorder in children and adolescents. *Arch. Gen. Psychiat., 46:*335–341.

Swift, W. J. (1982), The long term outcome of early onset anorexia nervosa: A critical review. *J. Am. Acad. Child & Adol. Psychiat., 21:*38–46.

Swift, W. J. (1985), Assessment of the bulimic patient. *Am. J. Orthopsychiat., 55*(3):384–396.

Swift, W. J., Andrews, D. & Barklage, N. E. (1986), The relationship between affective disorder and eating disorders: A review of the literature. *Am. J. Psychiat., 141:*290–299.

Swift, W. J. & Letven, R. (1984), Bulimia and the basic fault: A psychoanalytic interpretation of the binging-vomiting syndrome. *J. Am. Acad. Child Psychiat., 23:*489–497.

Szmulker, G. I., McCance, C., McCrone, L. & Hunter, D. (1986), Anorexia nervosa: A psychiatric case register study from Aberdeen. *Psychol. Med., 16:*49–58.

Tabin, J. (1985), *On the Way to Self: Ego and Early Oedipal Development.* New York: Columbia University Press.

Teitelbaum, P. (1957), Random and food-directed activity in hyperphagic and normal rats. *J. Comp. Physiol. Psychol., 50:*489–490.

Teusch, R. (1988), Level of ego development and bulimics' conceptualizations of their disorder. *Int. J. Eat. Dis., 7:*607–615.

Thirer, J., Zackheim, M. A., & Summers, D. A. (1987), The influence of depression on selected motor performance tasks by college athletes and nonathletes. *Educational Psychological Res., 7:*75–89.

Thompson, D. A., Berg, K. M. & Shatford, L. A. (1987), The heterogeneity of bulimic symtomology: Cognitive and behavioral dimensions. *Int. J. Eat. Dis., 6:*215–234.

Thompson, P. D., Stern, M. P., Williams, P., Duncan, K., Haskell, W. L. & Wood, P. D. (1979), Death during jogging or running: A study of 18 cases. *J.A.M.A., 242:*1265–1267.

Timko, C., Striegel-Moore, R. H., Silberstein, L. R. & Rodin, J. (1987), Femininity/Masculinity and disordered eating in women: How are they related? *Int. J. Eat. Dis., 6:*701–712.

Torras De Bea, E. (1987), Body schema and identity. *Int. J. Psychoanal.*, 68:175–184.

Touyz, S. W., Beumont, P. J. V. & Hook, S. (1987), Exercise anorexia: A new dimension in anorexia nervosa? In: *Handbook of Eating Disorders, Part I.* G. D. Burrows, P. J. V. Beumont, & R.C. Casper, (eds.). New York: Elsevier Science Publishers.

Tucker, L. A. (1987), Effect of weight training on body attitudes: Who benefits most? *J. Sports Med.*, 27:70–78.

Turnbull, I., Freeman, C. P. L., Barry, F. & Henderson, A., (1989), The clinical characteristics of bulimic women. *Int. J. Eat. Dis.*, 8:399–409.

Vaillant, G. (1977), *Adaptation to Life.* Boston: Little, Brown.

Van den Broucke, S. & Vandereycken, W. (1986), Risk factors for the development of eating disorders in adolescent exchange students: An exploratory survey. *J. Adol.*, 9(2):45–50.

Vanderheyden, D. A. & Boland, F. J. (1987), A comparison of normals, mild, moderate, and severe binge eaters, and binge vomiters using discriminant function analysis. *Int. J. Eat. Dis.*, 6:331–337.

Vanderheyden, D. A., Fekken, G. C. & Boland, F. J. (1988), Critical variables associated with binging and bulimia in a university population: A factor analytic study. *Int. J. Eat. Dis.*, 7:321–329.

Van der Kolk, B. A. (1987), The separation cry and the trauma response: Developmental issues in the psychobiology of attachment and separation. In: *Psychological Trauma.* Washington, D.C.: American Psychiatric Press.

Van-Gend, M. A. & Noakes, T. D. (1987), Menstrual patterns in ultramarathon runners. *So. African Med. J.*, 5:788–793.

Veroff, J., Douvan, E. & Kulka, R. A. (1981), *The Inner American: A Self Portrait from 1957–1976.* New York: Basic Books.

Wadden, T. A., Foster, G. D., Stunkard, A. J., & Linowitz, J. R. (1989), Dissatisfaction with weight and figure in obese girls: Discontent but not depression. *Int. J. Obes.*, 13: 89–97.

Waller, B. F. & Roberts, W. C. (1980), Sudden death while running in conditioned runners aged 40 or over. *Am. J. Cardiology*, 45:1292–1300.

Walsh, B. T., Katz, J. L., Levin, J., Kream, J., Fukushima, D. K., Weiner, H., and Zumoff, B., (1981), The production rate of cortisol declines during recovery from anorexia nervosa. *J. Clin. Endocrinol. Metab.*, 53:203–205.

Walsh, B. T., Kissileff, H. R., Cassidy, S. M., & Dantzic, S. (1989), Eating behavior of women with bulimia. *Arch. Gen. Psychiat.*, 46:54–58.

Walsh, B. T., Roose, S. P., Glassman, Stewart, J. W., et al., (1985), Bulimia and depression. *Psychosom. Med.*, 47:123–131.

Wardle, J., & Foley, E. (1989), Body image: Stability and sensitivity of body satisfaction and body size estimation. *Int. J. Eating Dis.*, 8:55–62.

Wazeter, M. & Lewis, G. (1989), *Dark Marathon: The Mary Wazeter Story.* Grand Rapids, MI: Zonderlean.

Weinraub, M., Yaeger, E. & Hoffman, L. W. (1988), Predicting infant outcomes in families of employed and unemployed mothers. *Early Childhood Res. Quart.*, 3:361–378.

Weinstein, H. M. & Richman, A. (1984), The group treatment of bulimia. *J. Am. Coll. Health Assoc.*, 32:208–213.

Wellman, H. M. (1988), First steps in the child's theorizing about the mind. In: *Developing Theories of Minds*, J. Astington, P. Harris & O. Olson (eds.). New York: Cambridge University Press.

Wells, J. E., Coope, P. A., Gabb, D. C. & Pears, R. K. (1985), The factor structure of the Eating Attitudes Test with adolescent school girls. *Psychol. Med.*, 15:141–146.

Wheeler, G. D., Wall, S. R., Belcastro, A. N., Conger, P. & Cumming, D. C. (1986), Are anorexic tendencies prevalent in the habitual runner? *Br. J. Sports Med.*, 20:77–81.

Wiener, S. G., Johnson, D. F. & Levine, S. (1987), Influence of postnatal rearing conditions on the response of squirrel monkey infants to brief perturbations in mother-infant relationships. *Physiol. & Behav.*, 39:21–26.

Wilmore, J. H. & Behnke, A. R. (1969), An anthropometric estimation of body density and lean body weight in young men. *J. Appl. Physiol*, 27:25–31.

Wilmore, J. H., Brown, C. H. & Davis, J. A. (1977), Body physique and composition of the female distance runner. *Ann. N.Y. Acad. Sci.*, 301:764–776.

Winnicott, D. W. (1965a), Psychiatric disorders in terms of infantile maturational processes. In: *The Maturational Processes and the Facilitating Environment: Studies in the Theory of Emotional Development*. New York: International Universities Press.

Winnicott, D. W. (1965b), The capacity to be alone. In: *The Maturational Processes and the Facilitating Environment: Studies in the Theory of Emotional Development*. New York: International Universities Press.

Winnicott, D. W. (1971), *Playing and Reality*. London: Tavistock Publications.

Wolpe, J. (1958), *Psychotherapy and Reciprocal Inhibition*. Stanford, CA: Stanford University Press.

Wood, E., & Paley, S. (1988), Some female psychiatrists ignore own advice. *The Psychiatric Times*, December.

Woodall, C. (1987), The body as a transitional object in bulimia: A critique of the concept. *Adolescent Psychiat.*, 14:179–184.

Wooley, S. & Wooley, W. (1979), Obesity, and women—I: A closer look at the facts. *Women's Studies International Quarterly*, 2:69–79.

Wooley, S. C., & Wooley, O. W. (1985), Intensive outpatient and residential treatment for bulimia. In: *Handbook of Psychotherapy for Anorexia Nervosa and Bulimia*, D. M. Garner, & P. E. Garfinkel (eds.). New York: Guilford Press.

Yager, J. (1984), Bulimia. *Resident & Staff Physician*, 30(2):44–58.

Yager, J., Kurtzman, F., Landsverk, J. & Wiesmeier, E. (1988), Behaviors and attitudes related to eating disorders in homosexual male college students. *Am. J. Psychiat.*, 145:495–497.

Yager, J., Landsverk, J. & Edelstein, C. K. (1987), A 20-month follow-up study of 628 women with eating disorders. I: Course and severity. *Am. J. Psychiat.*, 144: 1172–1177.

Yager, J. & Strober, M. (1985), Family aspects of eating disorders. In: *American Psychiatric Association Annual Review (Vol. 4)*, R. E. Hales & A. J. Frances, (eds.). Washington: American Psychiatric Press.

Yates, A. (1987), Eating disorders and long distance running: The ascetic condition. *Integr. Psychiat.*, 5:201–211.

Yates, A. (1989), Current perspectives on the eating disorders: I. History, psychological and biological aspects. *J. Am. Acad. Child & Adol. Psychiat.*, 28(6): 813–828.

Yates, A. (1990), Current perspectives on the eating disorders: II. Treatment, outcome and research directions. *J. Am. Acad. Child & Adol. Psychiat.*, 29(1): 1–9.

Yates, A., Leehey, K. & Shisslak, C. M. (1983), Running: An analogue of anorexia? *N. Engl. J. Med.*, 308:251–255.

Yates, A. J. & Sambrailo, F. (1984), Bulimia nervosa: A descriptive and therapeutic study. *Behav. Res. Therapy*, 22:501–517.

Zakin, D. F. (1989), Eating disturbance, emotional separation, and body image. *Int. J. Eat. Dis.*, 8:411–416.

Zaslow, M. J. (1987), Sex differences in children's response to maternal employment. Unpublished manuscript prepared for the Committee on Child Development Research and Public Policy, National Research Council, Washington, D.C.

Zimmerman, B. J. (1986), Development of self-regulated learning. Which are the key subprocesses? *Contemp. Ed. Psychol.*, 16:307–313.

Zimmerman, B. J. (1989), A social cognitive view of self-regulated academic learning. *J. Ed. Psychol.*, 81(3):329–339.

Zohar, J., Insel, T. R., Zohar-Kadouch, R. C., Hill, J. L. & Murphy, D. L. (1988), Serotoninergic responsivity in obsessive compulsive disorder. *Arch. Gen. Psychiat.*, 45:167–172.

Author Index

Yaeger, E., 161
Yager, J., 77, 103, 104, 113, 199
Yates, A., 4, 7, 8, 10, 17, 25, 77, 107, 122, 148
Yee, D. K., 100
Young, T., 78

Zackheim, M. A., 106
Zajicek, E., 162
Zakin, D. F., 148
Zaslow, M. J., 161
Zimmer, B., 55, 148
Zimmerman, B. J., 153
Zohar, J., 189

Subject Index